THE OFFICIAL® IDENTIFICATION
AND PRICE GUIDE TO

Costume Jewelry

THE OFFICIAL® IDENTIFICATION
AND PRICE GUIDE TO

Costume Jewelry

HARRICE SIMONS MILLER

PHOTOGRAPHY BY KENNETH CHEN

FIRST EDITION

HOUSE OF COLLECTIBLES • NEW YORK

© 1990 by Harrice Miller

This is a registered trademark of Random House, Inc.

All rights reserved under International and Pan-American Copyright Conventions.

Published by: The House of Collectibles
201 East 50th Street
New York, New York 10022

Distributed by Ballantine Books, a division of Random House, Inc., New York, and simultaneously in Canada by Random House of Canada Limited, Toronto.

Manufactured in the United States of America

ISBN: 0-876-37787-8

First Edition: March 1990

10 9 8 7 6 5 4 3

To my parents, to whom I owe all my collecting urges—Betty Simons, who would have been a great co-author of this book, and Bernard Dine Simons, who recently became an actor at seventy-eight, proving to me that anyone can do anything, at any time.

TABLE OF CONTENTS

ACKNOWLEDGMENTS

One of the most exciting things about costume jewelry is that it is a comparatively new field of collecting, and there's a lot of information still to be discovered. Almost every collector we interviewed has been collecting *seriously* for less than five years. Many people, including this author, have been collecting and wearing vintage costume jewelry for the past twenty years but always have treated it in a very casual way. Now, with prices sometimes surpassing real-jewelry prices, people are taking a different view of the things that have been sitting in their jewelry boxes for years.

When we hear from dealers that people such as Catherine Deneuve, Diane Keaton, Shirlee Fonda, Norma Kamali, and Michael Jackson are collecting costume jewelry, that many top jewelry designers use vintage costume jewelry for inspiration, and that there is an incredible rise in prices, we know that this field is growing in importance every day.

However, there has not been a lot of academic research in the field as yet. Curators of costume collections in museums are usually interested in jewelry only as an adjunct to the costumes and don't give it the same kind of attention. Important auction houses have held very few costume jewelry sales, giving financial considerations as their reason; the prices don't give them the kinds of commissions precious jewelry does. So most of the help we've gotten in writing this book has been from individuals who care enough about the field to give us their time.

Manufacturing: We started our research in Providence, Rhode Island, where Peter DiCristofaro is founding The Jewelers Museum and has been a great source of technical and manufacturing information.

Designers and manufacturers: Kenneth Jay Lane and Genevieve Mitchell Dawson of Kenneth Jay Lane; Maria V. Niscemi Romanoff of Mimi di N; Erwin Pearl, Debra Pearl Heller, and Suzanne Pearl of Erwin Pearl; Cindy Shulga and Beth Miller of The Napier Co.; Patti Cohen of Donna Karan; Diane McLoone of Monet; Betty Terry and Margie Lefcourt of Pauline Trigère; Sandra Leander and Barbara E. Raleigh of Trifari; Sanford Moss of Miriam Haskell; Joan Castle Joseff of Joseff-Hollywood; Pat Hill of Ciner; Sandra Boucher; Donald Hobé of Hobé Cie Ltd.; Claire Kellam of Bijoux Christian Dior; Wendy Gell; Amadeo Panetta of Panetta; Isabell von Flugge of Robert Lee Morris; Maria Snyder; Anita and Steve Vaubel; Basil Nasto of Basil & Co.; Frances Patiky Stein; Laura Miller of the Yves St. Laurent Collection; Carolee; and Karen Erickson of Showroom Seven.

Dealers: Norman Crider of Norman Crider Antiques, New York; Charles France of Divine Idea, New York; Carol Caver of Jóia, New York; Ross Berman of Muriel Karasik Gallery, New York; Terry Rodgers of Terry Rodgers, New York; Only Yesterday, Hudson, NY; Barbara Strand of The Good, the Bad and the Ugly, New York; Matthew Burkholz, Past Perfect, New York; Diane Petipas, Mood Indigo, New York; Barbara Flood of Flood's Closet, New York; Beverly Birks, New York; and Tania Santé of Tania Santé's Classic Collectables, Miami.

Fashion editors, collectors, and others who gave generously of their time and knowledge: Candy Pratts Price, Fashion Director, Accessories and Shoes, *Vogue;* Diane Smith, Senior Editor, Sittings, *Glamour;* Phyllis Magidson, Associate Curator of the Costume Collection, Museum of the City of New York; June Burns Bové, freelance costume curator; Steffan Aletti, President of the Jewelry Industry Council; Kathryn Dwyer, Judith Bumberg, Dorothy Torem, Andrew Spingarn, Otto Hoffer, Andrew Salvadore, Joseph Terino, Al Weissberg, and Raymond Cuminale.

Some of the people who gave us information and advice prefer to remain anonymous—thanks to the conservators, dealers, and collectors who answered all of our questions in a generous manner.

Thanks to Kenneth Chen for taking wonderful pictures and having great fortitude.

Thanks to my daughter, Sloane Miller, for her enthusiasm and help with everything, including photography, and for being very independent this year.

Thanks to my sister, Susie Simons Fasbinder, for her spirited encouragement and assistance with the photography.

To my grandmother Judith Levenson, in Boston, who still has the same verve and style that has inspired me since childhood.

Thanks to the entire Miller family for being there—particularly Robin

Miller Feldman, Carol Miller Hershaft, and Gary and Patty—and to all my friends who haven't heard from me in ages but haven't given me up.

Thanks to my friend, writer Joan Duncan Oliver, who got this whole thing going, and writer Harriet Ross, who is always one of my staunchest supporters.

Special thanks to Pam Smith, my research assistant, who doubled as cheerleader, bloodhound, hand-holder, illustrator, photography stylist, and both fair- and foul-weather friend, particularly since every time we had to borrow or return jewelry there seemed to be a torrential downpour; and thanks to her children Amy, Laura, and Craig for being so understanding.

To my agent, Ruth Nathan, who brought me to House of Collectibles and Ballantine Books and to Dottie Harris, Editor-in-Chief, whose talent, understanding, and simpatico got me through a couple of touch-and-go moments—thanks to two terrific women.

To Philip Scharper, who had the unenviable job of trying to keep me on track but did it well and with humor and patience, thanks, and I'll miss our daily chats.

To Barbara Goldstein, who was always available to answer my questions, thanks.

A great big dose of gratitude to Cindy Berman, who is as much a perfectionist as I am!

And thanks to the whole production staff, copyeditor, proofreader, and everyone who helped get all the details right.

1

An Overview

INTRODUCTION

When we started the research on this book, we thought we knew a fair amount about collectible costume jewelry. We found out there is an almost limitless body of knowledge because there have been so many manufacturers and designers over the years who revived older styles, kept popular designs in their lines for years, and "knocked off" each other like crazy. Each time we thought we had a dating system pinned down, we'd uncover new information that made us not quite so sure. When we talked to the manufacturers and designers who actually made the pieces in the Forties and Fifties and *they* couldn't always date a piece exactly, we realized that often an educated guess is all that we could expect. Often, even when manufacturers have been "known" to use a certain logo during certain years, when we questioned them more closely, we found out that if those little tags that had been soldered on in the Forties were still hanging around the factory in the early Fifties, of course they were used. Stampings that were first manufactured in the Twenties are actually still available now—just because there was a change in the decade didn't mean that certain styles ended abruptly. Costume jewelry design evolved, and it has always been a series of revivals—Victorian, Egyptian, Gypsy, tailored, Art Deco, Art Nouveau, it all comes around again—and then again.

Most manufacturers of costume jewelry did not chronicle their product. Very few companies have kept advertising, photographs, or publicity material from the past. The majority of companies didn't even put their name on their jewelry. Many companies no longer exist, and without extensive

3

research in the Patent Office or in the cities where the businesses were registered, much of the information has to be word of mouth. One of the most exciting aspects of researching this book was talking to the people who had been in the industry years ago.

Peter DiCristofaro, president of Providence Machinery Exchange and the head of the new Jewelers Museum in Providence, invited us to lunch with his uncle, Andrew Salvadore of Salvadore Tool; Joseph Terino of Tercat Tool & Die; and Al Weissberg of Technic, an electroplating company. Talk ranged from stone-setting "home work" that women and children did in the Thirties to style cycles to stories about how the original British and "Yankee" jewelry companies in Attleboro, Massachusetts, hired Italian and Jewish immigrants during World War I to make stampings and findings. It was at this luncheon that a belief we held that a piece of costume jewelry could be dated by the color of the plating was blown apart by Mr. Weissberg, who told us that color is solely up to the manufacturer. Often manufacturers used the same name to describe many different colors. He gave us an example of a color that was popular in 1932, "Russian Antique," that could be done for a company today if requested.

Collecting costume jewelry takes the collector into so many worlds. On one level it's about a love for beautiful or unusual or whimsical objects. But then some collectors get interested in how the jewelry is made, who the designers were, how they lived, how they were trained, what the manufacturing process was, who wore the jewelry, and what was happening in the world at that time. We've touched upon all these areas of interest in this book. Many of the manufacturers and designers are no longer around to tell us their histories firsthand. What information we could gather is presented in the following manner.

First we trace the birth of costume jewelry in Paris in the Twenties to the manufacturers in Providence and New York through to the Eighties. Manufacturing methods are outlined, including a section on imitation stones.

The next section highlights the designers and manufacturers we were able to get information about, including direct quotes and anecdotes whenever possible. Replicas of some other manufacturers' marks are shown to aid in identifying other important collectible jewelry.

The ins and outs of collecting, including care and repair of costume jewelry and how to spot fakes and forgeries, are also covered. Collectors and dealers contributed greatly to this section.

A chapter is devoted to each decade from the 1920s through the 1980s, surveying the fashions of the day and other influences on costume jewelry and featuring photographs with detailed descriptions, including prices. Pieces that were not photographed are also described and evaluated. When available, we've reprinted the original advertisements from the manufacturers. There are also some photographs showing costume jewelry worn by Hollywood movie stars. In the center of the book is a group of color pictures with descriptions and prices.

An interesting chapter for collectors who have an eye to the future is the one called "The Eighties." Established designers, manufacturers, and rising new stars in the costume jewelry world are featured, with photographs and descriptions of their work. (Mainly, we've shown the work of New York designers because that's whom we've had access to.) This section illustrates some new trends and new materials being used, as well as the classic looks.

Promoters, dealers, and antiques malls are separated by states in listings at the end of the book. We canvassed hundreds of collectors and store owners to find those who carry significant costume jewelry, in both quantity and quality.

For readers who are interested in doing further research, there is a bibliography and suggestions for additional resources.

A WORD ABOUT PRICING

The reader will notice that most pieces of costume jewelry depicted or described in the book have fairly high price ranges. The reason is that many of the pieces were borrowed from dealers who have shops in New York City (where overhead prices are high), the pieces are usually in excellent condition, and the market there will bear the prices. These prices are far from the final word—it doesn't mean that the sharp-eyed collector can't go to a local church fair and find something fabulous at a much lower price.

Recently, at a street fair in our neighborhood in Manhattan, we bought the following pieces, all from one vendor: six unused, carved-Bakelite buckles from the 1930s, for $25.00 the lot, one in highly-sought-after red; a clear Lucite bangle from the 1950s with imbedded straw flowers and leaves, for $7.00; a 1930s plastic necklace with red carved flowers on plastic links, for $22.00; an unused gold-plated Coro cuff from the 1950s with red rhinestones set into little star shapes in the metal, for $17.00; and a 1950s pin and earrings set of copper in the shape of an African mask with an aqua ceramic face, for $30.00 the set. From another dealer we bought a pin from the 1950s made of clear Lucite with a pink rose imbedded, hanging from a silver-colored bow, for $12.00. These prices are all within a resalable range, but if we were buying them to collect or wear, we'd consider them bargains.

Dealers everywhere will agree that pricing is usually based on a number of factors, collectibility being the most important. What makes a piece collectible is usually its beauty, workmanship, quality of materials, age, rarity—and sometimes most important, the fad of the moment. For example, we've heard from a couple of dealers that "jelly bellies," the animals with clear crystal bodies, aren't selling as quickly this year as they were last year. This year everyone is looking for Trifari sets from the 1940s and Bakelite. By the time this book is published, enameled copper sets or 1950s glitter may be the rage.

In which part of the country you do your buying, from whom you buy, whether you buy from the best dealer in town or at a neighbor's yard sale all affect the price you'll pay. The best thing you can do is educate your eye, handle the jewelry so that you get to know weight and feel of different materials, examine it for signatures or marks, notice carefully if stones are missing or have been replaced badly and if there are obvious changes or alterations, such as cut marks, that may indicate major modifications in the piece.

When there is just a single price given, not a range, it's because that particular piece at that particular store at the moment it was researched had a price tag with that price. Some dealers sell their jewelry at the exact price quoted, some give a 10 to 20 percent discount to other dealers or to "frequent buyers." Some of the prices—for example, those on the Pauline Trigère pieces—were given to us by the designers who've kept archives. Since we did not have much of a basis for comparison, we used their estimates. For the pieces lent to us by sources that were not selling them (the Museum of the City of New York, for example) we estimated the prices based on similar pieces we've seen.

You must remember that dealers usually at least double their purchase prices, so in selling to a dealer you won't be able to ask more than half of what the retail price is to be.

Factors that affect pricing are the following: aesthetics, condition, materials, popularity, geographical differences, and the "flea market/antique store" variable. We've attempted to give fair estimates based on looking at thousands of pieces at street fairs, flea markets, private collections, and antique shops of all types. These prices are not gospel; they are to be used as a guide.

HOW OLD IS YOUR JEWELRY?

To find out how to date a piece of costume jewelry, we went directly to the source—to Providence, Rhode Island. There we learned that a fairly reliable method is to examine the functional parts—the closures, pin backs, earring backs, and clasps. That works as long as the parts haven't been repaired or replaced. We also were shown how various manufacturing methods have changed over the years, but the same day we saw machinery that was over 100 years old still producing stampings! We also saw stampings that were designed even before the Twenties still available to be made into jewelry. Settings have undergone changes. Pavé-set, prong-set, gluing, nicking in— all can denote different eras. But although we were told that no one hand-sets anything today, we found many contemporary companies that do set by hand! Just to confuse things further, it is well known that manufacturers constantly revive earlier styles. Some never take the original ones out of their lines; the decision rests on how well the piece sells. In the Twenties, Thirties, Forties, and Fifties there were Victorian revivals. Today there are companies that specialize in an antique look, using the original stampings. In the photo shown on the next page, the bottom bracelet looks like a Thirties style, but we were told by our Providence sources that the manufac-turing methods show it definitely to have been made in the Fifties. The bracelet on the top has a distinct Art Deco design, and we were told by its owner that it is from the Twenties or Thirties, but something about it looks off. We could definitely be wrong. Of course, in these cases, the bracelets are more valuable if they're older rather than of more recent vintage.

We've been told the wrong years by some of the best-informed dealers in this country. Sometimes they've been off by two decades! We've inter-viewed manufacturers who aren't sure of the dates on their own jewelry;

9

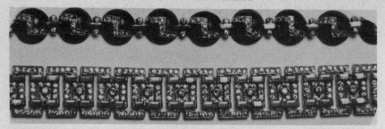

Unsigned Art Deco–design bracelets. *Photo by Kenneth Chen, jewelry courtesy of Charles France and Clare Feldman.* (See descriptions and prices in the 1950s chapter.)

we've talked to others who've given us very specific dates on certain pieces, and then we found similar pieces in books lent by those same manufacturers—with totally different dates! Some manufacturers, such as Hollycraft, Christian Dior, and Mimi di N (recently), actually stamp dates into their logos. Others, like Hobé, Napier, Monet, and Trifari, keep careful records for their archival collections. Much of dating is hearsay, and much of it is wrong.

The savvy collector knows that, like prices, dates given in books are to be used as indicators. We've noticed that for real jewelry dates are sometimes given by *centuries.* Because costume is comparatively new, we're supposed to be more precise. When we know the exact date of manufacture, either through advertisements or manufacturers' records, we note that. If we're quite sure of the decade, it is stated. However, when our fairly extensive research has not turned up a definite date, we've used "circa," followed by the decade we believe it to be.

An excellent way to learn dates is to look at old advertisements in newspapers and fashion magazines at the library. Look at the materials, get to know the companies and when they were in business, study the "working parts," and ask the age whenever you buy a piece.

*   *   *

Recently we heard about a research company that specializes in antiques. Unfortunately, there was not enough time to test the company's skills before publication. They specialize in retrieving information relating to provenance, genealogy, and other information concerning all categories of antiques. They call themselves "research detectives" and do not buy, sell, or appraise antiques. The results are presented in report form, with a list of sources and a photocopy of relevant data if possible. The fee is $35.00 per hour with a three-hour minimum.

For information, call or write: *Antique Researchers,* P.O. Box 79, Waban, MA 02168–(617)969-6238.

COSTUME JEWELRY
IS "THE LOOK"

June Burns Bové is a textile conservator whose specialty is costume. She works exclusively for museums, mounting costume exhibits for major museums of the United States. She discusses impressions of the recent history of costume jewelry in the following manner:

All people in all societies are attracted to jewelry. In primitive societies personal adornment comes before clothing. The act of adorning oneself is very deep-seated in the human psyche of whatever race, region, or religious persuasion.

Certain historical groups reject certain types of adornment because they are rejecting the values of a society. They use clothing and adornment to express these feelings. In the 1960s there was a great deal of pain in families due to the "generation gap." It was very clear in people's style of dressing. A person's political and social affinities could be discerned by the way he or she dressed. Young men decked themselves out in ways they hadn't done in a hundred years.

Chanel was the first important designer who made costume jewelry not only acceptable but fashionable. Sixty years later we're still influenced by some of her designs—easy jackets and skirts, wonderful chains, long necklaces, bold crosses, and bracelets—all very stunning. As the apocryphal story goes, as she became successful she acquired gorgeous pearls and liked to wear them. They became a security problem, and she began to wear fakes quite openly. She made use of the one bold statement. She wasn't burdened down by wearing everything at once. The look now is to wear multiple chains, but often she chose to wear one, big, bold piece that was in proportion and in order.

11

Women liked large, fake pearl earrings at the edge of their cloche hats and later peeping from the softer hairstyle of the 1930s. For the average woman pieces were more restrained than Chanel's cross.

In the Twenties there was a freedom and playfulness to adornment that had as much to do with design as it had to do with a generation that had been terribly marked by World War I. Long beads were around before the Twenties, but in the latter half of the decade they were worn prominently, sometimes with a knot in them, with short skirts, long, dangly earrings, bands across the brow, and coiled upper arm bracelets. It was a new and youthful look.

In the Thirties things became more refined and defined, and jewelry was used to make a statement. It was bolder because the woman of the Thirties was more mature. She had her bust back and her curves, and often a dramatic pin on the lapel of her suit.

In the late Thirties and early Forties, during World War II, the open neckline took a sweetheart or square shape, and a pair of matching clips was a signature of this era. Sometimes their function was to keep the wearer's underwear in place.

In the Fifties to the early Sixties, the signature was the charm bracelet, a collection of amulets of a society. Often the pieces marked different events in the wearer's life. They became both a personal and fashion statement.

Later, in the Seventies, the charm bracelets evolved into horseshoe-shaped pendants with charms hanging from them. Perhaps because women were now working in greater numbers and it wasn't practical to wear a clanking charm bracelet to the office, it became a "fashion."

Jewelry designers often worked closely with clothing designers. Poiret in Paris in the Twenties was friendly with Bakst and Diaghilev, and they went from one design discipline to another. Sonia Delauney was a perfect example of crossover design, from textiles to objects to clothing. Now practically every designer makes costume jewelry to go with a collection and to be sold in his or her boutique. There's always been a "trickle down" effect, with mass producers copying the clothing designers' jewelry.

There is "nothing new under the sun" in fashion, and jewelry is definitely bound to fashion. In the Western world, as well as in Islamic, Chinese, or primitive societies, adornment never stays static; it is always changing, always reflecting the temperament of the culture.

WHY COSTUME JEWELRY?

We asked dozens of dealers and collectors what the appeal of costume jewelry is. We found out that the people who collect costume jewelry do so because of the wide range of color, objects, and designs that are represented, but the most pervasive reason is probably the fantasy and glamour it embodies. On really good costume jewelry, the work is as good as on real jewelry. Many of the early designers were trained in fine jewelry and continued to use the same techniques in manufacturing costume. Today's designers and manufacturers seem to come from three distinct camps: those who are trained as designers and artisans, manufacturers who are basically merchandisers, and artists who turn to costume jewelry for freedom in the use of materials and designs.

In the Thirties, when costume jewelry came into its own, the Depression and the shadow of the war to come brought about a feeling of bleakness in Americans. Hollywood responded with movies on a grand scale: opulent settings, beautiful women, handsome men, glamorous clothing, impeccable diction, and gorgeous jewelry. Everything was bigger and certainly better than real life. Gowns by Adrian were worn with rows of "diamond" bracelets. A person could spend a couple of dollars on a piece of jewelry and bring a little piece of Hollywood home. Costume jewelry made people feel they were part of the magic they saw on the silver screen.

As the nation moved into war, costume jewelry was perhaps the only bright spot in a woman's wardrobe. Everything was rationed except hats. Jewelry was designed to uplift the spirit and make the wearer feel safeguarded. Pieces were large and heavy, with happy designs and exuberant colors. Women across the nation could buy cheap clothes and furs, but there was no such thing as a cheap diamond. Costume jewelry, particularly the well-made imitations of Cartier and other fine jewelers, satisfied the universal need to have beautiful things.

Today, with our economy inflated once again, people are turning to costume jewelry, both vintage and contemporary, to feel good. An appreciation of the wonderful designs of Schiaparelli, Miriam Haskell, Eisenberg, or DeRosa has developed among people who might ordinarily wear precious jewelry. The true test of costume jewelry's popularity is that it is being reproduced fraudulently, giving authentic vintage costume jewelry a certain cachet.

THE PROCESS

Costume jewelry is appealing on many levels. Ever since the 18th century, when paste and cut steel were used as a substitute for diamonds, pinchbeck was substituted for gold and Wedgwood for cameos so that milady wouldn't be prey to larcenous highwaymen, women have tucked costume jewelry into their travel bags. In the same way that costume jewelry allows the designer greater artistic freedom by using a wide range of materials, it allows the wearer eccentricity of taste and more flexibility of personal expression.

In the evolution of the United States as the world's leading mass mer-
chandiser, costume jewelry reflected the country's style of mass production
and marketing. Fine jewelry was made one piece at a time; imitation or
costume jewelry could be made in multiples. The mill workers in Providence who couldn't afford the real jewelry that was made there could buy
gold-filled and sterling silver jewelry and still own examples of fine workmanship.

Definitions of costume jewelry range from the one given in *An Illustrated Dictionary of Jewellry*, "Mass produced jewelry made of non-precious metals and is not designed to last—made for a prevailing fashion,"
to that of some of today's designers, who are often artists and see costume
jewelry as a transformation of materials that combines form, function, and
design in a way that satisfies the wearer's soul.

In the beginning, costume jewelry closely imitated real jewelry, following the designs and styles of Tiffany, Cartier, and Van Cleef and Arpels. The
materials were usually sterling silver or plated base metal, set with pastes
and marcasites. Before the Twenties everything was made of stampings;
there were no castings until the Twenties. The stampings were put together,
soldered, manipulated, and designed with different settings and with places
for stones and enamel. They were assembled in much the same way a
building is.

According to Peter DiCristofaro, stamping is the true art form of costume
jewelry because the piece has to be rendered or sculpted into steel. If a piece
is chipped off in the making, it has to be redone; there's no way to replace
it. "The workmanship in steel is equivalent to the workmanship in marble,
in sculpture," says Peter. In the early days everything was hand-carved into
steel; there were no electric tools. The identification process was not important until now, with the new boom in collecting costume jewelry. The artists
didn't sign the dies; they might have been fired for such an act. Sometimes
if the owner of the company created the dies, he signed them. Even now,
designers and manufacturers from New York go to Providence, find the
stampings, take them back to their factories, glue in stones, enamel them,
solder them together, and sell them.

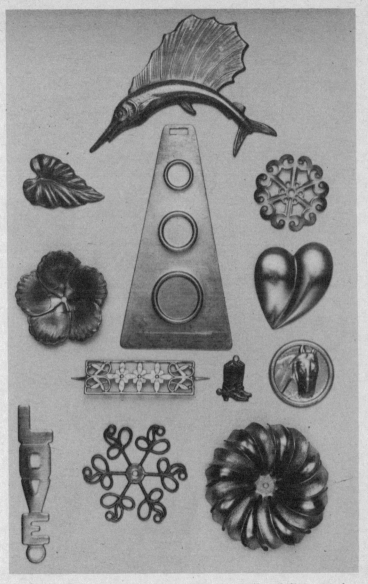

Brass stampings from the 1920s through the 1970s. *Photo by Kenneth Chen, original stampings courtesy of Andrew Salvadore, Salvadore Tool & Findings.*

Brass stampings from the 1920s through the 1970s. *Photo by Kenneth Chen, original stampings courtesy of Andrew Salvadore, Salvadore Tool & Findings.*

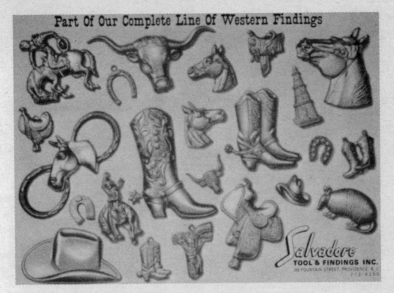

Photograph of stampings courtesy of Salvadore Tool & Findings.

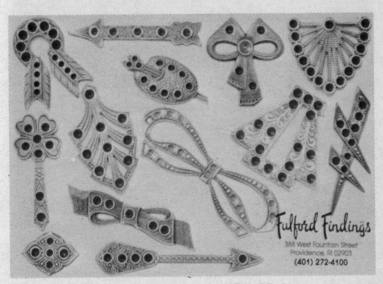

Photograph of stampings courtesy of Fulford Findings.

VICTORIANA
Classic Findings,
Forever in Style

Fulford Findings

388 West Fountain Street
Providence, RI 02903
(401) 272-4100

Photograph of stampings courtesy of Fulford Findings.

A BRIEF HISTORY OF IMITATION GEMSTONES

From the "random personal reminiscences" of Otto Hoffer, exporter, 1980:

For several centuries, glass factories abound in the wooded sections of northern Bohemia. They have very little contact with one another and produce consumer goods on the premises from the glass they manufacture. A glassmaker named Josef Riedel decides to produce straight glass rods that can be transported easily, in addition to his usual vases and glasses.

Handling glass rods and using them to produce beads, buttons, and stones for jewelry turns out to be a much simpler operation than running a glass factory, so many small companies develop. Mr. Riedel expands his stock and offers a larger range of colors, to satisfy the market's needs. Manufacturers quickly explore the great number of refinements that are possible with glass, leading to specialization and increased production. Factories begin producing heavily leaded glass with higher brillance and more diversity of effects, including "compositions," which are used to make finer imitation semiprecious and precious stones. By the early Twenties there are approximately fifty factories and about one thousand small glass and stone bead-making businesses.

Generally, a *Lieferant* or "factor," orders the glass from the factory; turns it over to pressers who make the "rough"; takes the rough to the shearers (mostly women), who shear the overflow of glass from the edges; then takes the stones to the beveler. The stones then go to the fire-polisher and to the cutter of tables. A table is the flat surface on top of a gem-cut stone or the flat back of a flat-back stone if polished. The cutters distribute the stones still further to their home workers to cut and polish either the top surface only (halftin) or all of the facets on the front and back of the stone (fulltin). Next, painting or foiling is done. Foiling is the process of attaching a silver mirror or foil to the back of the stones for more brilliance. Finally, the factor selects stones for quality and ships them to the exporter.

The terms *halftin* and *fulltin* originate with the use of a tin alloy wheel used for polishing the facets, which produces a sharper polish than wood or rubber wheels. Today the expression "tintable" is used for doublets made in Germany, by Swarovski in Austria, and in Czechoslovakia by the nationalized stone industry, even though a tin wheel has not been used for more than fifty years.

In the 1920s in Czechoslovakia the cutters are mostly farmers who work at home in between sowing and harvesting. Prior to World War I, cutters often take shortcuts and finish stones on a wooden wheel to save time, rather than use the more precise, but slower, tin wheel. Sometimes, after using a sandstone, the stones are sent directly to the fire-polisher instead of polishing each facet individually. The fire-polisher heats the stones so that the glass melts on the surface and becomes shiny. Often this technique is used on larger stones with larger facets, producing an intermediate quality. These stones are used in pendants and brooches and in the chandelier industry after World War II.

Producing the stone by hand is a complicated and delicate process. The way the glass is heated, the temperature of the die, and the side of the stone that is chosen to be faceted are all important choices made by each glassworker. Minute cracks, uneven cooling, hollow facets, or unevenness of the stone can occur if not handled properly. At this point only the rough stone is produced; it still has to undergo many steps before it is ready to be set.

Machine-cut stones and beads are cut and polished on elaborate machines. Less expensive machine-made beads and buttons are made by tumbling and fire-polished in large quantities.

Around the town of Gablonz is a cluster of small communities whose main activity is fancy lamp work, using glass chips and combinations of glass rods laminated or twisted together. This method produces good imitations of opaque semiprecious stones such as jade, jasper, tigereye, moonstone, opal, turquoise, and coral. Nearby is a concentration of the jewelry industry, whose settings and findings manufacturers are called *Estampeure*.

At this time, the 1920s, in the town of Gablonz there is a factory making celluloid items and another that makes galalith (a casein formaldehyde product). In Paris, Chanel is displaying crystal rhinestones—multifaceted, round, unfoiled, held in rims exposing the complete stone. They look like diamonds but are too large to be real. The buyer from Saks Fifth Avenue buys a dozen, and by noon of the first morning they are sold out at a price of $100 for each necklace. This leads to a great surge in the popularity of stones. By 1928 any kind of transparent stone is sold in huge quantities. In the 1920s Gablonz practically has a monopoly on glass stones and beads for jewelry. Swarovski in Austria is the big competitor.

At the end of the 1930s Japan is producing good-quality imitation pearls at competitive prices and begins to manufacture imitation stones as well.

War breaks out, and shipments across the Atlantic stop. In the years following the war, attempts are made at reestablishing the glass production business in Czechoslovakia. By the 1950s Austrian stones from the Swarovski factory are sold widely in the United States, but in the mid-Fifties business drops off; it picks up again when glass bead neckchains become fashionable. At this time stones are still made in Czechoslovakia, but they aren't as well made as the Austrian stones. Today (1980) there is a decline in the production of stones due to a shortage of skilled workers.

In the mid-Fifties in Paris some jewelry manufacturers are using iridescent Austrian stones. Ernest Lowenstein in New York calls them "Aurora Borealis," and other vacuum-plated coatings on the backs of stones are called Volcano and Vitrail, Light, Medium, and Dark; Bermuda Blue; and Heliotrope. All of the colored optical effects are produced by layers of different metals placed in sequence. Imitation hematites and vacuum-plated gold become popular products in the United States.

The name "rhinestone" has an interesting source. In the late 1800s tourist shops along the Rhine River in Austria sell jewelry with stones called *Rheinkiesel* (Rhine pebbles), which are water-clear stones cut like diamonds, with red, green, and blue colors fused inside the crystal glass. A businessman, perhaps an American importer, calls these imitation diamonds rhinestones, and the name is used from then on.

IMPORTANT DESIGNERS AND MANUFACTURERS

Actually, this chapter should be titled "Important Designers and Manufacturers We Could Find Information About" because there are many companies that are extremely important to collectors, such as Hattie Carnegie, R. DeRosa, Schiaparelli, Coro, Chanel, Jomaz and Mazer (same company), HAR, Hollycraft, Robert, Nettie Rosenstein, Schreiner, and others, that we couldn't find material on. Either the companies no longer exist or, as in some cases, wouldn't submit material to us for publication. If any readers have information about any designers or manufacturers of costume jewelry, please send it to the author in care of the publisher in New York.

Manufacturers' marks are depicted below their respective headings.

MARCEL BOUCHER

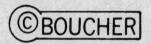

A history of the company as related by Sandra Boucher, noted jewelry designer and teacher, widow of Marcel:

In 1925 Marcel Boucher arrives in New York from France and goes to work for Cartier as a jeweler. Eventually, he leaves there and makes shoe buckles, possibly for Trifari. At this time jewelry is all flat, without high modulation. Marcel starts his own firm in the Thirties, and his first line is an extraordinary group of bird pins, made with colored stones and bright enamels. Nothing like this has ever been done before. The pins are three-dimensional and include an ornate bird of paradise. With just six different designs Marcel takes an order from Saks Fifth Avenue for $20,000 to $30,000!

Marcel keeps his company small in order to maintain quality control. He has about eighty employees. He does the designing, and his partner does the model making and selling.

In 1947 Sandra leaves France and comes to New York. Her background is also in fine jewelry. After two years she becomes interested in learning about costume jewelry, so she joins the firm of Marcel Boucher in 1949 and stays there until 1958, designing jewelry and selecting stones. In 1960 she leaves to become the head designer at Tiffany, later to return to Boucher and "marry the boss."

After Marcel's death Sandra sells the company to a firm that makes Lucite watches. They, in turn, sell the company to another firm, which now owns the name and doesn't use it for anything at the present time.

Sandra talks about designing jewelry:

It was not easy to work with the fashion designers because they always kept their designs secret. Sometimes if we came out with bangle bracelets, the designers would have very tight, long sleeves for that season; or if we designed necklaces, they might come out with high necklines. There was not much communication or cooperation. You needed at least six months in advance to be able to produce jewelry that would complement the fashions. Many of the articles in the jewelry trade magazines came out too late for the jewelry designers to act on. Usually, the clothing designers gave us the runaround when we asked for advance information. It would have been very helpful, for example, if we had known that silk blouses would be popular that season: women don't wear heavy pins on silk blouses because they would pull. We tried to follow colors and styles when it was possible, but it was difficult.

Designers are influenced by other events besides clothing design. Barbara Bush is shown wearing pearls, so we know that once again pearls will be popular. Movie stars and famous women definitely influence costume jewelry trends.

In jewelry design, first comes the design, then the model. At Marcel Boucher I used to design a new line twice a year, with about 300 models each year. Every week we had to make at least thirty to forty designs. But my designs always had a look; refined, sensuous, recognizable.

CINER

In 1892 Ciner is founded by Emanuel Ciner, the grandfather of current owner Pat Hill. Ciner's first location is on Maiden Lane in New York City. Until the 1930s the company works only in gold and platinum, using precious stones. Then they switch to costume jewelry, using sterling silver and later white metal. The same approach to design and manufacturing is used in costume as in real jewelry. The Ciner look has always been that of "real" jewelry that could be from any of the finest jewelry stores. Mr. Ciner runs the company until he is ninety-four years old and then turns it over to sons Irwin and Charles. In the late Seventies Pat and David Hill take over the business, and now their two children work with them.

Everything is manufactured at their current location, which is in the costume jewelry district in midtown New York City. There the designing, model making, casting, finishing, and selling take place. The Hills and their sales manager create new designs, along with a freelance designer who renders the ideas so that the model maker can work from them. Over the years they've used freelance designers and bought designs from France.

Many of the original designs from Pat's father's time are still in the line. Some go back to the Forties and Fifties. If something is beautiful and classic, it will stay in the line for as long as it is appropriate. The styles range from tailored lines to very elaborate pieces with glitter and rhinestones. Ciner puts a tremendous effort into maintaining the quality of the line. All of the materials are the finest they can find, including Austrian rhinestones, European glass cabochons, and simulated pearls that are made to their specifications. They use no plastic. Every piece is signed "Ciner," with the same logo they have used since they started.

The current Ciner customer is upscale and classic, not funky or trendy. Often it's the woman who owns real jewelry but doesn't take it with her when she travels. They sell to finer department stores and specialty stores. The story goes that Elizabeth Taylor once bought $20,000 worth of Ciner jewelry at one time.

BIJOUX CHRISTIAN DIOR

Henkel and Grossé, a company that begins in 1907 in West Germany, first makes fine jewelry and then expands into the fashion jewelry field, using more affordable materials. Paris couturiers, hearing of their reputation for fine work, commission jewelry from Grossé to accessorize their fashions.

In 1947 Christian Dior revolutionizes the fashion world with his "New Look." It is characterized by long, flaring skirts, fitted waists, and softly rounded shoulders and hips. It heralds a return to femininity that is very different from the short, narrow skirts that are worn during the war years.

In 1955 Christian Dior signs a licensing agreement with the Grossé family to manufacture jewelry that bears his name. He has a reputation for seeking out only the highest-quality products. Grossé pieces made for Christian Dior are much sought after. They are stamped with the Christian Dior logo and have the year of their manufacture after the name.

EISENBERG

Eisenberg and Sons Originals starts out as a dress manufacturer in Chicago, founded by Jonas Eisenberg in 1914. Beautifully jeweled pins, using the finest Austrian rhinestones from Swarovski, adorn the dresses. It soon becomes apparent that there is enough interest in the dress clips and pins to manufacture and market them on their own because customers are walking off with them.

In the 1930s the company starts producing jewelry, mostly unmarked except for sterling stamps. The workmanship and stones are of exceptionally high quality. In the mid-Thirties and for about ten years the pieces are stamped "Eisenberg Original," and in the early Forties, a script E is often there, in addition or alone. Because of the ban on materials during the war, the pins are usually sterling in the early Forties. Most of the collectible pins are marked "Eisenberg Original" or E and are heavy in feeling and in weight. In the latter part of the Forties the pieces are marked "Eisenberg" and are often heavy white metal. "Eisenberg Ice" is also used in the late Forties and early Fifties. From then on, until the Seventies, no stamp is used at all. From the Seventies until the present, "Eisenberg Ice" in script is on the pieces.

Eisenberg pins command very high prices in today's collectibles market. They are big and bold, with a look of importance and value.

MIRIAM HASKELL

In 1924 petite, attractive Miriam Haskell creates a new concept—that fashion jewelry should be an accessory to fashion and become part of a woman's total appearance. At this time most fashionable women resist wearing "fake" jewelry. Miriam is influenced by her friend Coco Chanel, who paves the way for costume jewelry to be accepted by the stylish women of Paris. Her friends in the fashion world are impressed with her designs and encourage her to open a small shop in the modish McAlpin Hotel in New York City. Some of New York's best-known and best-dressed women buy her beautiful designs, which she packages in jewelry boxes with her name inscribed in an Art Deco style. Her designs are innovative and feminine and often are created on themes taken from nature. Her success at the McAlpin leads her to open a second shop in another hotel. By now she has developed a following among the "chic" women of New York.

By 1926 Miriam's designs are sought by retailers, and the firm of Miriam Haskell is established in order to manufacture her designs on the wholesale level. From the start and to this day Miriam's designs are not mass-

Original illustration by Miriam Haskell, showing the early logo that appeared on jewelry boxes, circa 1920s. *Photo by Kenneth Chen, original photo courtesy of Miriam Haskell.*

produced. Everything that bears the Miriam Haskell logo is made by hand. Most pieces made before 1948 are unsigned but are often recognizable by the beautiful workmanship and materials, as well as by their design motifs. Beads and tiny seed pearls are manipulated on highly tensile brass wire to form delicate flowers. The finest cut stones, beads, and findings are brought back from Europe. Miriam becomes famous for her use of beautifully simulated pearls that are painstakingly produced in Japan for her. When Miriam designs, there are definite "seasons," and she often uses shell motifs for cruise and summer. She is very patriotic and loves to use red, white, and blue in addition to her favorite flower motifs.

In 1953 Miriam becomes ill, and her protégé and assistant, Frank Hess, continues to design in her detailed, feminine, innovative style. Successive designers adhere strictly to Miriam's design concepts.

In 1958 Sanford Moss joins Haskell Jewels Ltd. as manager. In 1983 he becomes vice president, and in 1984 he purchases the company from Morris Kinsler, who had bought it from Miriam's brother Joe.

The current line is developed through the concerted efforts of Sanford Moss, the designer, the sales organization, and the fashion coordinators. They gain knowledge by attending museums, reading fashion publications, seeing exhibitions, and traveling to Europe frequently to observe the fashion trends. Each year 4,000 pieces of jewelry are created.

Many materials used in costume jewelry design have peaks of acceptance. There may be a period when shell is important, and another when customers don't want to see shells, or pearls, for example.

Producing the seed pearls that are the company's signature is a tedious, time-consuming job. They are handmade in Japan and are less than 2mm in diameter. It's quite possible that when the current inventory is exhausted, there may be none available. Haskell Jewels never uses castings, preferring fine filigree stampings that have a delicate feeling. There is currently a selection of 25,000 stampings from all over the world. The glass beads come from Europe, mostly Germany, but some come from Paris, Austria, and Czechoslovakia. The company always has total control of its operations. Design, production, sales, and shipping are all under one roof. Recently, both the New York and London productions of *The Phantom of the Opera* have had jewelry designed by Haskell. The finest stores in the country carry the current Haskell line. Haskell Jewels Limited is actively designing and manufacturing high-quality, high-fashion, manipulated jewelry, for which they have always been famous.

The personal memories of a man who had a fifty-year friendship with Miriam:

The best way to describe Miriam Haskell would be to say she was a wonderful woman who loved beautiful things. She often attended auctions in New York and bought superb art, furniture, and paintings. She lived in an attractive

Red-headed mannequins in Saks Fifth Avenue windows wearing necklaces from Miriam Haskell's Tutankhamen Collection, 1970s. *Photo by Kenneth Chen, original photo courtesy of Miriam Haskell.*

apartment on Central Park South, facing the park, that she had decorated herself with fine furniture and objects. She dressed appealingly but was not the typical American woman. She was good-looking in a European way. A man I knew who came from a very well known family in New York used to bid against her at auctions. He would always ask me questions about her and wanted very badly to meet her. She was very elusive and had a sense of mystery about her. She was not an outgoing person. I never did introduce them.

Miriam was a great lover of things in nature. I think her creativity was nurtured by her love of flowers, stones, rocks, and shells. Most of her early designs were flowers. She once gave me a very beautiful book on seashells that I treasured.

She was an interesting woman, traveling extensively for business and pleasure. She would often go to Europe by ship. Prior to World War II she traveled to Middle Europe, Czechoslovakia, and Austria to buy stones. I know she was friendly with important designers in Europe, but she never told me about them.

Miriam was conscious of those in need and was very generous and benevolent. She always helped people in some way. She was forever giving presents of her work to those she loved. She would never visit someone without bringing a bracelet or a pin or something she had designed.

Miriam was a sensitive young lady, not trained at all in jewelry design. I would compare her to a painter like Goya, who never had a lesson but had natural talent. She was also a good businesswoman, with the ability to get retailers to take on her jewelry wherever she was. Saks Fifth Avenue had an exclusive right to sell her jewelry in New York City. In the Thirties there was a large showcase right near the entrance that contained only her jewelry. She used to spend part of the winter at the Roney Plaza in Miami Beach, where she gave Burdine's the exclusive right to sell her jewelry there. She dressed very well and always wore her own designs.

Frank Hess, her right-hand man, was a talented designer. I understand she wasn't easy to work for. She was demanding and wanted everything to be perfect. But she had many outside interests in the arts, and I admired her for her compassion for the forgotten, the poor, and the sick. I always found her charming.

HOBÉ

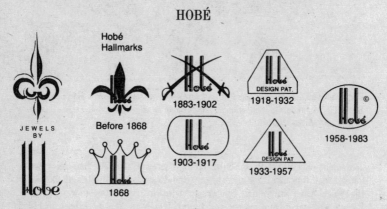

Hobé
Hallmarks

JEWELS BY

Before 1868

1868

1883-1902

1903-1917

DESIGN PAT.
1918-1932

DESIGN PAT
1933-1957

©
1958-1983

It's Paris in the late 1800s. The Eiffel Tower is completed, and Jacques Hobé, a master craftsman and fine jewelrymaker, has a revolutionary new concept in jewelry. At this time only the very rich own quality jewelry. Jacques decides to manufacture fine jewelry at affordable prices, using newly efficient manufacturing techniques.

His son William continues in his tradition and brings his art and craftsmanship to America, where it is well received from New York to Hollywood. Stars and producers appreciate his creativity in both costume and jewelry design. The jewelry is designed by members of the family except for one man, Lou Vici, who is with the company from the Thirties through the early

Seventies. Today William's sons Donald, Robert, and grandson, James, continue to produce fine Hobé jewelry.

Don Hobé shares an interesting anecdote about his father, William, and the first time the term "costume jewelry" was used:

> Jacques Fath, Philip Mangone, and Pierre Hobé had a company in Germany in the Twenties. They manufactured bugle robes, which are sequined robes. They wrote a letter to Florenz Ziegfeld to set up an appointment for William to sell him the robes for his lavish productions. William came to the United States with two huge steamer trunks filled with robes.
>
> Ziegfeld gave him a huge order, for the next five or six shows, for over $200,000. He asked if the company could also supply jewelry to match the robes. When William returned with the samples of the robes, Flo asked him where the "costume jewelry" was, referring to the jewelry he was making to go with the costumes.
>
> At that time each piece of jewelry was very expensive, perhaps $12 to $15. In comparison, a good steak dinner cost about $2.25.
>
> It was also at that time that William began a lifelong friendship with a young chorine he once shared his sandwich with when he was calling on Ziegfeld. Her name was Carole Lombard.
>
> William never returned to Europe. Instead he stayed in the United States and opened a jewelry company in competition with Hobé Cie; he called it Hobé Cie Limited. Twenty years later he bought out Hobé Cie, which was a French company owned by his father and grandfather.

The story of Hobé, the "Man of Jewels," as featured in *Mayfair* (a pamphlet distributed by Hobé, undated but reported to be 1936):

Jewels for the Madonna

A cynical French philosopher once remarked that jewels should be worn either by courtesans or madonnas—no in-betweens. Jewels lend to courtesans the sacred aura of the madonna and lend to madonnas some of the wicked fires of the courtesan.

Mr. William Hobé, internationally famous jewelry designer, improved on this philosophy by designing jewelry of fine craftsmanship within the budgets of madonnas, courtesans, and the classes in between. His workmanship runs from the finest sterling silver, priced at $10, to bracelet masterpieces of star sapphires and diamonds priced at many thousands of dollars. A connoisseur of antique jewelry, Hobé interprets historical designs into modern settings, forgoing none of the original artistry, no matter the price.

For the past four decades Hobé has studied period design in world-famous art museums. Today he enjoys the confidence of the Hollywood Colony as a historical authority. He designs settings for many of our finest epic pictures. It was in his spare time that he created original jewels inspired by his romantic delving into the fashion modes of yesterday. His spare-time hobby proved so successful that before long Hobé the Hobbyist became Hobé the Man of Jewels.

Hobé creates costume jewel pieces encrusted with fine imported stones. Some of his pieces have the flavor of Oriental art and Hindu motifs. Each piece of jewelry is individually made by hand and involves an elaborate process often consisting of several hundred individual parts. His jewels of legendary splendor are timeless in fashion—classics—reminiscent of rare museum antiques.

Another illustration of Hobé's artistry is his famous "Hobé Porcelains." This master artisan traveled to Dresden and Meissen to learn for himself the intricacies of the fine art of porcelain making.

Hobé jewels and porcelains are nationally distributed and can be found at the finest stores throughout the country.

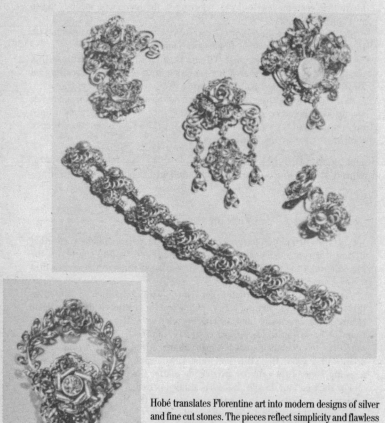

Hobé translates Florentine art into modern designs of silver and fine cut stones. The pieces reflect simplicity and flawless craftsmanship.

Jewel-encrusted evening bag of fine French faille with matching bracelet and earrings make an exquisite ensemble by Hobé.

JOSEFF-HOLLYWOOD

Joseff   JOSEFF
                            HOLLYWOOD

Note: According to Mrs. Joseff, Joseff-Hollywood stamped their jewelry "Joseff-Hollywood" through the Forties. After the Forties it was marked "Joseff." The above mark, "Joseff Hollywood" on two lines, was on an early piece, but there was no hyphen.

In the early Thirties Eugene Joseff works in the advertising field and dabbles in jewelry design. He makes his own models out of paste and tries, unsuccessfully, to sell his designs to the movie studios. It takes a year and a half to make his first sale—a rhinestone bracelet and four buttons.

By the end of the Thirties Joseff's designs have become so sought after he can hardly keep up with the orders. Sometimes costume designers build entire costumes around his fabulous jewelry. He is known for doing extensive research on ancient jewelry designs in order to create accurate pieces for historical films.

Joseff uses the best stones from Czechoslovakia and Austria. His skilled craftspeople work with wood, glass, tin, platinum, gold, silver, and precious stones, as well as plastics. He formulates a special antiqued gold and silver plating that doesn't reflect the movie lights. By using injection-molded acetate he reproduces carved ebony and ivory antique jewelry. For the very ornate pieces it's often necessary to use a plastic compound because metal would be too heavy to be worn. Virginia Bruce's fourteen-pound headdress in MGM's *The Great Ziegfeld* is made of pear-shape jewels of cast transparent resin. In the same film a chorus girl wears a $2,000 costume designed by Adrian that consists of a thousand pear-shape transparent cast-resin drops.

Eugene Joseff with jeweled armor he created for Douglas Fairbanks, Jr., in *Sinbad the Sailor. Photo by Seawell, Paul A. Hesse Studios, Hollywood, courtesy of Joan Castle Joseff.*

Joseff cleverly works out a plan to rent, rather than sell his jewelry, in order to maintain extensive archives. Over three million pieces are in the current rental library.

In 1937 Joseff develops a commercial line to be sold in retail stores, based partly on pieces he's made for motion pictures.

At his peak Joseff is producing 90 percent of Hollywood's jewelry for films. He is influenced by forms that occur in nature, as well as Renaissance designs. Seashells, flowers, and animals often appear as pins and earrings.

Joseff's untimely death in 1948 does not end his imaginative line of costume jewelry. His wife, Joan Castle Joseff, or J.C. as she is known, continues to produce and sell pieces to fine department stores in the United States to the present time. She does so well that *Fortune* singles her out as an outstanding woman executive, and in 1955 she receives a lifetime membership in the Women of the Motion Picture Industry. Her citation reads in part: "For the contribution she has made to the entire motion picture industry through her creative ability, conscientious research, and historical accuracy."

Old designs using the original molds and stampings, as well as new, often Renaissance-period styles, are sold today. The jewelry is cast and stamped from brass and hand-soldered and hand-set in the same way precious metals and real jewels are. The pieces that were designed on a massive scale in order to be visible to movie audiences are appealing to today's collectors. Not only movies but also television shows, such as "Murder, She Wrote," "Dynasty," and "Mission Impossible," have used Joseff jewelry. Jewelry is just 5 percent of the company's output; manufacturing precision parts for aircraft and missiles is the company's main business.

KENNETH JAY LANE

Kenneth Jay Lane's name is synonymous with glamour. His philosophy: "Elegance, luxury, and good taste never go out of style. I believe that every woman has the right to live up to her potential to be glamorous. I try to help her achieve that by creating affordable, beautiful jewelry that enhances her femininity."

Kenneth was born in Detroit and earned a degree in advertising design from the Rhode Island School of Design. Even though his experiments in jewelry started as a result of embellishing shoes with rhinestone ornaments, one leading manufacturer says that Kenneth has done more for the costume jewelry industry than any other designer. Some of the most elegant, beautiful women in the world wear Kenneth's jewelry—Jackie Onassis, Elizabeth Taylor, Audrey Hepburn, Nancy Reagan, the British royal family, and Barbara Bush. A leading expert in costume often calls on Kenneth to reproduce famous jewelry for exhibits at the Metropolitan Museum of Art in New York.

Kenneth was awarded the Coty American Fashion Critics Special Award for "Outstanding Contribution to Fashion," followed by awards from Neiman Marcus, *Harper's Bazaar,* and Tobé Coburn, as well as numerous industry citations.

Kenneth's personal style reflects the social world of the women who wear his jewelry, and he has been on the international list of best-dressed men for many years.

Taken from an interview with Kenneth Jay Lane at his showroom:

I knew very little about making jewelry when I first started. Mostly I fiddled around with making samples. At the time I was working for Genesco as the head of Christian Dior shoes.

I started my own company in 1963 and learned from absolutely everything I did. Sometimes my designs didn't take off immediately. In the early Seventies I started to revive Art Deco by "putting together plastic bits and stones." It took five or six years before anyone was interested in buying it. I persevered because I liked it.

I'm not very influenced by current fashions. Of course, if there are a lot of suits and jackets, they can take pins better than softer clothing does. I saw that brooches came back into style when young people bought them at thrift shops and found them in their mothers' drawers. They started wearing them in combinations on their coats. It's a whole generation that never saw brooches for sale in the stores.

Fashionable women, except for the Chanel days in the Twenties and Thirties, have always worn real jewelry. Costume was made for the couture houses to show with the collections, particularly in Paris, so they'd have very elaborate necklaces and earrings. I don't think contemporary fashionable women wore costume jewelry until I started making it. At first I made big, outrageous earrings. I knew many of the attractive women in New York—Chessy Rayner, Mica Ertegun, Diana Vreeland, who was always a friend, Dede Ryan, and others—and they all started wearing my earrings. Babe Paley and the Duchess of Windsor both wore lots of my jewelry. For an official photograph in *Vogue,* the Duke of Windsor was in kilts, and the duchess was wearing my big hoop earrings and long beads with rondelles around her neck. I made many pieces just for her.

Today, Brooke Astor wears costume jewelry because even though she has some wonderful fine jewelry, she has worn it for several years and likes new things now. Wearing costume jewelry makes a woman feel younger, particularly women who have had money and good jewelry for a long time and who like a change. Mrs. Bush is giving me such lovely publicity with her pearls.

Film stars wear a lot of fake jewelry. The soaps have been a big thing for the last several years, "Dynasty" and others. I supplied lots of them from my collection, from my Beverly Hills shops. Joan Collins is a friend of mine. In London there's a Ken Lane shop in the Burlington Arcade in addition to two shops that sell vintage costume jewelry. They have things of mine that sell for 300 to 400 pounds!

I find that the Chanel look is easy to wear. I first did her bracelets with crosses for a show at the Costume Institute of the Metropolitan Museum, at Diana Vreeland's request. I'm still making them exactly the same way I did then. I used the K.J.L. logo at the very beginning of my business and for about ten years.

My inspiration? I do whatever amuses me, even if it means I won't be following the trends.

MIMI DI N

Mimi di Niscemi, originally from Palermo, Sicily, from the same family as the famous jeweler Fulco di Verdura, is graduated from the Philadelphia Museum School with a degree in silversmithing and jewelry. While she is in school in the early Fifties, she studies ecclesiastical silversmithing with the renowned Dutch artist, Rudolf Bröm, who invites her to be his assistant when he teaches at the Wichita Art Association.

In 1954 Mimi enters a competition for foreign art students who want to study in Paris and, along with a German student, wins a scholarship to study for one year at L'Ecole National Superior des Arts Décoratifs, a well-known secondary art school. There she earns a diploma in silversmithing and jewelry and studies wrought iron, metalworking design, and rendering.

While still a student in Philadelphia, Mimi is hired to work for a manufacturer who has the license to produce Schiaparelli jewelry, where she learns the techniques of manipulation. When Mimi finishes school and goes to New York, she attracts the attention of Diana Vreeland, who introduces her to clothing designer Arnold Scaasi for the purpose of starting a jewelry company together. In the late Fifties, Mimi and Scaasi become partners in Jewels by Scaasi. Next Mimi works for Brania, a New York bead house, and for a while there is a Brania/Mimi di N label. In 1962 Mimi starts her own company, Mimi di N.

Mimi's concept is to start a company that will be run like a European concern; building a library of designs from which she can draw all the time. In her factory she has designs and molds and samples that accumulate year after year, in the same way that English or French, or other continental companies function. The designs are not created for one season and then discarded. Mimi creates a body of work, not throwaway chic. She produces what she calls "artisanal" designs.

Mimi di N talks about one of her favorite subjects—costume jewelry:

An original design is not a novelty, it's worth infinitely more than that; it's a minor work of art. I adore costume jewelry but I do not enjoy a flashy novelty. The philosophy of transiency is a merchandising and advertising gimmick. It's not a true workshop or artisan's type of activity. Someone who really works at something seriously puts a tremendous amount of effort and love into it. It's like Tiffany glass or the work of a Swedish silversmith like Count Bernadotte. It doesn't matter if the material is precious or not, clay isn't precious. It's what the artisan does with the material that counts.

There's a healthy trend in fashion now in America. Some of the better sportswear designers have adopted a theme, which is to use good fabric in a simple way, producing 'investment dressing'. There is a cumulative and longer-lasting philosophy behind it rather than the flashy, trendy, instantaneous, and then deader-than-a-doornail-in-five-minute method. By producing something well-made and beautiful, and intrinsically valuable in the way the materials are handled, and by using genuine fibers and fabrics, they have brought stability into the product and the market.

I aspire to and try to achieve the same philosophy in making jewelry out of base metals. It is beautifully made and could just as easily be cast in sterling silver or gold. The material has no bearing on the workmanship. My jewelry is polished, enameled, finished, refined, and put together by hand after the molding process. It has an 'investment' feel about it.

Costume jewelry is so indicative of the moment in time it is created. It evolves because, although the criteria for making the product remains the same, the interpretation of the product changes with the evolution of the era. Costume jewelry becomes a marvelous reflection of the time. Since glass, plastic, tin, and other materials are not as expensive as precious metal and real jewels, they allow the designer to exaggerate a bit and be more lavish without fear of exceeding the purchaser's budget. The designer can be more *au courant* and expressive of the period. Collectors enjoy jewelry from the past because they are truly mirrors of the moment.

Two distinct types of manufacturers are emerging. One is more distinctive and collectible because of the individual creator's own mark, vision, and type of design. The other is the skillful *copiste,* who makes copies and furnishes well-made imitations.

I predict more joyfulness in the future of costume jewelry! What was good about it in the past is even better now. It's always valid as a form and as an expression of the wearer. Humankind has always sought adornment, and costume jewelry is not as expensive as precious metals and stones and is an art form that will never die.

MONET

MONET

Brothers Michael and Jay Chernow start Monocraft in 1929 in Providence, Rhode Island, manufacturing metal monograms to adorn handbags. They rapidly develop a reputation for quality manufacturing, and frequently their initials outlast the merchandise they're attached to. In 1937, encouraged by their success, the Chernows begin producing jewelry with the same fine gold-plating their monograms have, and they call their new company Monet. Their goal is to make a collection of jewelry that gives fashionable women the look and feel of real jewelry at a reasonable price. It becomes the first jewelry house in the industry to have its tradename stamped on every piece of jewelry.

It's the 1940s, and Monet as well as the rest of the country is influenced by Hollywood glamour and the reality of World War II. Monet features bold chain links, amusing enamel pins, and equestrian motifs.

In the 1950s, when America's postwar youth is once again having fun, Monet's charm bracelets, poodle pins, and white jewelry perk up the young at heart.

Mini-skirts and hip-huggers of the Sixties look great with Monet's hoop earrings and bold drops, and their adventurous pins, pendants, and bangles enhance brilliant colors, prints, and ethnic motifs. In 1968 Monet is acquired by General Mills as its first entry into the fashion business.

In the quality-conscious Seventies Monet's multistatus chains, modern sculptural shapes, and authentic styling accent tailored designs.

Yves St. Laurent jewelry is launched by Monet in 1981 and is an outstanding example of "frankly fake" costume jewelry.

Monet now has three Rhode Island factories and still produces a high-quality product. From model making to hand-setting stones to hand-twisting bi-metal chains to final inspection, great attention is still paid to details.

NAPIER

Napier, the oldest fashion jewelry house in the United States, is founded in 1875 by Whitney & Rice in North Attleboro, Massachusetts. Its first products are watch chains, chatelaines, and silverplate matchboxes. The company is purchased by salesman E. A. Bliss and a Mr. Carpenter, and the name becomes Carpenter and Bliss.

By 1882 Mr. Bliss's efforts are rewarded with success, and when Mr. Carpenter retires, the company becomes the E. A. Bliss Company, moving to its present home in Meriden, Connecticut. There had been a New York office since 1883.

Miss America 1956, Sharon Kay Ritchie, with Napier's gift to the winner, a complete wardrobe of fashion jewelry. *Photo courtesy of The Napier Co.*

In 1893 the talented silversmith William R. Rettenmeyer, who had completed his apprenticeship at Tiffany & Co. and studied design at Cooper Union, joins the company as chief designer. The company has just become the first concern to manufacture sterling silver merchandise in Meriden, which is now known as "the silver city." Mr. Bliss travels extensively through Europe to research European fashions and to purchase stones, beads, and other materials to use in manufacturing jewelry. At this time the Bliss Company is a pioneer in the new field of fashion jewelry. When Mr. Bliss dies, his son William becomes the active head, continuing in the direction his father had begun.

In 1913 Mr. Rettenmeyer retires, and his son Frederick becomes the head of the design department. The following year James H. Napier becomes the general manager and director, setting off a tremendous period of growth, with new employees, new machinery, new products, and a big push for advertising and sales.

During World War I the company is one of the first in Meriden to turn over its plant to the manufacture of war materials, including bayonet scabbards, gas masks, trench mirrors, and vane braces. Again, in World War II, the company turns over its facilities to manufacture war materials, with contracts from every branch of the services. Since the company is highly skilled in doing precision work for jewelry, they specialize in doing the "impossible": bronze silver-clad bushings, flying boat landing frames, belt buckles for officers, stainless steel moisture traps, radar panels, and identification tags.

After World War I Mr. Napier is elected president and general manager, and the company becomes Napier-Bliss. Two years later, in 1922, in honor of his contribution to the growth of the company, the name is changed to The Napier Co. Upon Mr. Napier's death in 1960, Frederick Rettenmeyer is elected president and chairman of the board, and in 1962 John A. Shulga is elected vice president. He becomes president in 1964 when Mr. Rettenmeyer retires.

By this time the Napier line consists of more than 1,200 designs with two major line changes each year, spring and fall, with more than 50 percent new designs each change. The plant at Napier Park contains a press room where flatstock is blanked, drawn, formed, or swaged. In the wire bending department, bending, shaping, adjusting, and cutting take place. The soldering department performs both machine- and hand-soldering operations. Buffing and polishing are also done by both machine and hand, depending on the intricacy of the piece. The plating room plates copper, nickel, silver, gold, and rhodium. A lacquer room applies clear or colored lacquer to various pieces. The tool room creates and maintains tools, blanking forms, and embossing machines. Many inspection points between critical operations preserve the high quality standards. The Meriden plant is able to handle the total production of an item from its concept to the finished product.

In 1982 Mr. Shulga retires, and in 1985 Ronald J. Meoni is appointed president and chief executive officer. Napier is the largest privately owned manufacturer of fashion jewelry in the United States. Napier jewelry is carried by major department and specialty stores.

PANETTA

Panetta was started right after World War II, in November 1945, by Beneditto Panetta, who was originally a "platinum jeweler" from Naples, Italy. In Naples Mr. Panetta had his own jewelry store. When he came to the United States, he continued to work as a platinum jeweler in New York City. During the Depression he began making costume jewelry, using white metal. His two sons, Amadeo and Armand, who were born in New York, were always involved with jewelry—talking about it, handling it, examining it—so it was natural that when their father wanted them to learn a trade, they turned to jewelry manufacturing. Every day after high school they worked at learning to be jewelers.

From 1935, when he was graduated from high school, until 1941, Amadeo worked as a stone setter and model maker. His brother Armand set diamonds. After the war they decided they knew more about making jewelry than anyone they worked for, so they started their own company.

At first Panetta made sterling silver jewelry with hand-set stones. When sterling became too costly, they used white metal but kept their same level of high-quality workmanship and design. They found there was more freedom of expression in costume jewelry.

Everything is manufactured by Panetta on their premises in New York City's jewelry district and sold to fine stores all over the world. They've made necklaces, pins, earrings, rings, and clasps for pearls. Many of their designs are original copyrights; some are inspired by other pieces of jewelry they see in their research. The line has a conservative but stylish "real" look. Every piece of jewelry is signed "Panetta," the same way it was done in the Forties, often on the catch. There have been approximately 10,000 pieces in the line. Some of their current styles go back thirty years.

The design is carved directly into the metal, as in sculpture. It is not made first in wax. It takes about one week to finish a model; then castings are made from the original. When stones are set, Panetta takes care to match and space the stones carefully in order to maintain quality and give the piece a "real" look. Each stone, which is always first quality, is hand-set individually, as diamonds are. They use very strong gold and rhodium plating and take great care in polishing each piece. Rhodium is the "first cousin" to platinum and is actually more expensive than platinum.

Both Panetta brothers can do every operation in the shop: model making, casting, soldering, setting, and polishing. They set strict guidelines for quality for all of their workers. They say, "It has to look real or out it goes." They recently sold the company to one of their best customers in Japan, who knows the jewelry business well.

TRIFARI

Trifari and Krussman is founded in 1918 by Gustavo Trifari, Sr., and Leo F. Krussman. Mr. Trifari has been in the business of manufacturing bar pins and hair ornaments made out of tortoise shell and rhinestones. In the new company Trifari makes the jewelry, and Krussman sells it.

In 1925 Carl Fishel, a young hair ornament salesman, joins them, and the company becomes Trifari, Krussman & Fishel.

In 1930 the well-known European designer Alfred Philippe joins the company as chief designer. His work has been sold in Cartier and Van Cleef and Arpels. Through Mr. Philippe's use of multicolored Austrian crystals in wonderful new designs, Trifari, Krussman and Fishel become known as the "Rhinestone Kings." Stones are hand-set and made with the same workmanship as real jewelry, giving the pieces the look of the finest precious jewelry.

Starting in the 1930s and continuing through the 1960s, Trifari creates exclusive designs for Broadway productions, among them *The Great Waltz*, *Roberta*, and *Jubilee* with Ethel Merman. Sophie Tucker, Lena Horne, and Rosalind Russell wear specially designed jewelry by Trifari.

The famous "Crown Pin" is introduced in 1941. It is made of sterling silver and vermeil, with real-looking cabochons plus rhinestones and baguettes. It is highly collectible today.

During World War II Trifari produces patriotic jewelry, including pins depicting the American flag and the eagle, in honor of the American armed forces.

From 1942 to 1945 Trifari uses sterling silver in their jewelry collections because the metals that make up white metal are banned for use by private industry.

In 1953 Mamie Eisenhower commissions Trifari to design her inaugural ball jewels. For the occasion Alfred Philippe designs a triple-strand pearl choker, matching bracelet, and earrings. Three sets are produced, one for Mrs. Eisenhower, one for the Smithsonian Institution, and one for Trifari's archives. In 1957 Mrs. Eisenhower again asks Trifari to design her jewels, for her second inaugural ball. This time the set consists of a triple strand of graduated pearls with small rhinestone rondelles, a matching bracelet, and cluster earrings. Pearl drops extend from the bottom strand of the necklace.

In 1954, in a landmark federal copyright case, Trifari is awarded a judgment that establishes fashion jewelry design as a work of art, therefore able to be copyrighted.

In 1964 sons Gustavo Trifari, Louis F. Krussman, and Carlton M. Fishel succeed their fathers and witness a renewed interest in fashion, inspired by the young First Lady, Jacqueline Kennedy.

Hallmark Cards, Inc., acquires Trifari in 1975, and in 1982 Trifari acquires Marvella, which specializes in simulated pearls.

In 1988 Crystal Brands, Inc., acquires both companies, and in 1989 they join Monet to form Crystal Brands Jewelry Group, a division of Crystal Brands, Inc.

MANUFACTURERS' MARKS

Manufacturers' marks are usually found on the back of a pin, on the clasp of a necklace or bracelet, and on the clips of earrings. Often they are on a little tag that is soldered on or hanging from the back of a necklace. Numbers that are thought to be the stone-setter's imprint are occasionally stamped into the piece of jewelry. A loupe should be used to see the marks, because often they have worn away partially, or are too small to be seen with the naked eye, particularly the sterling- or gold-filled stamps.

The illustrations for this section are by Pam Smith.

*Coro pieces are also marked "Coro" in the same script as the "Coro Craft" mark.

43

De NICOLA ©

EUGENE

FLORENZA©

Hattie Carnegie

HOLLYCRAFT COPR. 1955

HH

KRAMER

*Matisse**

*Renoir**

Rebaje

PAULINE RADER

REGENCY

REJA

Nettie Rosenstein

Original BY © Robert

©
SARAH COV

Schiaparelli

SCHREINER NEW YORK

WEISS

*Renoir and Matisse are marks for the same company that manufactured copper jewelry in the Fifties.

BUILDING A COLLECTION

"People are addicted to it," states a prominent shopowner in New York City. It's fashionable. It's popular. It's exciting to collect. One astute collector sees costume jewelry as an important form of American art, not yet fully appreciated.

A well-known and respected collector talks about his collection:

About twenty years ago in London I happened upon a dealer with a great cache of 18th-century and Georgian paste, set in silver. I bought some and started wearing it for fun when I'd go out to the theater. Every time I went to London, I'd buy more because prices were so high in New York. About five years ago I was poking around at the Manhattan Art and Antiques Center and wandered into Rita Sacks's shop. There was the most extraordinary collection of costume jewelry, made by Schreiner, Hattie Carnegie, Trifari, Dior, and Coro, that she rented out for photography shoots and films. Then I went to Karasik Gallery and bought a large Hobé spray brooch with topaz and citrines. I was getting very interested in costume jewelry. I went back to Rita Sacks, and we talked a lot and I learned a lot, and became friends. Then I started buying pieces from her. I went around to all the flea markets and other stores in New York. Norman Crider, who has a wonderful sense of adventure, was an important source for good-quality pieces. Dealers at several Manhattan flea markets, such as Roberta Pankey (E. 67th St., W. 77th St.), Beverly Austrian (W. 77th St.), Elaine Bestmann (W. 77th St.), and Nancy Elby (W. 77th St.), are the most fun and the most knowledgeable.

By then I was out collecting all the time I wasn't working. I bought whatever was beautiful or had great design or was from a period that I liked and, most important, was in good condition. I have no patience for resetting stones. At some point I was "overflowing" and began to sell some pieces.

Since then my collection has become more refined and more specific. I particularly love the Thirties, Forties, and Fifties. I look for DeRosa, unusual Coro sterling novelty pins, Trifari that's beautifully made and looks like real jewelry, Miriam Haskell if it's exceptional, and unsigned pieces if they are very outstanding. A few weeks ago I bought a bracelet that needed some regilding. After I picked it up and brought it home, I noticed it had an "HC" inside a diamond shape, which is the signature for an older Hattie Carnegie piece. Neither the dealer nor I had seen it. That's the kind of thing that makes it all fun. Those old pieces of hers are very hard to find.

As Chanel supposedly once said, "The real jewels you have should look like costume jewelry, and the costume jewelry you have should look real." You can find something that has the design, the color, the workmanship of fine jewelry—every element that's beautiful and thrilling—but it's fake! You may pay $500 for it, but if it were from Tiffany's, it would be $5,000. There's a certain "chic" about costume jewelry. It has an intention that is not defined completely by the object. It's more extravagant; it speaks to people in a different way; it always draws people's attention. No one notices a tiny piece of precious jewelry in the same way that they see a large, important piece of costume jewelry. There's a sense of fantasy and a freedom in the use of materials that you don't find in real jewelry.

It's true that prices are going way up, but I recently bought something for $1,400 that I fully expect to make my money back on, and then some. When I buy, I'm interested in only the best pieces in any given category, and I'll pay a high price. If I sell them, I'm happy making a small profit. I make bigger markups on the low-end pieces. I usually buy from dealers in New York rather than seek out the original source.

I predict that pieces made in the Thirties, Forties, and Fifties by major companies are going to continue to rise in price. I imagine one of these days a major museum will mount a great costume jewelry exhibit, or something will happen that will make people focus on this area as an art. Eisenberg, Trifari, Coro, Nettie Rosenstein, Schiaparelli are all pieces that collectors will continue to want.

Unfortunately, there are many reproductions and fakes on the market today. People are copying the most famous creations of the best-known designers. Most dealers are aware of this and know what to look for. A new collector must go out and look at a lot of jewelry and educate himself or herself about the field. Learn the difference between a piece that sells for $60 and one that's marked $750.

Collecting costume jewelry is a pastime with many climaxes. There's always great excitement; and when a dealer calls and says he or she is saving a special piece for you, and you go there and lift the lid of the jewelry box, and there is an extraordinary piece that you wouldn't have dreamed existed, it's heart-stopping.

Norman Crider of Norman Crider Antiques, New York, discusses collecting antique costume jewelry:

You have to have a feeling for the old, a sophisticated level of taste to appreciate the workmanship, the materials, the design. Many pieces are copies of real jewelry, and they are wonderfully executed, which is why they have value today and why prices are going up. It's about the last area in the antiques business that hasn't yet been brought to its peak in value. There is still room for prices to go higher. There are collectors who will pay more for a piece made of pot metal than for gold and diamonds because it was made during a certain time period or by a sought-after designer. Take, for example, the Staret company, which made all kinds of funny things in the Forties. It becomes a challenge to the collector to discover everything the company made. He or she will pay an outrageous price in order to add a piece of Staret to the collection. At that point it's not about cost; it's about relating it to the others they have in their collection. It has nothing to do with the integral value of the materials used in the piece; it's the design and the era in which it was made that makes it valuable.

Right now the most collectible jewelry was made by Miriam Haskell, Trifari, Boucher, Eisenberg, and Hobé. For a new collector I recommend buying what you like, learning as you go, finding your own taste. You might find you like animals, or bracelets, or Chanel, or Schiaparelli—it could go in any direction, and it's all fun. Buy what pleases you, and in the process find out about all of the different styles and designers.

Before you buy something that seems very expensive, you should look around and compare prices for that piece if you can find it or something similar. I usually sell Trifari crown pins for between $150 and $250, depending on their condition and whether or not they're sterling. At the last show I did, there was a dealer whose collection of sterling Trifari crowns was priced at $400 to $500 each. At the end of the show the overpriced ones were still there, and I had sold many of mine. There is a small group of dealers who, either through ignorance or in an attempt to take advantage of buyers, put prices on things that are way out of line. Most dealers are professional, and you can count on their prices to be fair. It's a good idea to get to know the dealers in your city, and they will often work with you.

Sandra Boucher, jewelry designer, on collecting:

As a jewelry designer, it's difficult to suggest jewelry to collect. I create it, so I don't look at the past; I look to the future. During the war, in the first half of the Forties, there was no material to make jewelry. After the war, from 1945 to 1947, many Europeans came here, and there was a big renaissance in the industry. In the Fifties there was a basic elegance. The pieces were well made, well designed, well executed. I remember doing cover layouts for *Vogue* and *Harper's Bazaar,* and we had to take two pairs of earrings and solder them together so they would look special. Sometimes we would take a pin and use it as an earring.

I would recommend collecting Ciner, Panetta, Monet, and Trifari from twenty to twenty-five years ago, old Mazer and Jomaz (same company, now owned by Japanese), and Kenneth Jay Lane, whose jewelry is worn by many important women. If you want to collect something special, find something that cannot be done any more. Objects are not always collectible because of their beauty. The more expensive jewelry is often made better and will probably last longer.

CARE OF COSTUME JEWELRY

It's happened to every collector or dealer. We bought a beautiful amethyst and pearl Victorian-revival 1940s bracelet and necklace set at a flea market. As we unwrapped it from the tissue at home, the pearls fell apart, losing their outer "pearlized" casings, exposing the inner bead. Unfortunately, the jewelry had reached its "critical threshold" somewhere between the flea market and our apartment.

An expert in costume and associate curator of a New York Museum says that prevention is the key, rather than trying to repair something after the damage has been done. If a collector plans to keep costume jewelry more than ten or fifteen years, and it's been exposed to normal wear and tear and temperature changes that may affect stones, materials, and plating, certain measures should be taken to protect it.

Any extreme that any material is exposed to will cause expansion and contraction, from either heat or moisture. All substances that are incorporated into a piece are affected. If rhinestone jewelry that had an adhesive used in setting the stones is discovered in Grandma's attic, chances are the stones will be loose. Even if there's no evidence of it at first, it should be checked very carefully before it's worn or sold. When it's brought into a different environment, the change in temperature may trigger a loosening of the stones. Jewelry may be perfectly fine up to a certain point, and then whatever has been accumulating hits it. Changing the environment may just be the one factor that causes it to break down.

A noted conservator who works freelance for major museums observes that since people originally considered costume jewelry as a "cheap throw-away" in both manufacturing and buying, it has an "inherent vice" that can give it a time bomb quality. Sometimes the material will fail on its own, no matter how it is treated. Some of the early plastics were made with an unstable formulation, which is also true of early adhesives. Always check prongs, if they exist, to make sure they are restraining the stones in case the adhesive gives out. Pieces with adhesives should not be dipped or cleaned with water. If the electroplating is not done well originally, delami-nation of the outer plating can occur, or there can be migration of the precious-metal exterior plating (gold or silver) into the base metal. Rub-bing, through wear or by using an abrasive cleaner, can harm the thin coating. The metal parts of costume jewelry are actually damaged more easily than fine jewelry and require more care, not less.

Costume jewelry is particularly vulnerable to hostile environments. Lead was often used in its manufacture, making it susceptible to corrosion. Even something as seemingly harmless as storing lead-based jewelry in an oak drawer can lead to corrosion because of the interaction of the high-acid oak with lead. When pieces are placed in a closed showcase for storage, it must be determined whether the case is generating volatile acids that can harm the jewelry.

All metals should be protected from acid environments. Self-closing plastic bags are fairly efficient in keeping out moisture. Silica gel is a further protection from dampness. Some plastics, however, exude fumes. The best way to store costume jewelry is to cover it with a soft material, such as washed muslin that does not have sizing, starch, or surface finishes or acid-free tissue. Then either wrap it loosely in plastic or store it in boxes. Acid-free tissue is made of abaca fiber and does not interact with materials used in jewelry. To buy it, either contact your local museum or call Ar-chivart, Process Materials, Rutherford, NJ, (800) 631-0193. In addition to preservation, if a piece is wrapped in this manner and a stone should fall out, it will be easily found.

In general, don't wear costume jewelry on bare skin that's just been sprayed with perfume. Oils and chemicals in the perfume can cause damage to any kind of metal. When handling important pieces or ones that are designated to be preserved, use either white cotton gloves that are readily laundered (they can be purchased at photography supply stores, or pallbear-ers' gloves can be used) or plastic gloves that aren't treated with oil or lanolin-based emollients. In this way, no traces of body oils or perspiration are transferred to the various materials that make up the jewelry.

Natural body chemistry can affect all of the materials adversely. Plastic pearls or stones cannot take much abuse and are damaged by exposure to excessive light and ultraviolet rays, which can cause them to yellow. When glass is manufactured, it is produced under high temperatures, then annealed. If it is not annealed properly, it can fracture very easily due to internal stress. In costume jewelry, glass is cut and then polished, which adds duress to the stone. If it is annealed incorrectly and then manipulated, the stones can be damaged by a slight bump or even a change in temperature, so glass stones should be well protected. If a piece is harmed, it's a good idea to backtrack and try to figure out what caused it in order to prevent a recurrence. Incorrect storage, a hostile environment, or mishandling can lead to serious damage to a piece that cannot be replaced.

REPAIR OF COSTUME JEWELRY

To fix or not to fix is often the question. Each piece has to be looked at individually, and a decision has to be made about how damaged it is and what the collector is trying to preserve. From simply replacing missing stones to soldering, replating, or re-enameling, the answer depends on many variables. If a piece needs professional attention, see a professional conservator, who normally charges upward of $25 per hour. Contact your local historical society or museum for a list of conservators in your area.

The first rule is, don't buy it if it's broken unless you intend to wear it as is. The materials used in costume jewelry are more difficult to handle and more fragile than in precious jewelry, and repairs are more complicated. Generally, it is difficult to find someone to solder a broken piece of costume jewelry because repairs on base metal are risky. Replating can be done, but a good plating job can be costly because it is necessary to clean the piece thoroughly and check for failures in the original plating. Few people today do repainting or re-enameling, and it's very hard to match the original colors.

Costume jewelry now has two functions: adornment and investment. Today's rising prices verify that often it's not a casual purchase. Making major repairs changes aspects of the jewelry that may change the value.

After interviewing many conservation and restoration experts, we offer the following advice:

Always use a conservative approach. Look at something carefully before you do anything. For example, when cleaning a piece with an enamel finish, an

53

unnoticed chip can get caught and pulled off, ruining the enamel. Buy a loupe (magnifier) at either a jewelers' or photographers' supply store and use it to examine every piece.

Replacing missing stones is usually not a problem if it entails round, square, or marquis shapes. They can be found at hobby shops or, if you live in a large city, at a supplier in the costume jewelry wholesale district. An easy way to build up your own storehouse of rhinestones is to buy inexpensive bits and pieces of broken jewelry at yard sales or flea markets and save them for the stones. When you replace stones, be careful to match both size and color because, even with white stones, if a stone is too gray or too yellow it stands out and will decrease the value of the piece. Many dealers use cyanoacrylate (Krazy Glue®), which is not very good in an alkaline environment such as glass; so eventually it breaks down, and the glass stone will fall out. Epoxy is longer-lasting, although it tends to yellow. Better-quality epoxies discolor less. Two common mistakes are using too much adhesive and not cleaning it up properly afterward. Use acetone or a solvent after setting the stone to remove any excess. If plastics are involved, test the acetone on a part that doesn't show to make sure it doesn't ruin it. Do not use acetone on Bakelite.

To replace a stone use either a pair of jeweler's tweezers or wet the tip of your finger, pick up the stone, and carefully drop it into its setting, which already has a drop of glue or epoxy in it. For foil-backed stones whose foil has begun to erode, don't attempt to remove or replace the foil. When the original foil is in place, even if damaged, there is an indication of what the original craftsmanship had been.

For metal that is tarnished, first try polishing it by using a clean cotton cloth. An old, clean, soft T-shirt is perfect. A lot of dirt and tarnish will come off by just gently rubbing it. Use restraint, and don't handle silver too much. Don't use an instant dip; it might be slightly acid and harmful to the metal. If delamination of the plating has occurred and solution gets into that area, it can further destroy the plating and create corrosion. If for some reason a dip is used, wash the piece immediately afterward with distilled water and dry it thoroughly. Use a hair dryer on the lowest setting. Use the least abrasive silver cleaners. Baking soda or other abrasives can put tiny lines into the surface, which ultimately gives a buffed or satin finish rather than a shiny one.

When jewelry has a patina, it is a sign that part of the surface has oxidized; if it is removed, part of the actual piece is being removed. The more often an oxidized piece is cleaned, the more surface metal is being removed.

If a piece shows some corrosion, use dental tools, a loupe, and either an eraser or a cotton swab to lightly brush the surface and knock off some grains. Next, with a slightly damp cotton swab, use distilled or filtered water or alcohol and go over it again. Dry it at once with the other end of the swab. When using a cotton swab, keep one side dry and one side wet so that the piece can be worked on with the wet side and dried immediately.

Major repairs may change aspects of a piece that change the value. As collecting costume jewelry becomes more important and more highly regarded, the original marks of wear may add value rather than detract from it. In the future, as more superior and technically advanced ways are developed to repair and restore pieces, we may find that what we are doing today is irreversible. However, if someone buys a fabulous Forties pin to go with a new suit, it should be treated one way regarding storage and repair. If a person is interested in establishing a collection for investment, as a legacy for future generations, or as a donation to the costume department of a museum, a different approach should be taken. At this moment costume jewelry is making the transition from use to value, so a different standard of approach to preservation and restoration may have to be explored and adopted. Some pieces may transcend their functional or decorative use and be put away as collectibles.

Norman Crider says that he never re-enamels or regilds a piece of costume jewelry. He either doesn't buy a piece that's not in good condition or he leaves it in the state it's in. He doesn't think there's anything wrong in re-enameling if it makes the piece look more attractive and the buyer wants to wear it. Mr. Crider says costume jewelry is to wear and to enjoy. But when it comes to reselling it, it would be less valuable if it's been redone. He lets things keep their original patina, but he does replace stones, which are constantly falling out. Again, your point of view on repair depends on your frame of reference for costume jewelry—adornment or investment.

Note: Some manufacturers will repair or replate their own jewelry no matter how old it is. If a company is not listed here, contact its customer service department to inquire about their repair policy. Most manufacturers are in Providence, Rhode Island; Attleboro, Massachusetts; and New York City.

Napier
Customer Service
Napier Park
Meriden, CT 06450

Monet
2 Lonsdale Avenue
Pawtucket, RI 02860
Attn: Customer Service

Robert Lee Morris
409 West Broadway
New York, NY 10012
(212) 431-9405

Cluster Jewelry
125 West 45th Street
New York, NY 10036
(212) 382-0033
Berj, Robin, Kevin Zavian
(repair, reconditioning, appraising)

Trifari
Repair Department
3400 Pawtucket Avenue
E. Providence, RI 02915

FAKES, REPRODUCTIONS,
AND OTHER TRAPS

Recently we were at a flea market, and a very reputable, well-known vendor pointed to an enameled animal pin and told us that although it was unsigned, it was probably a Kenneth Jay Lane piece from the Forties. We gently pointed out to her that he didn't start his company until the Sixties, and in the Forties he was probably in elementary school. She was, deservedly, embarrassed. Knowing her reputation, we chalked it off to its being the end of a long day. Kenneth Jay Lane told us he once saw a piece of his at an antique shop, and the would-be seller told him it was from the Fifties. Kenneth remarked that it must have been from Mr. Lane's early period and laughed at his own little joke.

Very often even the most experienced dealer makes a mistake. What we are concerned with is the occasional person who will try to sell new, made-in-the-Far-East marcasite jewelry as old, or take a signed clasp from a Miriam Haskell piece and string on new pearls or beads and sell it as an original. While doing research on this book, we were told by more than one dealer that a company in California is reproducing "old" Eisenberg pins. Other dealers told us that the Joseff-Hollywood company is using the original old findings and reissuing the pieces. We have since found out that the Joseff-Hollywood company is indeed alive and well and manufacturing jewelry, using both the original castings and stampings as well as new ones. One dealer we know in Philadelphia sells them as new/old Joseff-Hollywood, being sure to explain the situation to customers. That's fine. It's the unscrupulous dealer or manufacturer that collectors have to avoid.

Many original findings and castings from the Twenties through the Seventies still exist in Providence (see the photographs and drawings of stampings in "Costume Jewelry Is 'The Look' "). Anyone can buy them or have the original dies restruck in any material, from brass to sterling silver to gold, and sell them. Indeed, a number of manufacturers we interviewed keep their most popular sellers in their line—sometimes for forty years! So what's a collector to do?

First and last, educate yourself. Study books with photographs and price guides. Go to all of the antiques shows, street fairs, and flea markets in your area. Ask questions. Get to know the dealers. Pick up pieces so that you get to know their feel and their weight. Examine the way the stones are set, the colors of the enamel, the manufacturers' marks. Marks change over the years. Joseff-Hollywood was stamped "Joseff-Hollywood" through the Forties, after that "Joseff." Hobé changed their logo approximately every twenty years (see the Hobé section in "Important Designers and Manufacturers"). Hollycraft and Christian Dior/Grossé stamped the date in each individual piece. Look at a lot of pieces made by the same manufacturer.

In an attempt to date his pieces accurately, we showed some pins marked K.J.L. to Kenneth Jay Lane. He said that one of them was never made by his company. It had the K.J.L. mark on the back, but the spacing between the initials was different, and something about the plating didn't look right. It was a subtle difference, one that we hadn't noticed until he pointed it out. Only by knowing the style of the period and of the particular manufacturer can you be aware of a similar situation.

If the materials or the workmanship don't look as though they are from the period the piece is purported to be from, investigate it very carefully. For example, if a seller presents a brass piece as being from the early Forties, there's a good chance that it's being misrepresented. It was illegal to use brass to make jewelry in the early Forties because it was reserved to make bullet casings for the war. We've heard that there was some black-market brass used, but it was minimal. That's why you see so many pieces made of sterling silver from the Forties.

Rhinestones from Czechoslovakia and Austria weren't imported here in the Forties, nor was there any jewelry from France and much of Europe. Celluloid and other early plastics used in the Twenties were much lighter and thinner than the Bakelite that was used in the Thirties, which again is much different from plastics used in the Fifties and Sixties. Only by familiarity with a design, material, or manufacturer can a collector begin to recognize a fake or a reproduction. If a piece is bought for adornment or decorative purposes only, its provenance may not matter too much. If, however, it is to be preserved as part of a collection or for investment purposes, its authenticity is integral to its value.

2

Costume Jewelry
Through the Decades

Miriam Haskell's first shop, 1920s, New York City. *Photo by Kenneth Chen, original photo courtesy of Miriam Haskell.*

THE TWENTIES

The Twenties—when the nation comes alive after a devastating war and women hike up their skirts, bob their hair, and smoke in public. In Paris, Paul Poiret bans corsets and petticoats. Chanel shows sailors' jackets and men's pullovers for women in her shop at Deauville. The new silhouette is long and flat without feminine curves.

Androgynous dressing is quite the rage. Women wear men's smoking jackets and affect short, short haircuts. They even wear men's blazers, shirts, ties, and cuff links with their pleated skirts. It's seen as the ultimate statement made by the newly emancipated woman.

Art Deco is launched in 1925 at the Paris Exposition Internationale des Arts Décoratifs et Industriels Modernes. The "wild years," The Jazz Age officially begins. The geometric shapes and brilliant colors of Art Deco permeate art, fashion, furniture, and industrial design. Skyscrapers reflect Babylonian ziggurats and stepped Mayan and Aztec temples. Jewelry designers have a heyday with the materials of Indian art—obsidian, onyx, rock crystal, and jade. They experiment with German silver, marcasites, pewter, and rhinestones. Noted designer Auguste Bonaz introduces a galalith necklace in 1923, and newly inexpensive chrome is used in combination with Bakelite and other new plastics for jewelry. Jewelry takes on the shapes of Art Deco motifs, simple geometric forms that overlap and repeat.

In fine art the Twenties spawns avant-garde movements in every European country. Picasso's Cubism, the Italian poet Marinetti's "Futurist Manifesto," and Holland's Piet Mondrian's Neo-plasticism paintings all echo the "modernistic" style. The interest is in the *new*. The Fokine ballet, Hunt Diederich's sculptures, Leon Bakst's costume sketch exhibit, the Gish sisters of the cinema, Edna St. Vincent Millay's romantic poetry, and Ziegfeld and his Follies have far-reaching effects. Fashion designers are inspired by Martha Graham, Paul Manship's *Salome,* Isadora Duncan's dancers in Paris and Greece, and Pavlova, who is pictured in a Gypsy costume. King Tut's tomb is opened in 1922, and it inspires Egyptian designs in jewelry for the rest of the decade.

In Paris, Chanel's to-be-legendary jersey suits and dresses are easy to wear for women who now have freer, more active lives. Women are shown in advertisements wearing tennis and golf outfits and driving cars! Pearl chokers, pearl and coral bracelets, and long necklaces are suggested for "sports costume and evening wear" in a magazine advertisement. Chanel accessorizes pleated skirts and sweaters with triangle scarves and chunky glass bead necklaces. Vionnet shows supple fashions worn without underclothing. In 1926 short skirts and beaded sheaths are worn for evening, as are evening gowns made of gold and silver embroidery with sequins over lace and chiffon. Designer Louiseboulanger creates an elegant chiffon dress, short in front and gracefully long in back. Shoes are made of black satin with cut-steel buckles. Longer skirts and the slim profile encourage women to wear long strings of beads, and they adorn their turbans and cloches with clips or brooches.

Before Chanel boldy mixes imitation stones with real gems, jewelry worn by the fashionable 1920s woman is mostly pearls in every variety of size and length, bracelets with links made of precious stones, and brooches, brooches everywhere. For evening loose strands of pearls are worn, with pearl-studded medallions that stop above the elbow. Long, dangling necklaces fill in plunging necklines and decorate bared backs. The demand for pearls is so great that Japan accelerates its production of cultured pearls for export.

After World War I women's traditional role changes drastically. They take over men's jobs and often stay in the workforce when the war ends. Heavy fabrics are needed at the front, so women get used to wearing lighter rayon and muslin. Lighter fabrics mean lighter jewelry. Women no longer wear gloves for every occasion, and rings become more important. Usually they're large pearls, combinations of materials in geometric patterns, and machine-inspired designs. By the end of the Twenties, jewelry evolves into large daring motifs with distinct outlines.

Bracelets are wide, and earrings are long. In 1923 hatpins decorate cloches. Women cut their hair short and expose their ears, hence the popularity of long, dangly earrings. In the late Twenties, earrings are so long they touch the shoulders. Sautoirs are now strings of beads in every material from wood to semiprecious stones. No longer are they worn just in the front; they hang down over the back, across one shoulder, or wrapped around one leg. The long necklaces that complement flappers' short tunic dresses have pendants and tassels that hang down to the stomach or even to the knees. The ups and downs of the hemlines in the Twenties create a constant need for new jewelry. Besides, the spirit of the day encourages women to look for excitement in something new and a little bit daring.

Brooches sparkle on hats, shoulders, dress straps, and belts. Sleeveless dresses stimulate great interest in bracelets, which range from four or five flat, flexible narrow bands decorated with rhinestones in floral and geometric shapes and worn on the wrist to bangles or slave bracelets worn several at a time on the upper arm. The elongated, sleek silhouette requires new-looking jewelry with simple lines, minimal design, and bright colors. Advertisements in fashion magazines show plastic cameos, rhinestone bar pins, and bracelets in white metal; artificial pearls of all lengths; and reproductions of Victorian jewelry.

From 1925 to 1929 what's chic is short skirts, short hair, cloche hats, fox furs, vivid colors, jazzy patterns, simplicity in evening wear, and rhinestone shoe buckles or satin T-straps.

Everything changes by the end of the Twenties. Skirts are long again, with a narrow silhouette and harder lines; colors are navy, brown, black, and gray, with fur trim on suits and coats. Hats are small and worn at an angle; handbags are envelopes or *pochettes* with gold metal clasps. Women are wearing Art Deco jewelry, real pendants, and diamond clips at each side of the decolletage. In 1929 Schiaparelli opens her salon in Paris and introduces "shocking," a bright magenta pink.

Twenties jewelry is not as collectible today as that of the Thirties through the Fifties. It's a bit delicate for modern tastes. What has survived are the rigid and flexible sterling silver or white metal bangles set with colored rhinestones—usually white, blue, green, and red—and Art Deco designs in necklaces, bracelets, pins, and earrings. The outstanding motifs are the rose; Oriental symbols such as pagodas, urns, and dragons; Egyptian designs, particularly in early plastics; delicate necklaces; and beads with tassels.

NAMES FOR COSTUME JEWELRY SUGGESTED BY NAPIER FOR THEIR SPRING 1929 LINE

Chrystobal—for chrysoprase and silver

Suntan—bronze finish, "an excellent tie-up with the popular vogue for being sun-browned"

Aloma—sapphire and amber effects; blues and yellow beige are leading colors for spring, blue skies and yellow sunshine, a tropical
combination

Hawaiian moonlight—jade and sapphire and jade and amethyst

Georgian silver—light antique silver finish

Contemporary art—"modernistic" effects

Asymmetric necklines—off-to-one side choker, "conceived to harmonize
with the out-of-proportion necklines"

Circular ruffle collars—filigree chokers to go with new dresses that have
ruffles or pleats

Solaray—amber and gold

Montmartre—amethyst and pearl combinations

Heirloom jewelry—same as amethyst reproductions

Vignette-filigree, ancient scrollwork—"giving grace to the severely simple dress creations"

Coral—pink for spring and summer

Capucine—color sponsored by Patou, contrasts with Chinese jade
jewelry

The

Laurel Wreath
Necklet

as presented by

Lucien Lelong

now on display

Signifies
A Triumph in Chic

Reproductions will be
available shortly

JEWELRY—FIRST FLOOR

Lucien Lelong necklet. *Ad courtesy of The Napier Co.*

Lucien Lelong Necklet. Laurel wreath, 1920s. $300.00–$450.00

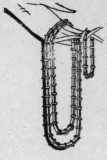

Lucien Lelong link necklace and bracelet set. *Ad courtesy of The Napier Co.*

Lucien Lelong Necklace and Bracelet Set. Barbaric tubular links strung on a coil chain, gold or silver finish, 1920s.   *$150.00–$275.00 the set*

Miriam Haskell floral-motif bracelets. *Photo by Kenneth Chen, jewelry courtesy of Miriam Haskell.*

Left to Right.

Miriam Haskell Wrap Bracelet. Large floral design made of seed pearls with a gold-plated filigree center with round white rhinestones and elongated seed pearls on the wristband, unsigned, 1920s.   *$250.00–$350.00*

Miriam Haskell Wrap Bracelet. Floral motif, turquoise glass beads and pearls on brass wire, gold-plated leaves, unsigned, 1920s.

$300.00–$400.00

Miriam Haskell Wrap Bracelet. Gold-wrapped wristbands with matching ball ends made of small white, round prong-set rhinestones in florets, unsigned, 1920s. $175.00–$250.00

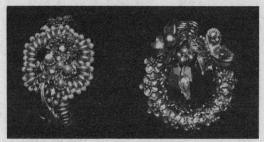

Miriam Haskell pearl wrap bracelets. *Photo by Kenneth Chen, jewelry courtesy of Miriam Haskell.*

Left to Right.

Miriam Haskell Bracelet. Large flower with oval pearls, florets with white rhinestone and pearl centers, oval pearls on the expandable mesh wristband, unsigned, gold-plated, circa 1920s. $450.00–$600.00

Miriam Haskell Bracelet. Large floral medallion, florets with seed pearl centers, central black cabochon with a flower and butterfly, oval pearls on the flexible mesh wristband, unsigned, gold-plated, 1920s. $450.00–$600.00

Miriam Haskell glass and Bakelite wrap bracelets. *Photo by Kenneth Chen, jewelry courtesy of Miriam Haskell.*

Left to Right.

Miriam Haskell Wrap Bracelet. Blue marbleized-glass center with coral glass beads alternating with pearls, two florets in brass leaves, star-shaped leaves, coral beads and pearl separators covering the wristband, unsigned, 1920s. $300.00–$400.00

Miriam Haskell Wrap Bracelet. Red, white, and blue Bakelite stars with Bakelite ball centers on a blue elastic wristband, unsigned, 1920s. $150.00–$250.00

Advertisement for Hobé ivory jeweled Thibetan [sic] pin, 1920s. *Photo by Kenneth Chen, jewelry courtesy of Don Hobé, Hobé Cie Ltd.*

Hobé Pin. Carved-ivory Thibetan [*sic*], bezel-set dentelles in a foliate setting, sterling silver, 1920s.   *$250.00–$400.00.*

Advertisement for Hobé "charm pin" chatelaine, 1920s. *Photo by Kenneth Chen, jewelry courtesy of Don Hobé, Hobé Cie Ltd.*

Hobé Pin. Chatelaine type with partially jeweled ornaments, sterling silver, 1920s.   *$250.00–$400.00*

Napier sterling silver bracelet and earrings, Hobé sterling floral pin. *Photo by Kenneth Chen, jewelry courtesy of The Napier Co. and Norman Crider Antiques, New York.*

Top to Bottom.

Napier Bracelet. Open cuff, crown design with bezel-set amethysts in a foliate-design wristband, sterling silver, unsigned, circa 1920s. *$750.00*

Hobé Pin. Leaves, flowers, and bows with large aquamarine center, gold-plated sterling silver, 1920s. *$400.00*

Napier Earrings. Overlapping circles with bezel-set multicolored stones in textured sterling silver, unsigned, circa 1920s. *$300.00*

Napier Earrings. Shield shape with bezel-set multicolored stones in textured sterling silver, unsigned, circa 1920s. *$300.00*

Napier Earrings. Fan-shaped articulated drops with bezel-set multicolored stones in sterling silver, circa 1920s. *$300.00*

Advertisement for Napier Art Deco, African, and medieval-inspired jewelry in *Fashionable Dress*, January 1929. *Courtesy of The Napier Co.*

Top to Bottom, Left to Right.

Napier Necklace and Bracelet Set. Square Premet link chain with an Art Deco pendant in brown and beige, gold metal, 1929.

$250.00–$325.00 the set

Napier Necklace, Bracelet, and Ear Drops Set. Ultramodernistic Molyneux design in jade and two tones of gold, 1929.   *$300.00–$450.00 the set*

Napier Necklace, Bracelet, and Earrings Set. African-inspired gold and tourmaline set with pendants, 1929.   *$300.00–$450.00 the set*

Napier Necklace and Earrings Set. Medieval motif taken from a suit of armor, polished steel, 1929.   *$250.00–$325.00 the set*

Advertisement for modernistic coral Napier jewelry in *The New York Times*, April 2, 1929. *Courtesy of The Napier Co.*

Napier Necklace, Bracelet, and Earrings Set. "Casanova Coral" beads in a modernistic design inspired by the 18th century, antique silver-finished metal, 1929.   *$300.00–$450.00 the set*

Advertisement for Napier Art Deco modernistic jewelry in *Giftwares*, August 1928. *Courtesy of The Napier Co.*

Napier Necklaces. Art Deco pendants on snake and herringbone chains, 1928.   *$175.00–$325.00*

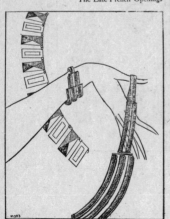

Advertisement for Napier geometric-motif jewelry, 1920s. *Courtesy of The Napier Co.*

Napier "Collarette." Open oblongs and polished pyramids of gold metal, 1920s.   *$150.00–$200.00*

Napier Necklace and Bracelet Set. Triple strands, stepping down to double and then a single strand in the back, attributed to Premet, gold metal, 1920s. *$250.00–$325.00 the set*

Advertisement for Egyptian-style Napier jewelry to appear in *Giftwares*, 1920s. *Courtesy of The Napier Co.*

Napier Necklaces. Gold cobra necklace, amulet necklace, and Egyptian-style beads, 1920s. *$175.00–$350.00*

Napier Bracelets. Art Deco links, snake chain, sterling silver, 1920s. *$125.00–$250.00*

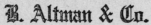

B. Altman & Co.

FIFTH AVENUE AT THIRTY-FOURTH STREET

TELEPHONE: MURRAY HILL 7000

A Very New
PARIS BRACELET

Sponsored by no less than three
important couturiers

Worth   Paquin   Agnes

Ladder links alternating gold
and silver finishes

Copies, $10.00

JEWELRY—FIRST FLOOR

Advertisement for Paris-in-
spired costume jewelry, 1920.
Courtesy of The Napier Co.

Unsigned Bracelet. Ladder links, alternating gold and silver finishes, sponsored by Worth, Paquin, Agnes, 1920s.   *$150.00–$225.00*

Unsigned figural celluloid and brass pins. *Photo by Kenneth Chen, jewelry courtesy of Charles France.*

Unsigned Pins. Group of celluloid animals on brass, all in bright painted colors on white, set with small multicolored rhinestones, 1920s.

$20.00–$30.00 each

Unsigned Art Deco clips and pins. *Photo by Kenneth Chen, jewelry courtesy of Terry Rodgers, New York.*

Left to Right.

Unsigned Pair of Clips. Art Deco, triangular, with white round and baguette rhinestones and jet beads in a geometric pattern, white metal, 1920s.

$60.00

Unsigned Pin. Large bird with pavé-set white rhinestones, green rhinestone eye, green and purple rhinestones in tail plumage, white metal, 1920s.

$75.00

Unsigned Pin. Arrow made of large clear rhinestones, marked *sterling 935, Austria,* 1920s.   *$200.00*

Unsigned Pin. Art Deco, frosted glass with square sapphire rhinestones in the center, surrounded by white rhinestones, white metal, 1920s.

          $68.00

Unsigned chrome and enamel "machine age" necklaces. *Photo by Kenneth Chen, jewelry courtesy of Muriel Karasik Gallery, New York.*

Top to Bottom.

Unsigned Necklace. Collar, red enamel on chrome with decorative turned posts, front closure with two red beads on a silver chain, 1920s.

          $575.00

Unsigned Necklace. Collar, red and blue enamel on interlocking chrome links, 1920s.   *$450.00*

Unsigned Necklace. Red and black enamel on chrome with turned spiral posts, 1920s.   *$400.00*

Unsigned Art Deco earrings and necklace. *Photo by Kenneth Chen, jewelry from the author's collection.*

Top to Bottom.

Unsigned Earrings. Art Deco, red and black Bakelite with chrome trim in a triangular geometric design, pierced earwires, 1920s.   *$65.00–$85.00*

Unsigned Necklace. Art Deco, square carnelian links alternating with blue and white enameled "clouds" on brass, 1920s.   *$150.00–$175.00*

Unsigned celluloid and rhinestone bracelets. *Photo by Kenneth Chen, jewelry courtesy of The Good, the Bad and the Ugly, New York.*

Left to Right.

Unsigned Bracelet. White celluloid bangle with red and white rhinestones, 1920s.

Unsigned Bracelet. Translucent celluloid bangle with white rhinestones in a geometric design, 1920s.

Unsigned Bracelet. White celluloid bangle with red and white rhinestones, 1920s.

Unsigned Bracelet. Translucent celluloid bangle with white rhinestones in circles, 1920s.

Unsigned Bracelet. White celluloid bangle with red and white rhinestones, 1920s.

Unsigned Bracelet. Translucent celluloid bangle with white rhinestones in a geometric design, 1920s.

Note: The celluloid bracelets pictured above range from $110.00 to $225.00.

. . . MORE TWENTIES

Hobé Pin. Diamond shape, blue central stone surrounded by large and small round blue dentelles, edged with round white dentelles, bezel-set in thin gold-plated rope curlicues, sterling silver, circa 1920s.

$500.00–$750.00

Kaywin Pin. Four vertical flower blossoms with pale blue enameled trim and florets with pink rhinestones, white metal, circa 1920s.

$75.00–$120.00

Unsigned Pin. Blue and red enameled kissing birds, yellow cabochon center, round white pavé-set rhinestones on the tails and wings, white metal, circa 1920s.   *$40.00–$60.00*

Unsigned Bracelet. Links of three rows of white paste stones in circles, swirl jeweled clasp, sterling silver, marked *S110,* 1920s.

$295.00–$375.00

Unsigned Pin. Small bird with black and white enameled trim on the tail and wings, round white pavé-set rhinestones on the body, sterling silver, 1920s.   *$175.00–$225.00*

Unsigned Pin. Taj Mahal with emerald green and white paste stones, sterling silver, 1920s.   *$150.00–$175.00*

Unsigned Bracelet. Channel-set sapphire and white paste stones in three rows, white stones in the center row, sterling silver, 1920s.

$225.00–$275.00

Unsigned Pin. Bar shape with a large central faceted red rhinestone surrounded by enameled blue flowers with green stems in a carved frame, 1920s. $50.00–$75.00

Unsigned Pin. Celluloid woman with an Afghan dog, painted blue and cream, 1920s. $75.00–$125.00

Unsigned Pin. Square pearlescent ivory celluloid with silhouetted scene of Venice, circa 1920s. $35.00–$60.00

Unsigned Bracelet. Round white pavé-set rhinestone links, sterling silver, 1920s. $125.00–$175.00

Unsigned Bracelet. Single row of blue square-cut rhinestones in flexible links, sterling silver, 1920s. $85.00–$125.00

Unsigned Pin. French, bar shape, two unfoiled green cabochons at either end, white frosted-glass center stone surrounded by marcasites, sterling silver, 1920s. $200.00–$275.00

Unsigned Pin. Yellow oval cabochon surrounded by round white prong-set rhinestones, circa 1920s. $35.00–$75.00

Unsigned Pin. Intaglio-carved glass rose, green enameled trim, marcasites set in the four corners, sterling silver, circa 1920s. $65.00–$95.00

Unsigned Pin. African drum player, black metal with white accents, 1920s.
$90.00–$120.00

Unsigned Necklace and Bracelet Set. Links of black onyx and crystal beads set in sterling silver, three teardrop, faceted-crystal drops on the necklace, matching link bracelet, 1920s. $275.00–$350.00 the set

Unsigned Bracelet. Small lozenge-shaped links with an enameled orange and black geometric design and a yellow dragon on each link, brass, circa 1920s. $25.00–$40.00.

Unsigned Bracelet. Small oval frame links with an oak leaf inside each frame, brass, circa 1920s. $15.00–$25.00

Unsigned Bracelet. Bangle with alternating blue and white square-cut rhinestones, safety chain, sterling silver, 1920s. $95.00–$110.00

Unsigned Necklace. Choker, various green glass beads, with jet rondelles and crystal, green, and black swirled beads, tiny white spacers, brass barrel fastening, 1920s. $35.00–$50.00

An MGM photo of Marlene Dietrich, 1930s. *Photo courtesy of The Lester Glassner Collection.*

THE THIRTIES

The Thirties glitter with glamour. Sinuous, bare-backed, body-clinging satin evening gowns are worn seductively by Hollywood's most captivating women. In Paris, Vionnet creates the figure-flattering bias cut and becomes known as the "architect among dressmakers."

Schiaparelli, the rebel, shows padded, squared-off shoulders in *Vogue* magazine in 1933. In Hollywood she dresses Anita Loos, Marlene Dietrich, Gloria Swanson, and Lauren Bacall. Adrian creates fashions for many of the most glamorous stars. Clara Bow has "it" in 1930, and everyone else tries to get it. Ginger Rogers, Joan Crawford, Greta Garbo, Vivien Leigh, and Bette Davis are filmdom's leading women. In Hollywood Greta Garbo's slouch hat, Katharine Hepburn's loose trousers, Joan Crawford's ankle-strap shoes, and Marlene Dietrich's men's attire influence women all over the country. Marlene Dietrich shocks *haute couture* when she wears a man's trouser suit on a film set.

People flock to Broadway to see Ethel Merman in *Anything Goes*. In Paris, Josephine Baker and Colette gather avid followers, and Eleanor Roosevelt inspires women the world over. Everyone's eyes are on Joe Louis and Jesse Owens. Salvadore Dali jolts the art world with his dreamscapes, and Fred Astaire is the epitome of the debonair gentleman. "Chain letters" circle the globe, African art is the new collectible, and dinner at the Rainbow Room in New York City is $3.50 with $1.50 *couvert*.

Sports clothes are designed for women, reflecting their newly active lives. Schiaparelli designs knitted T-shirts and blouses to wear with tailored skirts. She launches culottes and shows tweeds for evening, and her hand-knitted jumpers have African, Cubist, and Surrealist art motifs. In New York women are wearing denim wrap skirts. Nautical motifs appear on everything. Fabrics are covered with Art Deco designs.

For fashionable women the flapper silhouette is finished. The Chrysler tower, built in 1930, is "zigzag moderne." Art Deco jewelry is now mostly brooches and clips. "Mad little hats" and hats with brims folded back are worn with everything and go everywhere. In 1933 Patou shows zebra stripes that echo the infamous El Morocco's decor.

By the mid-Thirties skirts flare out gracefully from a slim waist and hips. Alice Marble wears shorts while playing tennis at Wimbledon in 1936, and the public is aghast. From 1935 to 1939 women are showing their defiance by their choice of clothing. In 1938 the fitted silhouette is popular, with wider shoulders, a more definite waistline, and a higher hemline that now brushes the knees. Colors are darker, and hair is either coiled at the nape or swept up. Hats are perched atop the head, and snoods control shoulder-length hair.

By the end of the Thirties, Balenciaga in Spain is showing broader shoulders, shorter skirts, eccentric hats with veils, and elbow-length gloves. Vionnet retires in 1939, and her pupil, Mad Carpentier, takes over her couture house, showing body-clinging satin and crepe de chine dresses without fastenings.

Costume jewelry becomes even more popular during the Depression. Established designers of precious-metal jewelry turn to costume jewelry out of economic necessity. They experiment with metals, plastics, glass, imitation stones, ceramics, enamels, shells, wood, and leather. Women are buying Miriam Haskell's ultrafeminine designs and Schiaparelli's whimsical creations, as well as rhinestones from the five-and-ten. Large rhinestone pins and clips are created to accessorize Eisenberg & Sons dresses, and women find them more appealing than the dresses themselves. Hobé uses semiprecious stones and sterling silver in floral and Oriental motifs. The well-known European fine-jewelry designer Alfred Philippe joins Trifari and creates real-looking costume jewelry. Joseff is creating fabulous, historically accurate pieces for most of the movies made in Hollywood and in 1937 begins producing a commercial line to be sold in fine stores. Marcel Boucher leaves Cartier and precious jewels to start his own company and designs his first line of costume jewelry.

Rita Hayworth wearing jewelry by Joseff-Hollywood, late 1930s. *Photo by A. L. Schafer, Columbia Pictures, courtesy of Joan Castle Joseff.*

Beads of all kinds are worn as long strings, often with combinations of colored rhinestones, beads, and pearls, à la Chanel. Black and white evening gowns are worn with crystal and pearl ensembles to match. Earrings are now studs instead of long drops. Curves and flowers are favored over the harder geometric lines of the Twenties. Every woman has to have an enameled flower pin for her favorite jacket lapel. Clips are worn on hats, at the end of the V in a V-neckline, and at each corner of a square neckline. These clips are often triangles set with clear or colored rhinestones.

Mrs. Carmen Cuminale of Jo Copeland wearing a dress clip pictured in the color section. *Photo courtesy of Raymond Cuminale.*

The "chunky" look is popular, rather than the delicate and dainty designs of the Twenties. Art Deco and Art Moderne still have a strong influence on costume jewelry. Schiaparelli designs necklaces, bracelets, and earrings of "silver latticework studded with exotic dark woods" and necklaces of ivy leaves with pearls.

There's great interest in African and Cubist jewelry in gold and silver plate, enamel, and tortoise shell. Pearl chokers, "Duettes," machine-age metal creations, bulky pins, East Indian influences, and even Gypsy coin necklaces are part of the "look" of the Thirties.

Coro Craft enamel-and-rhinestone
sterling silver Josephine Baker pin
and earrings set. *Photo by Kenneth
Chen, jewelry courtesy of Charles
France.*

Coro Craft Pin and Earrings Set. Josephine Baker, brown enameled face,
red and green feathers in her headdress, round, white pavé-set rhinestones
in alternating feathers and as accents on her headband and green enameled
necklace, matching smaller earrings, gold-plated sterling silver, 1930s.
$1000.00–$1500.00 the set

Coro flying goose pin and an unsigned fiddle-playing grasshopper.
*Photo by Kenneth Chen, jewelry
courtesy of Charles France.*

Left to Right.

Coro Pin. Flying goose with pink translucent stones, marked *Pat. No.
Pend.*, gold-plated, 1930s. $195.00–$275.00

Unsigned Pin. Green enameled grasshopper playing the fiddle, round white
pavé-set rhinestones on the fiddle and on lower *tremblant* legs, red stone
eyes, gold-plated, 1930s. $75.00–$100.00

Eisenberg Original bow and floral clips and pin. *Photo by Kenneth Chen, jewelry courtesy of Charles France.*

Top to Bottom, Left to Right.

Eisenberg Original Pin. Bow with large pink faceted rhinestones, small round white rhinestones, and small coral stones in dark pot metal, circa 1930s.   *$175.00–$225.00*

Eisenberg Original Clip. Floral motif with a large red faceted rhinestone at the base, red rhinestones and small turquoise stones in the flowers and small round white rhinestones on the stems, bronze-plated metal, circa 1930s.   *$250.00–$300.00*

Eisenberg Original Clip. Bow cascade with a large emerald-cut, pink faceted rhinestone, small turquoise stones and pink cabochons on the ribbon ties, with oval and marquis pink faceted rhinestones in prongs, marked *34*, pot metal, circa 1930s.   *$250.00–$300.00*

Eisenberg Original bow pins. *Photo by Kenneth Chen, jewelry courtesy of Charles France.*

Top to Bottom.

Eisenberg Original Pin. Bow with large white rounded, square-cut center rhinestone, pear-shaped and marquis white rhinestones on the loops, small white pavé-set rhinestone trim, pot metal, circa 1930s.

$195.00–$225.00

Eisenberg Original Pin. Bow with large round white-center rhinestone, faceted red and white rhinestones on the loops, sterling silver, circa 1930s.

$400.00–$500.00

Eisenberg Original Pin. Bow with large emerald-cut, white-center rhinestone, white round graduated rhinestones on the loops, small white pavé-set rhinestone trim, sterling silver, circa 1930s. *$400.00–$500.00*

Eisenberg rhinestone clip, unsigned Art Deco and rhinestone necklaces. *Photo by Jessica Michael, jewelry courtesy of Tania Santé's Classic Collectables, Miami.*

Top to Bottom.

Eisenberg Clip. Floral motif with green rhinestones and round white pavé-set rhinestones, white metal, 1930s. *$400.00*

Unsigned Necklace. Art Deco, green cabochons and round white rhinestone links, geometric-design pendant, white metal, 1930s.   *$180.00*

Unsigned Necklace. Rose faceted rhinestones in geometric links surrounded by round white pavé-set rhinestones, white bezel-set rhinestone spacers, 1930s.   *$450.00*

Advertisement for a Hobé heart bracelet, 1930s. *Courtesy of Don Hobé, Hobé Cie Ltd.*

Hobé Bracelet. Heart-shape links and aquamarines, sterling silver, 1930s.
$225.00–$300.00

Hobé sterling silver basket pin. *Photo by Kenneth Chen, jewelry courtesy of Charles France.*

Hobé Pin. Woven basket of flowers, with multicolored, bezel-set dentelles, marked *1/20 14K on sterling, Design Pat'd* (in circle), 1930s.
$375.00–$450.00

Jo Copeland rhinestone dress clips and a sterling silver crown pin. *Photo by Kenneth Chen, jewelry courtesy of Raymond Cuminale and Norman Crider Antiques, New York.*

Top to Bottom.

Jo Copeland Dress Clip. Round white rhinestones, green glass beads looped around two large unfoiled, white bezel-set rhinestones, unmarked, 1930s.
$75.00–$125.00

Pair of Jo Copeland Dress Clips. Bold curved design, round white pavé-set rhinestones and white baguettes, unmarked, 1930s. $200.00–$250.00

Jo Copeland Dress Clip. Tiny bug with pearl body, round white rhinestone trim and red rhinestone eyes, unmarked, 1930s. $50.00–$75.00

Unsigned Pin. Crown with round white prong-set rhinestones, florets on points, sterling silver, 1930s. $250.00

Jo Copeland Dress Clip. Floral spray, round white pavé-set rhinestones with large pear-shape white rhinestone tips, unmarked, 1930s.
$125.00–$175.00

Note: All of the dress clips in the photograph on the previous page belonged to Mr. Cuminale's mother, Carmen, who, along with Jo Copeland and Ann Sadowsky, worked for Patullo from 1928 to 1929. They left to form the Jo Copeland dress company, where Mrs. Cuminale worked from 1929 to 1939. The clips were designed to accessorize the dresses. For a brief time Lucille Ball worked for Jo Copeland as a model.

Advertisement for Joseff-Hollywood leaf pin at Bullock's, Los Angeles, 1938. *Courtesy of Joan Castle Joseff.*

Joseff-Hollywood Pin. Leaf motif, 1938.

$225.00–$325.00

Mazer rhinestone-and-pearl pin. *Photo by Kenneth Chen, jewelry courtesy of Charles France.*

Mazer Pin. Shield shape with round white pavé- and bezel-set rhinestones, large central baroque pearl, marked *Mazer Bros,* silver-plated, 1930s.

$575.00–$650.00

Miriam Haskell plastic-and-glass flower clips. *Photo by Kenneth Chen, jewelry courtesy of Charles France.*

Miriam Haskell Clips. A pair of red plastic flowers with red glass leaves, small red glass beads on brass wire, unsigned, 1930s.

$300.00–$350.00

Trifari necklace, bracelet, pin, and ear-rings set. *Photo by Kenneth Chen, jewelry courtesy of Norman Crider Antiques, New York.*

Trifari Necklace, Bracelet, Earrings, Pin, and Pendant (not shown) Set. Floral links with carved ruby rhinestone centers, sapphire cabochon rhinestone petals, round white pavé-set rhinestone trim in a Cartier-style design, marked *Pat. Pend. 61,* gold-plated, 1930s. $3500.00 the set

Unsigned enamel-and-rhinestone bird pin. *Photo by Kenneth Chen, jewelry courtesy of Norman Crider Antiques, New York.*

Unsigned Pin. Bird with large faceted clear blue stone body, painted red, yellow, and green tail and wings alternating with pavé-set white rhinestones, painted head, red stone eye, sitting on a black painted branch, 1930s.   *$185.00*

Unsigned Art Deco rhinestone sets. *Photo by Kenneth Chen, jewelry courtesy of Jóia, New York; and Muriel Karasik, New York.*

Top to Bottom.

Unsigned Necklace and Earrings Set. Art Deco, white rhinestones set in triangular, stepped, geometric pendants with matching drop earrings in white metal, marked *Made in France,* 1930s.   *$350.00 the set*

Unsigned Necklace, Bracelet, and Earrings Set. Art Deco, white rhinestones in stepped pattern with square, faceted aquamarine rhinestones in white metal. Matching pendant earrings are on a long white rhinestone drop.   *$750.00 the set*

Unsigned bracelet with rhinestone figures. *Photo by Kenneth Chen, jewelry courtesy of Charles France.*

Unsigned Bracelet. Glossy wide convex links with hand-set multicolored rhinestone figures, gold-plated, 1930s.   *$225.00–$300.00*

Unsigned marcasite bug and initial pin. *Photo by Kenneth Chen, jewelry courtesy of Mr. and Mrs. Frank Corio.*

Top to Bottom.

Unsigned Pin. Bug with a pink, faceted, unfoiled center stone, a green, faceted, unfoiled stone for the head, red faceted stone eyes, pavé-set marcasites, silver-plated, 1930s.   *$250.00–$300.00*

Unsigned Pin. Initials in a square frame surrounded by an Art Deco swirl pattern, all with pavé-set marcasites, silver-plated, 1930s.

$225.00–$250.00

Unsigned rhinestone-cluster pendant necklace. *Photo by Kenneth Chen, jewelry courtesy of Charles France.*

Unsigned Necklace. Five graduated leaf-shape cluster pendants with varied white prong-set rhinestones on a white metal chain (belonged to Carole Lombard), 1930s.　　　　　*$1000.00–$1500.00*

Unsigned and Trifari Cartier-style clips. *Photo by Kenneth Chen, jewelry courtesy of Norman Crider Antiques, New York.*

Left to Right.

Unsigned Clip. Molded ruby, sapphire, and emerald rhinestones with round white pavé-set rhinestones in "fruit salad" Cartier-style floral design, marked *Pat. Pend.*, silver-plated, 1930s.　　　　*$900.00*

Trifari Clip. Molded ruby, sapphire, and emerald rhinestones with round white pavé-set rhinestones and white baguettes in "fruit salad" Cartier floral and ribbon design, silver-plated, 1930s.　　　　*$750.00*

Unsigned pearl and glass-bead necklace. *Photo by Kenneth Chen, jewelry
courtesy of Charles France.*

Unsigned Necklace. French, multicolored glass beads and baroque pearls,
1930s.   *$175.00–$225.00*

Unsigned Bakelite figural pins. *Photo by Kenneth
Chen, jewelry courtesy of Only Yesterday, Hudson,
NY; and The Good, the Bad and the Ugly, New York.*

Top to Bottom, Left to Right.

Unsigned Pin. Two orange Bakelite bunnies peeking over a brown wooden
log, 1930s.   *$75.00–$95.00*

Unsigned Pin. Butterscotch Bakelite horse with a carved face and mane,
gold painted bridle, butterscotch boots and horseshoe charms suspended
from a brass chain, 1930s.   *$125.00*

Unsigned Pin. Butterscotch and red segmented Bakelite, Oriental man
with a painted face and shirt, brass fastenings on the shirt, 1930s.
                                                        $375.00

Unsigned Pin. Orange Bakelite carrots dangling on a brass chain from green Bakelite tops, 1930s. $450.00

Unsigned Pin. Clear yellow Bakelite (prystal) alligator with touches of green, red, and white paint, 1930s. $100.00–$125.00

Unsigned Pin. Cream-colored carved scottie dog with a painted red collar and glass eye, 1930s. $65.00

Unsigned Pin. Butterscotch Bakelite hat with cream polka dots, 1930s. $275.00

Unsigned Bakelite bracelets with geometric designs. *Photo by Kenneth Chen, jewelry courtesy of The Good, the Bad and the Ugly, New York.*

Top to Bottom.

Unsigned Bracelet. Cream-colored Bakelite bangle with black-rimmed cut-out holes, angled sides, 1930s. $165.00

Unsigned Bracelet. Cream-colored Bakelite bangle with black polka dots, 1930s. $275.00

Unsigned Bracelet. Cream-colored Bakelite bangle with black oval polka dots, 1930s. $265.00

Unsigned Bracelet. Cream-colored Bakelite bangle with a black geometric design, 1930s. $125.00

Unsigned Bracelet. Cream-colored Bakelite bangle with black wavy lines, 1930s. $85.00

Unsigned Bracelet. Black Bakelite bangle, carved flowers with yellow centers and yellow diagonal lines, 1930s. $225.00

Unsigned Bracelet. Black and cream-colored Bakelite bangle with a zigzag pattern, 1930s. $255.00

Unsigned Bakelite hatpin and two necklaces. *Photo by Kenneth Chen, jewelry from the author's collection and courtesy of The Good, the Bad and the Ugly, New York.*

Top to Bottom.

Unsigned Pin. Red Bakelite leaves with screw-tip pin for use on a hat, 1930s. $20.00–$30.00

Unsigned Necklace. Red, black, and ivory Bakelite strips on an ivory Bakelite chain, circa 1930s. $350.00

Unsigned Necklace. Stars and stripes of red, ivory, and blue Bakelite on an ivory Bakelite chain, circa 1930s. $450.00

Unsigned Art Deco chrome-and-Bakelite necklace. *Photo by Kenneth Chen, jewelry courtesy of The Good, the Bad and the Ugly, New York.*

Unsigned Necklace. Art Deco, chrome links with brown and green Bakelite rounded pieces in a geometric design, chrome ball separators, 1930s.

$225.00

Unsigned chrome-and-metal "novelty" pins. *Photo by Kenneth Chen, jewelry courtesy of Charles France.*

Left to Right.

Unsigned Pin. Chrome woman with a parasol, watering flowers, pastel enameled hat, flowers, and parasol, 1930s.   *$125.00–$150.00*

Unsigned Pin. Chrome train engine with red, white, and aqua stones, red and black enameled trim, 1930s.   *$150.00–$200.00*

. . . MORE THIRTIES

Coro Pin. Flower with white cabochon center, red enameled petals accented by white rhinestones, green enameled leaves, white metal, 1930s.
$30.00–$50.00

Eisenberg Original Clip. Flower with prong-set turquoise stone petals, pear-shape amber rhinestones and center cluster of prong-set white rhinestones surrounded by oval yellow rhinestones, white metal, late 1930s.
$350.00–$450.00

Eisenberg Original Pin. Floral design with white pavé- and prong-set rhinestones, black and green enameled leaves, white metal, late 1930s.
$200.00–$300.00

Hobé Pin. Floral design with round blue prong-set dentelles, two chain-link tassels, sterling silver, circa 1930s.   *$225.00–$300.00*

Joseff-Hollywood Pin. Flower with gray Bakelite petals, silver-plated, 1930s.   *$110.00*

Trifari Clip. Bird with round white pavé-set rhinestones, white metal, circa 1930s. $65.00–$100.00

Unsigned Clip. Cartier-style, shield shape, with a blue central cabochon, rope adornment with round white pavé-set rhinestones, edged with multi-colored prong-set rhinestones, 1930s. $125.00–$150.00

Unsigned Pin. Antennaed creature with red rhinestone eyes, painted red lips and trim, gold-plated, circa 1930s. $75.00–$95.00

Unsigned Pin. Reverse-carved clear Bakelite with green ends, yellow center, and spray of flowers, 1930s. $95.00–$125.00

Unsigned Earrings. Reverse-carved clear Bakelite buttons, flower in the center with yellow, orange, and green leaves, 1930s. $25.00–$45.00

Unsigned Pin. Bakelite hatpin with a screw-on fastening, two pointed, carved "wings," one butterscotch, one olive, 1930s. $15.00–$25.00

Unsigned Pin. Geometric design, orange and green Bakelite with three olive circles in the center, 1930s. $175.00–$225.00

Unsigned Clip. Shield shape, cutout geometric pattern of round white pavé-set rhinestones and white baguettes, pot metal, 1930s.

$50.00–$75.00

Unsigned Clip. Oriental queen's head, carved crown, large aquamarine rhinestone, white metal, 1930s. $50.00–$75.00

Unsigned Pin. Three birds on a branch, painted blue, orange, and yellow, round white pavé-set rhinestones on the wings and tail, red rhinestone eyes, white metal, 1930s. $50.00–$75.00

Unsigned Pin. Art Deco design, blue mirrored-glass center, gold-plated "wings," 1930s. $30.00–$50.00

Unsigned Necklace. Bakelite, large striped balls in black, red, yellow, green, and ivory on an ivory Bakelite chain, 1930s. $50.00–$75.00

Unsigned Pin. King's head with black enameled hair and beard, red lips, blue rhinestone eyes, crown with round red and blue rhinestones, cape with oval prong-set amethyst rhinestones, pot metal, 1930s. $45.00–$65.00

Unsigned Pin. Large floral branch with prong-set turquoise stones and large round white rhinestones, white metal, 1930s. $135.00–$185.00

Unsigned Pin. Small bird with round white pavé-set rhinestones, a painted red eye, gold tail and beak, gold-plated sterling silver, 1930s.

$75.00–$100.00

Joan Crawford wearing a Joseff-Hollywood necklace of multiple strands of bells, made personally for her, 1946. Inscribed "With a heart full of gratitude to Joseff for his many kindnesses to Joan Crawford." *Photo courtesy of Joan Castle Joseff.*

THE FORTIES

The Forties—the time when people's minds are on war, not on fashion. Women working in industry are wearing pants and snoods to keep their hair out of their eyes and away from dangerous machinery. Practical shoulder bags, short "Eisenhower" jackets, tie-belted coats, and shorter skirts are in style. The typical wartime look is square-shouldered, severely tailored jackets worn with narrow, short skirts that aren't just a fashion whim but a necessity caused by severe rationing of material.

In the war years of 1939 to 1947 women's fashions are static. Hats are the only interesting expression of individuality and the only item of clothing that isn't rationed. Women are working in defense, and the masculine, no-nonsense look prevails, partly out of necessity, partly from an emotional identification with the war effort. Turbans mimic the head coverings factory workers wear. Shoes are usually some version of practical lace-up oxfords with open toes or sling backs.

Some brave designers such as Charles James, with his sculptured looks and elegant ball gowns, Norman Norell, and Mainbocher continue to introduce new American styles. Pauline Trigère from Paris shows her first New York collection in 1942. Claire McCardell introduces the "ballerina look" and in 1946 shows the "baby dress" with a Napoleonic Empire line. She uses double stitching and a tubelike top and presents a wraparound coverall dress. In 1947 Dior launches his "New Look," which opens the way for truly feminine elegance. Unpadded, rounded shoulders, a defined bustline, and a waistline accentuated by slightly padded hips and a full billowing skirt that falls below the calves is worn with wide, flounced petticoats. In 1948 Lana Turner is "The Sweater Girl," and everyone's watching Dorothy Lamour's and Veronica Lake's newest movies. Flattering looks are coming back. Once again shoes have sexier high heels, platform soles, and ankle straps. Hats are small pillboxes.

In the early Forties there are no imports from France, and imitation stones from Czechoslovakia and Austria are rationed or cut off completely. By now 85 to 90 percent of the total jewelry manufacturing is done in Providence, Rhode Island, where workers are known for fine metalwork, and in New York. Brass is outlawed for use in the jewelry industry, being reserved for bullet casings, so sterling silver is used instead for stampings and stone settings.

Peter DiCristofaro of Providence says that virtually no jewelry is made in the early Forties. When manufacturers get their allotment of metal, it is sterling silver and is used to make figural sterling pins—dogs, horses, palm trees, sailboats, swordfish, owls, and penguins and heavy, bold pins for coats and suits. Women wear what they have saved from the Thirties. Factories in Providence are practically shut down because there are no men to work in them. When the workers return from the war, Coro, Lisner, Monet and others go back into production.

Sterling link bracelets, sterling pins with crystal "bellies," multicolored gold plating on sterling, snake chains, mesh, and chunky chrome bracelets appeal to the Forties woman.

Tailored clothing calls for something elaborate, like a showy brooch with matching earrings, bold sunburst and "atomic" designs, and heavy bracelets worn in groups. Oversize bow and flower pins and clips have a single large real or imitation aquamarine, topaz, or amethyst because the finer, smaller stones aren't available. Novelty jewelry made of leather, shells, and wood and little Disney character pins show up on sweaters. War-related jewelry such as flags, airplanes, and other patriotic themes reflect the nation's sentiment. By the end of the Forties dressy jewelry comes back to accessorize the "New Look," and pearls reappear in necklaces of all lengths with matching bracelets. There's a Victorian revival in evening jewelry.

Today some of the most collectible jewelry was made in the Forties. Large pins, chunky link bracelets, amusing enameled figural designs, as well as Cartier-inspired "real-looking" jewelry, are all sought after. Trifari, Hobé, Staret, Hattie Carnegie, Joseff-Hollywood, Ciner, Coro, Eisenberg, Marcel Boucher, R. DeRosa, Monet, Napier, and Nettie Rosenstein are some of the most important designers and manufacturers of the Forties.

Christian Dior rhinestone necklace. *Photo by Kenneth Chen, jewelry courtesy of Charles France.*

Christian Dior Necklace. Round white prong-set rhinestones in domed flowers, marked *Christian Dior,* France, silver-plated, 1940s.   *$850.00*

Ciner, Trifari, Nettie Rosenstein, Kenneth Jay Lane, and Coro turtles. *Photo by Kenneth Chen, jewelry courtesy of Charles France.*

Clockwise, Starting at Upper Right.

Ciner Pin. Turtle with a knapsack, blue and green enameled back, round white pavé-set rhinestones on the head, feet, and tail, blue pavé-set rhinestones on the knapsack, blue stone eyes, gold-plated, 1960s.

$150.00–$175.00

Trifari Pin. Turtle with a large blue faceted rhinestone back, round white pavé-set rhinestones on the body, legs, tail, and head, red stone eyes, sterling silver, 1940s.   *$100.00–$150.00*

Note: This pin was also made with an amber rhinestone back and blue stone eyes.

Nettie Rosenstein Pins and Earrings Set. Turtle family, each with large faceted-crystal back, white pavé-set rhinestone feet and head, red stone eyes, matching smaller earrings, only the largest turtle is signed, sterling silver, 1940s.   *$300.00 the set*

Kenneth Jay Lane Pin/Pendant/Watch. Turtle with faux lapis lazuli cabochons, white pavé-set rhinestones on the head with blue stone eyes, marked *K.J.L.,* opens to a watch marked *Geneva,* 17 jewels, gold-plated with silver-plated feet, 1960s.   *$200.00*

Coro Pin (Center). Large turtle with round white pavé-set rhinestones, red prong-set rhinestones in a ring on the back, red stone eyes and red enameled dots on the feet, silver-plated, 1940s.   *$350.00–$450.00*

Cini sterling silver pin and earrings set, Hobé sterling silver bow pin, Eisenberg sterling silver pin and earrings set. *Photo by Jessica Michael, jewelry courtesy of Tania Santé's Classic Collectables, Miami.*

Left to Right, Top to Bottom.

Cini Pin and Earrings Set. Floral cluster with black Bakelite drops, matching earrings, sterling silver, 1940s.   *$450.00 the set*

Hobé Pin. Bow floral design, aqua, pink, and purple bezel-set dentelles, sterling silver, 1940s.   *$350.00*

Eisenberg Pin and Earrings Set. Flower with royal blue pear-shape rhinestones, round white central rhinestone, round white pavé-set rhinestones around the petals, matching earrings, marked *E,* sterling silver, early 1940s.   *$550.00 the set*

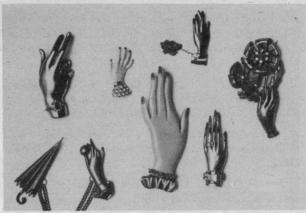

Collection of hand pins. *Photo by Kenneth Chen, jewelry courtesy of Only Yesterday, Hudson, NY.*

Collection of Hand Pins. Unsigned and Coro Craft, gold-plated, sterling silver, and Bakelite, 1930s and 1940s.   *$25.00–$125.00*

Coro "Duette" pins, unsigned double clip/pins, and a Trifari "Clip Mates" pin. *Photo by Kenneth Chen, jewelry courtesy of Charles France.*

Top to Bottom, Left to Right.

Coro Duette Pin. Flowers with large center topaz rhinestones, surrounded by round white pavé-set rhinestones, green enameled leaves, gold-plated sterling silver, 1940s.

Coro Duette Pin. Abstract swirls, moonstone centers in round white pavé-set rhinestones, pink prong-set rhinestones and pink rhinestones at the tip of each swirl, marked *Coro Craft, Pat. No. 1798867,* gold-plated sterling silver, 1940s.

Unsigned Double Clip/Pin. Flowers with pink and green unfoiled rhinestone petals, a white pavé-set rhinestone connection, green rhinestone centers, marked *Pat. No. 2.143.538,* gold-plated, 1930s.

Trifari Clip-Mates Pin. Art Deco, blue glass beads with dark blue centers, round white pavé-set rhinestone design, marked *Pat. No. 2050804,* silver-plated, 1930s.

Unsigned Double Clip/Pin. Art Deco flowers with coral and turquoise opaque carved-glass petals, round white pavé-set rhinestones, black centers with white bezel-set rhinestone, 1930s.

Coro Duette Pin. Feathers, pink round and square-cut rhinestones, silver-plated, 1940s.

Coro "Duette" pins. *Photo by Kenneth Chen, jewelry courtesy of Charles France.*

Top to Bottom.

Coro Duette Pin. Acorns with red square-cut, invisibly set rhinestones, round white pavé-set rhinestones on the crowns, white baguettes on the leaves, matching earrings, marked *Coro Craft,* gold-plated, 1940s.

Coro Duette Pin. Triplet owls, red rhinestone bodies, green stone eyes, round white pavé-set rhinestones on the heads and branches, marked *Coro Craft,* gold-plated sterling silver, 1940s.

Coro Duette Pin. Monkeys, large purple rhinestone bodies, purple rhinestone ears, glass bead eyes, round white pavé-set rhinestone accents, rose-gold-plated sterling silver, 1940s.

Coro Duette Pin. Carved ivory Oriental man and woman, coral and turquoise beads, pearls, 1950s.

Coro Duette Pin. Large birds, enameled red, green, yellow, and black with round white pavé-set rhinestones on chests, wings, and tails, marked *Coro Craft,* sterling silver, 1940s.

Coro Duette Pin. Lovebirds with spread wings on a white pavé-set rhinestone heart, pink unfoiled opalescent bodies, blue and green enameled tails, dark pink enameled wings, black beaks, red stone eyes, and white rhinestone trim, sterling silver, 1940s.

Note: The above double clip/pins range from $125.00 to $600.00 depending on their materials, workmanship, condition, and scarcity. Duette is Coro's name for a pair of clips that becomes a pin when placed in a device that has a pin back. Other companies manufactured them under various names, but they are usually known as Duettes whoever the manufacturer was.

Coro enamel-and-rhinestone bracelet, earrings, and "Duette" pins. *Photo by Kenneth Chen, jewelry courtesy of Flood's Closet, New York.*

Top to Bottom.

Coro Earrings. Flowers with red marquis rhinestones and white rhinestone centers, gold-plated, 1940s. *$65.00–$85.00*

Coro Bracelet. Tremblant flower links with white baguette rhinestone petals and red rhinestone centers, green enameled leaves with connecting links of red baguettes and round white pavé-set rhinestone trim, unsigned, gold-plated, 1940s.   *$300.00–$375.00*

Coro Duette Pins. Each pin has two *tremblant* flower clips that become a pin with a device that holds the clips together. The top pin has white enameled flowers and leaves, red marquis rhinestone petals with white rhinestone centers, round white pavé-set rhinestones on the leaves, silver-plated with gold-plated flowers and clip holder, 1940s.

$180.00–$250.00

The bottom pin has green enameled leaves, red baguette leaves, and white baguette petals with red rhinestone centers, round white pavé-set rhinestone trim, silver-plated with gold-plated flowers, marked *Pat. No. 1798867* on the pin, 1940s.   *$225.00–$295.00*

Coro Mexican-style bracelet. *Photo by Kenneth Chen, jewelry courtesy of Beverly Birks, New York.*

Coro Bracelet. Links of Mexican-style birds, antiqued silver-plate, 1940s.
$100.00–$150.00

Coro scroll pin and earrings set. *Photo by Kenneth Chen, jewelry from the author's collection.*

Coro Pin and Earrings Set. Horizontal scroll motif with large central faux amethyst, matching earrings, gold-plated, 1940s.   *$95.00–$135.00*

Coro sterling silver enamel "people" pins. *Photo by Kenneth Chen, jewelry courtesy of Charles France.*

Top to Bottom.

Coro Craft Pin. Mexican woman and son with enameled clothing in red, yellow, green, black, and white, round white pavé-set rhinestones on the water jug, gold-plated sterling silver, 1940s. $275.00–$350.00

Coro Pin. Mexican woman carrying a flower basket, multicolored enameled flowers and dress, gold-plated sterling silver, marked *Sterling Craft Coro,* 1940s. $275.00–$350.00

Coro Craft Pin. Egyptian man on horseback with round white pavé-set rhinestones on the horse's body, blue, white, and red enameled outfit, brown skin, black horse with yellow and green trim, gold-plated sterling silver, 1940s. $375.00–$450.00

Coro Craft Pin. Egyptian woman playing a musical instrument, brown enameled skin, bright blue skirt and black, white, and red touches, with round white pavé-set rhinestone trim, gold-plated sterling silver, 1940s. $300.00–$375.00

Coro Craft sterling silver lyre pin and earrings set. *Photo by Kenneth Chen, jewelry courtesy of Charles France.*

Coro Craft Pin and Earrings Set. Jeweled lyre, round white pavé-set rhinestones, red faceted rhinestones at the base, aqua marquis rhinestones at the center and top, matching smaller earrings, gold-plated sterling, 1940s.

$325.00–$400.00 the set

Eisenberg clips, pin, and earrings. *Photo by Kenneth Chen, jewelry courtesy of Muriel Karasik Gallery, New York; and Terry Rodgers, New York.*

Top to Bottom, Left to Right.

Eisenberg Clip. Vertical floral design, large white center rhinestones, round white bezel- and pavé-set rhinestones, sterling silver, 1940s.

$750.00

Eisenberg Clip. Large flower with round white prong-set rhinestones and small round, white pavé-set rhinestones, marked *E*, sterling silver, early 1940s. $550.00

Eisenberg Earrings. Large white pear-shape rhinestone drops surrounded by small prong-set rhinestones, marked *E*, sterling silver, early 1940s. $275.00

Eisenberg Original Pin. Large sheaf of flowers, white pear-shape rhinestone flowers, marquis red rhinestone leaves, white metal, 1940s. $775.00

Eisenberg Original Clip. Shield shape with varied clear rhinestones, white metal, 1940s. $375.00

Eisenberg Original Clip. Vertical design with a large blue rhinestone at the top, clear white and blue rhinestone cascade, white metal, 1940s. $525.00

Eisenberg Original rhinestone-and-pearl sterling silver floral clip, Eisenberg rhinestone-and-pearl sterling silver cornucopia pins and earrings set, Eisenberg rhinestone-and-pearl floral sterling silver clip. *Photo by Kenneth Chen, jewelry courtesy of Charles France.*

Top to Bottom, Left to Right.

Eisenberg Original Pin. Leaf swirl, large center pearl, a row of white pearls and a row of gray pearls with round white pavé-set rhinestones, sterling silver, 1940s. $350.00–$400.00

Eisenberg Pin and Earrings Set. Pair of cornucopias with pearl centers, round white pavé-set rhinestones and a spray of white bezel-set rhinestones, matching smaller earrings, sterling silver, 1940s. $575.00–$650.00 the set

Eisenberg Clip. Floral design with large teardrop pearls, round white pavé-set rhinestones and sprays of white bezel-set rhinestones, sterling silver, 1940s. $275.00–$350.00

Eisenberg Original floral spray and feather "comet" clips. *Photo by Kenneth Chen, jewelry courtesy of Charles France.*

Left to Right.

Eisenberg Original Clip. Large "comet" floral spray with oval white prong-set rhinestones, pear-shape white rhinestone petals and a square-cut central white rhinestone, 1940s.   *$275.00–$350.00*

Eisenberg Original Clip. Large "comet" with marquis white prong-set rhinestones in two feather shapes, a flower at the top with a square-cut central white rhinestone, 1940s.   *$275.00–$350.00*

Flag collection. *Photo by Kenneth Chen, jewelry courtesy of Marjorie Jaffe.*

Flag Collection. Pieces signed Trifari, Coro, Weiss, in various materials, mostly 1930s and 1940s.   *$20.00–$900.00*

Joseff-Hollywood Native American and seashell earrings. *Photo by Kenneth Chen, jewelry courtesy of Muriel Karasik Gallery, New York.*

Top to Bottom.

Joseff-Hollywood Earrings. Native American drops with feather headdresses, feather tops, antique gold-plated, circa 1940s. $450.00

Joseff-Hollywood Earrings. Scallop shell drops with a simulated pearl and round white rhinestones in a starfish, scallop tops, antique gold-plated, circa 1940s. $600.00

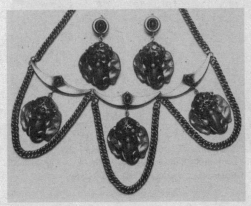

Joseff-Hollywood elephant necklace and earrings set. *Photo by Kenneth Chen, jewelry courtesy of Muriel Karasik Gallery, New York.*

Joseff-Hollywood Necklace and Earrings Set. Elephant pendants with multicolored faceted rhinestones and pearls in the headdress, red cabochons bezel-set in the crosspieces, matching drop earrings, antique gold-plated, circa 1940s. $2100.00 the set

Joseff-Hollywood bracelet and pin worn by Barbara Stanwyck in *Meet John Doe*, 1941.
Photo by Scotty Welbourne, Warner Bros., courtesy of Joan Castle Joseff.

Joseff-Hollywood Bracelet, Worn by Barbara Stanwyck. Leaf-motif links, each with a large center stone, 1941.   *$250.00–$350.00*

Joseff-Hollywood Pin, Worn by Barbara Stanwyck. Abstract floral cascade, 1941.   *$225.00–$300.00*

Joseff-Hollywood necklace, bracelet, and earrings worn by Jane Wyman in *My Love Came Back*, 1940. *Photo by Scotty Welbourne, Warner Bros., courtesy of Joan Castle Joseff.*

Joseff-Hollywood Necklace, Bracelet, and Earrings, Worn by Jane Wyman. Faux emeralds in floral settings, antique gold-plated, 1940.

Necklace	$500.00–$750.00
Bracelet	$225.00–$300.00
Earrings	$75.00–$125.00

Joseff-Hollywood pins and earrings set, worn by Marie Wilson. *Photo courtesy of Joan Castle Joseff.*

Joseff-Hollywood Pins and Earrings Set, Worn by Marie Wilson. Bee scatter pins and large flower pin, matching earrings, circa 1940s.

$350.00–$550.00

Joseff-Hollywood pin worn by Virginia Mayo. *Photo courtesy of Joan Castle Joseff.*

Joseff-Hollywood Pin, Worn by Virginia Mayo. Victorian-inspired bar pin with ornate pendant, chain tassels, antique gold-plated, circa 1940s.
$250.00–$350.00

Marcel Boucher sterling silver elephant clip, Hattie Carnegie mesh
bracelet, R. DeRosa sterling silver
flower pin. *Photo by Kenneth Chen,
jewelry courtesy of Charles France.*

Left to Right.

Marcel Boucher Clip. Elephant's head with square-cut, green faceted
rhinestones on the ears, round white pavé-set rhinestones on the head and
upper tusks, gold-plated sterling silver, marked *MB*, 1940s.

$300.00–$400.00

Hattie Carnegie Bracelet. Mesh link wristband with large center faceted
amethyst rhinestone, small round, white pavé-set rhinestones on the frame,
marked *HC*, 1940s. $225.00–$300.00

R. DeRosa Pin. Flower with large center faceted red rhinestone, small
round, white bezel-set rhinestone trim, gold-plated sterling silver, 1940s.

$150.00–$200.00

Miriam Haskell pearl necklaces
and a bracelet. *Photo by Kenneth Chen, jewelry courtesy of
Miriam Haskell.*

Left to Right.

Miriam Haskell Necklace. Triple strands of pearls with an ornate floral
pendant of seed pearls, rhinestone flowers, and leaves, gold-plated, circa
1940s. $325.00–$425.00

Miriam Haskell Necklace. Multiple strands of pearls and box chains, double floral pendant with seed pearls and rhinestones, gold-plated, circa 1940s.   *$350.00–$500.00*

Miriam Haskell Bracelet. Multiple strands of pearls and barleycorn chains with a floral clasp, circa 1940s.   *$275.00–$350.00*

Monet necklace, bracelet, and pins. *Photo by Kenneth Chen, jewelry courtesy of Monet.*

Left to Right.

Monet Pin and Earrings Set. Curved abstract floral motif, marked *Pat. No. 1967965,* sterling silver, 1940s.   *$100.00–$125.00 the set*

Monet Pin. Leaf motif, green enamel, gold-plated, 1940s.
                                                $40.00–$60.00

Monet Bracelet. Curved-scroll link bracelet, chrome, 1940s.
                                                $65.00–$85.00

Monet Pin. Oriental man with a tray of multicolored fruit on his head. Brown enameled face, yellow jacket, gold-plated, 1940s.   *$50.00–$75.00*

Monet Pin. Floral motif, pink enameled petals, blue ball design at the base, gold-plated, 1940s.   *$50.00–$75.00*

Monet Pin. Equestrian motif, horseshoe, gold-plated, 1940s.
                                                $45.00–$65.00

Monet Necklace. Equestrian motif links, gold-plated, 1940s.
                                                $75.00–$100.00

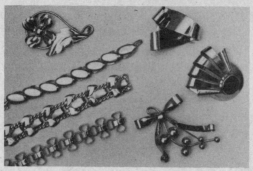

Napier sterling silver link bracelets and floral pins. *Photo by Kenneth Chen, jewelry courtesy of The Napier Co.*

Left to Right.

Napier Bracelets. Flat pellet links, ribbon links with circle spacers, abstract bow links on a double chain, sterling vermeil, circa 1940.

$200.00–$300.00 each

Napier Pins. Two flowers, two abstract "ribbon" designs, sterling vermeil, circa 1940.

$150.00–$300.00 each

Nettie Rosenstein sterling silver enamel rooster clip, Hattie Carnegie Bakelite rooster clip, Eisenberg sterling silver peacock pin. *Photo by Kenneth Chen, jewelry courtesy of Charles France.*

Top to Bottom.

Nettie Rosenstein Clip. Crowing rooster, orange and white enamel, round white pavé-set rhinestone trim, a red stone eye, pink-gold-plated sterling silver, 1940s.

$800.00–$1000.00

Hattie Carnegie Pin. Rooster with a red Bakelite head, yellow Bakelite body, black Bakelite tail, and a white rhinestone eye, sterling silver, 1940s.

$325.00–$400.00

Eisenberg Pin. Peacock with blue bezel-set rhinestones in the tail, a large blue faceted stone in the body, marked *E*, sterling silver, early 1940s.
$700.00–$800.00

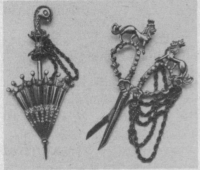

Nettie Rosenstein sterling silver "novelty" umbrella and scissors pins. *Photo by Kenneth Chen, jewelry courtesy of Norman Crider Antiques, New York.*

Left to Right.

Nettie Rosenstein Pin. Umbrella with bird handle, trimmed with round white pavé-set rhinestones and small pearls, gold-plated sterling silver, 1940s. $250.00

Nettie Rosenstein Pin. Scissors with lions on the handles, gold-plated sterling silver, 1940s. $380.00

Nina Wolf bracelets, pins, and a pin and earrings set. *Photo by Kenneth Chen, jewelry courtesy of the Costume Collection, Museum of the City of New York.*

Left to Right, Top to Bottom.

Nina Wolf Bracelet. Bangle with geometric circle design, unsigned, 24K-gold-plated plastic, 1940s. $125.00–$175.00

Nina Wolf Bracelet. Open braided cuff, unsigned, 24K-gold-plated plastic, 1945.   *$100.00–$150.00*

Nina Wolf Bracelet. Bangle with a vertically grooved design, unsigned, 24K-gold-plated plastic, 1945.   *$100.00–$125.00*

Note: Appeared in *Vogue,* October 1, 1945, and November 15, 1945.

Nina Wolf Bracelets. Two spiral twist bracelets, one with tiny pearls, unsigned, 24K-gold-plated plastic, 1945.   *$100.00–$125.00*

Nina Wolf Pin. Small gilded snail shell trimmed with turquoise glass cabochons, unsigned, mid-1940s.   *$75.00–$125.00*

Nina Wolf Pin. Gilded scallop shell with a faceted amethyst rhinestone circled by turquoise glass cabochons, edged with elongated turquoise stones, unsigned, 1945.   *$75.00–$125.00*

Nina Wolf Pin. Small gilded conch-type shell trimmed with turquoise glass cabochons, unsigned, mid-1940s.   *$75.00–$125.00*

Nina Wolf Pin and Earrings Set. Starburst with bi-level, stepped rays, a central star circled with rope, marked *Pat. Apl.,* gold-plated, unsigned, matching smaller earrings, 1945.   *$200.00–$250.00 the set*

Note: Appeared in *Vogue,* November 15, 1945.

Note: All Nina Wolf jewelry is a gift of William Wise (Nina W. Wise Trust) to the Costume Collection, Museum of the City of New York.

A note about Nina Wolf: We first heard about Nina Wolf when we went to see the jewelry at the Museum of the City of New York. She was a talented and prolific jewelry designer in the Forties who got wonderful coverage in all of the major fashion magazines. She did not sign her work, and although the gold-plated plastic bracelets are quite distinctive, we have not seen them in the antique marketplace.

Nina Wolf was awarded the American Fashion Critics Award by Coty in 1946. The year before, her designs were featured in advertisements for exclusive department stores in *Vogue, Harper's Bazaar,* and *The New York Times.* She made twisted metal loops, plastic spiral bracelets, chains, pins, and other jewelry from "chunky golden plastic with blue enamel-like decor."

The jewelry we photographed is made of gold-plated Lumarith, a Celanese cellulose acetate plastic. Ms. Wolf used stock extrusions fashioned in spirals and coils and combined extruded plastics with designs that were cut from sheet stock.

Besides jewelry, Ms Wolf designed innovative transparent packaging for Elizabeth Arden products.

R. DeRosa rhinestone flower clip. *Photo by Kenneth Chen, jewelry courtesy of Norman Crider Antiques, New York.*

R. DeRosa Clip. Floral design with large prong-set topaz and amethyst rhinestones, small round, white pavé-set rhinestones on the stem, gold-plated, 1940s. $900.00

Staret rhinestone-and-pearl squirrel pin. *Photo by Kenneth Chen, jewelry courtesy of Norman Crider Antiques, New York.*

Staret Pin. Squirrel holding a "pearl" acorn standing on an oak branch, round white pavé-set rhinestone trim, a red rhinestone eye, gold-plated, 1940s. $575.00

As Seen in MADEMOISELLE — August, 1948

Charm Pins . . . Wear them in groups of two, three, four on your suit collars and sweaters. Wear from desk to dusk, perched on a velvet neckband like Grandma used to wear. Exquisite little gems developed around amusing subjects close to your young heart. From $5.00 to $7.50 each at fine stores everywhere. Tax Extra.

Jewels by TRIFARI

Design Patents Pending

are authentic only if stamped on the back with the name Trifari.

Advertisement for Trifari "charm pins" in *Mademoiselle*, August 1948. *Photo of ad by Kenneth Chen, original ad courtesy of Trifari.*

Trifari Pins. Round white pavé-set and baguette rhinestone figural pins, blue enameled flower petals with rhinestone centers, gold-plated sterling silver and sterling silver, 1948.   *$50.00–$100.00 each*

Advertisement for Trifari sterling silver faux-moonstone and rhinestone bracelet, pins, and earrings set in *Harper's Bazaar*, May 1945, and *Vogue*, June 1945. *Photo of ad by Kenneth Chen, original ad courtesy of Trifari.*

Trifari Bracelet, Pins, and Earrings Set. Leaf motif, faux moonstones, red and white rhinestones, gold-plated sterling silver, 1945.

$500.00–$750.00 the set

Advertisement for Trifari starburst pin and earrings set in *Harper's Bazaar*, October 1944, and *Town and Country*, November 1944. *Photo of ad by Kenneth Chen, original ad courtesy of Trifari.*

Trifari Pin and Earrings Set. Starburst with large blue center rhinestone, red baguettes and round white rhinestone accents, gold-plated sterling silver, 1944.   *$150.00–$225.00 the set*

Advertisement for Trifari bow pins and earrings set in *Vogue*, October 1, 1946. *Photo of ad by Kenneth Chen, original ad courtesy of Trifari.*

Trifari Pins and Earrings Set. Bows with round white rhinestone trim, gold-plated sterling silver, 1946.   *$125.00–$175.00 the set*

Advertisement for Trifari sterling silver scroll pins and earrings set in *Vogue*, June 1944. *Photo of ad by Kenneth Chen, original ad courtesy of Trifari.*

Trifari Pins and Earrings Set. Pair of scrolls with large round red rhine-stones and round white rhinestone edging, gold-plated sterling silver, 1944.
$175.00–$250.00 the set

Advertisement for Trifari enamel flowers, "rhinestone encrusted," and a top hat, stick, and gloves pin in *Vogue*, 1940s. *Original ad courtesy of Trifari.*

Trifari Pins. Enamel and rhinestone flowers and a top hat, stick, and gloves pin, sterling silver, 1940s.   *$125.00–$225.00 each*

Advertisement for Trifari "lapel decoration" pins in *Vogue*, 1940s. *Original ad courtesy of Trifari.*

Trifari Pins. Flowers, fobs, a leaf, and a frog, pavé-set rhinestones and cabochons, sterling silver, 1940s.   *$125.00–$175.00 each*

Trifari sterling silver floral bracelet, topiary pins, and earrings set. *Photo by Kenneth Chen, jewelry courtesy of Muriel Karasik Gallery, New York.*

Trifari Bracelet, Earrings, and a Pair of Pins. Floral motif of faux rubies, sapphires, and diamonds in topiary pins, matching earrings and clasp of the open-design link bracelet, sterling silver, circa 1940s.   *$1200.00 the set*

Trifari sterling silver faux-topaz and rhinestone necklace, bracelet, and earrings set in the original box. *Photo by Kenneth Chen, jewelry courtesy of Charles France.*

Trifari Necklace, Bracelet, and Earrings Set. Links of faceted topaz prong-set rhinestones with tiny white bezel-set rhinestones, matching necklace and bracelet with floral earrings, sterling silver, 1940s.

$800.00–$1000.00 the set

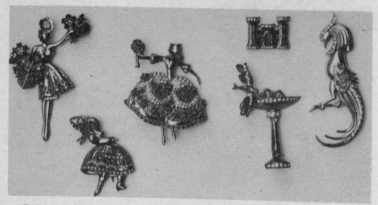

Trifari, Nettie Rosenstein, Coro Craft, Marcel Boucher, and unsigned pins. *Photo by Kenneth Chen, jewelry courtesy of Muriel Karasik Gallery, New York; Only Yesterday, Hudson, NY; and Terry Rodgers, New York.*

Left to Right.

Trifari Pin. Flower girl with ruby and sapphire rhinestone flowers, sterling silver, circa 1940s. **$900.00**

Nettie Rosenstein Clip. Russian dancing girl with blue, aqua, and white rhinestones in her skirt, a green faceted "jade" stone face, white rhinestones in the headdress, gold-plated sterling silver, circa 1940s.

$175.00–$225.00

Coro Craft Pin. Ballerina with tiny red rhinestone florets on her skirt with blue rhinestone centers, red and blue rhinestone bouquet, white faceted rhinestone face and white and red rhinestone accents on her skirt, gold-plated, 1940s. **$150.00–$225.00**

Trifari Pin. Castle with round white rhinestone trim, sterling silver, 1940s.

$110.00

Unsigned Pin. Birdbath with a fountain and bathing bird. Blue cabochons and round white rhinestone accents on the bird and birdbath, blue marquis rhinestones on the bird's wings, pink-gold-plated, 1940s.

$50.00–$75.00

Marcel Boucher Pin. Bird on a branch with a large plumed tail, round white rhinestones on the head, body, and tail, marked *MB*, gold-plated sterling silver. **$150.00**

Trifari and Coro "jelly belly" pins. *Photo by Kenneth Chen, jewelry courtesy of Jóia, New York.*

Left to Right, Top to Bottom.

Trifari Pin. Large bee with crystal "belly," round white pavé-set rhinestone trim, sterling silver, 1940s.   *$500.00*

Coro Craft Pin. Fox with crystal "belly," round white pavé-set rhinestone trim, gilded brass, 1940s.   *$650.00*

Trifari Pin. Small bee with crystal "belly," round white pavé-set rhinestone trim, sterling silver, 1940s.   *$250.00*

Trifari two-tone metal rhinestone flower clip. *Photo by Kenneth Chen, jewelry courtesy of Norman Crider Antiques, New York.*

Trifari Clip. Large flower with large pear-shape amber rhinestones, small round white pavé-set rhinestones and white baguettes, two-tone pink and yellow gold-plated leaves, 1940s.   *$1000.00*

Unsigned, Nettie Rosenstein, Coro, and Reja "faces" pins and a clip. *Photo by Kenneth Chen, jewelry courtesy of Charles France.*

Left to Right, Top to Bottom.

Unsigned Pin. African mask with pavé-set round white rhinestones in the crown and earrings, green, red, and blue cabochons in the headdress, gold-plated, circa 1930s. $100.00–$150.00

Nettie Rosenstein Pin. Ivory-headed Oriental woman playing the lute, gold-plated with pavé-set round white rhinestones, 1950s.
$200.00–$250.00

Coro Pin. Oriental man, allover pavé-set round white rhinestones with black enameled beard and eyes, green, red, and yellow enameled hat, 1930s.
$350.00–$450.00

Nettie Rosenstein Pin. Blackamoor, black enameled face, round green stones and round white pavé-set rhinestones in turban and breastplate, unsigned, 1950s. $250.00–$350.00

Coro Craft Pin. Woman with large yellow and brown enameled sunbonnet, flesh-colored face, brown hair, red ribbon ties, round white rhinestones, gold-plated sterling sterling, 1940s. $200.00–$250.00

Reja Pin. Blackamoor carrying a plate of pearls on his head, with black enameled face, turquoise stones in turban, round white rhinestone trim on sleeves and in eyes, gold-plated, unsigned, 1950s. $100.00–$150.00

Unsigned Pin. Woman with sculpted hair, round white pavé-set rhinestone face, bezel-set white rhinestone accents, gold-plated, 1940s.

$175.00–$250.00

Coro Craft Pin. Josephine Baker with brown enameled face, black hair, red trim on the feathers and necklace, blue cabochons at the feather tips, round white rhinestone trim, gold-plated sterling silver, 1930s.

$325.00–$400.00

Coro Pin. Genie with colored, varied rhinestones and white pavé-set rhinestone trim, gold-plated sterling silver, circa 1950s. $100.00–$175.00

Coro Craft Clip. Indian head with multicolored enameled feather headdress and band, multicolored, oval prong-set rhinestones in the headdress, band of round white pavé-set rhinestones, pink-gold-plated sterling, 1940s.

$350.00–$450.00

Coro Craft Pin. Nefertiti with brown enameled face, alternating band of round white rhinestones and red enamel on the elongated headdress, gold-plated sterling, 1940s. $150.00–$250.00

Unsigned, Coro, and Marcel Boucher enamel-and-rhinestone figural pins. *Photo by Kenneth Chen, jewelry courtesy of Flood's Closet, New York; Jóia, New York; Muriel Karasik Gallery, New York; Norman Crider Antiques, New York; and Judith Bumberg.*

Top to Bottom, Left to Right.

Unsigned Pin. Bird with a moonstone body, blue and black enameled tail and wings, red head, yellow beak, round white pavé-set rhinestones on the tail and wings, white metal, 1940s. $150.00–$175.00

Coro Craft Pin. Fish with blue and pink enameled fins, a blue and green tail, aquamarine rhinestone mouth, pink rhinestone eyes, and round white pavé-set rhinestones on the body, sterling silver, 1940s. $350.00

Coro Craft Pin. Bird with blue enameled feathers, yellow beak, blue face, and round white prong-set rhinestones in the tail, sterling silver, 1940s. $400.00

Coro Pin. Burgundy enameled tulip with green leaves, red baguette stamens, round white pavé-set rhinestones with red center rhinestone in the bow, 1940s. $350.00

Marcel Boucher Pin. Two birds and a nest with pearl eggs, blue and green iridescent enameled wings, green leaves, round white pavé- and bezel-set rhinestone trim, marked *MB*, 1940s. $1200.00–$1500.00

Unsigned faux moonstone and rhinestone swirl necklace and pin. *Photo by Kenneth Chen, jewelry from the author's collection.*

Top to Bottom.

Unsigned Necklace. Large topaz rhinestones, small round, white, pavé-set rhinestones in a swirled floral design, suspended from a flattened link chain, gold-plated, 1940s. $85.00–$125.00

Unsigned Pin. Large blue faux cabochon moonstones and white faceted, emerald-cut rhinestones, small round, white, pavé-set rhinestones in a swirled design, two-tone gold-plated, 1940s.   *$75.00–$100.00*

Unsigned enamel parrot clip and Garden of Eden pin, Coro sterling silver frog pin, and Trifari treble clef pin. *Photo by Kenneth Chen, jewelry courtesy of Norman Crider Antiques, New York.*

Top to Bottom, Left to Right.

Unsigned Clip. Parrot with aqua, yellow, and red iridescent enameled feathers, round white pavé-set rhinestones on the chest and tail, silver-plated, circa 1940s.   *$165.00*

Unsigned Pin. Garden of Eden, serpent has green rhinestones, a red rhine-stone eye, black tail, green enameled leaves, red apples, circa 1940s.
          $275.00

Coro Craft Pin. Green enameled frog with a gray stone eye, on lily pads with white pavé-set rhinestones, yellow and red enameled cat-o'-nine-tails, sterling silver, 1950s.   *$250.00*

Trifari Pin. Treble clef with red and blue cabochons, white pavé-set rhine-stones and an enameled staff, 1950s.   *$250.00*

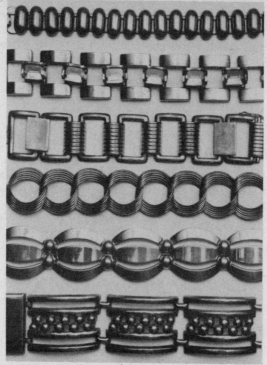

Unsigned metal link bracelets. *Photo by Kenneth Chen, jewelry courtesy of Terry Rodgers, New York.*

Top to Bottom.

Unsigned Bracelet. Pellet-shape links, brass, late 1940s.   *$40.00*

Unsigned Bracelet. Square links with square, faceted amber stones between them, silver-plated, 1940s.   *$50.00*

Unsigned Bracelet. Square links with ribbed spacers; the closing is a pin that fits into a holder, attached with a chain, brass, late 1940s.   *$60.00*

Unsigned Bracelet. Oval links of six hammered wires, marked 1/20 12K GF, 1940s.   *$55.00*

Unsigned Bracelet. Oval links with two balls between, brass, late 1940s.   *$45.00*

Unsigned Bracelet. Cast links with bar and geometric ball design, gold-plated, 1940s.   *$48.00*

Unsigned "South of the Border" and other tropical pins. *Photo by Kenneth Chen, jewelry courtesy of Only Yesterday, Hudson, NY.*

Top to Bottom, Left to Right.

Unsigned Pin. Mexican in sombrero sitting under a palm tree, painted green, red, and yellow plastic with rhinestone coconuts, 1940s.

$20.00–$30.00

Unsigned Pin. Palm tree with green enameled leaves, yellow and brown birds, marcasites in sterling silver, marked *Pat. No. 0108229,* 1940s.

$90.00–$110.00

Unsigned Pin. Palm trees, green plastic with yellow and brown painted leaves and trunk, 1940s. $15.00–$25.00

Unsigned Pin. Swordfish, white metal, 1940s. $10.00–$15.00

Unsigned Pin. Palm tree, white metal, 1940s. $10.00–$20.00

Unsigned Pin. Palm trees, enameled green and brown leaves, trunk, and ground, brass, late 1940s. $20.00–$30.00

Norma Pin. Mermaid with looking glass, red rhinestone in her hair, sterling silver, marked *Pat. Pen.,* 1940s. $45.00–$65.00

Unsigned Pin. Palm trees with green enameled leaves, blue enameled birds in flight in double oval frame, brass, late 1940s. $25.00–$35.00

Unsigned Pin. Mexican in sombrero with water jugs, enameled yellow hat and jugs, red serape, black boots, round white pavé-set rhinestone trim, silver-plated, 1940s.   *$30.00–$50.00*

Unsigned Pin. Mexican with sombrero and hoop earrings, red and black enameled trim and scarf, brass, late 1940s.   *$15.00–$25.00*

Unsigned Pin. Mexican playing guitar with yellow and red enameled sombrero, yellow, red, and black serape, blue trousers, black shoes, gold-plated metal, 1940s.   *$10.00–$25.00*

Unsigned Pin. Tremblant cowboy on horseback, red enameled outfit, black horse with a white rhinestone eye, silver-plated metal, 1940s.

$20.00–$30.00

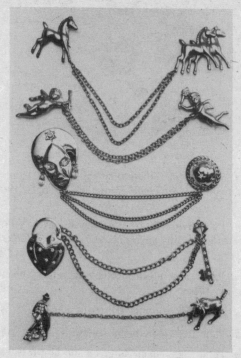

Unsigned chatelaines, or "sweater pins." *Photo by Kenneth Chen, jewelry courtesy of Only Yesterday, Hudson, NY.*

Unsigned Pins. Figural pins attached by a chain, some with rhinestone trim, silver, gold, and pink-gold-plated, 1940s.   *$15.00–$35.00*

LIST OF COLOR PLATES

Plate 1. Madame Gripoix necklace. Pink faux rose quartz beads, rhinestone rondelles, green crystal beads, green tracery carved glass pendant, unsigned, 1920s, $1500.00–$2000.00.

Plate 2. Left to right. Unsigned necklace. Large blue, oval, faceted, unfoiled rhinestones, geometric chain of round, baguette, and semi-circle white rhinestones, pendant ends in an oval blue rhinestone, sterling silver, 1920s, $300.00.

Unsigned necklace. Art Deco chrome and blue cabochons in a geometric design, chrome and blue ball and flat alternating link chain, 1920s, $135.00.

Unsigned necklace (bottom). Square-cut white rhinestone chain, triple strands of red glass beads, red glass floral carved pieces, and square-cut white rhinestones; clasp has bead and baguette drops, sterling silver, 1920s, $300.00.

Plate 3. Top to bottom. Unsigned pin. Oriental motif with an urn, pagoda, and dragon; round, white, pavé-set rhinestones, and red, green, and black enamel trim, silver-plated, 1920s, $48.00.

Unsigned pin. Oriental motif, pagoda and tree with green and black enamel; round, white, pavé-set and baguette rhinestones, silver-plated, 1920s, $175.00.

Unsigned pin. Bow tie with round, white, pavé-set rhinestones and red baguettes, sterling silver, 1920s, $135.00.

Unsigned pin. Red enameled roses with green leaves in a vase with round, white, pavé-set rhinestones, black enameled handles, silver-plated, 1920s, $110.00.

Unsigned bracelet. Flexible links of green, square-cut rhinestones and round, white rhinestones, sterling silver, 1920s, $140.00.

Unsigned bracelet. Flexible links of red and white round rhinestones, sterling silver, 1920s, $225.00.

Unsigned bracelet. Geometric floral links, round, white rhinestones, sterling silver, 1920s, $75.00.

Plate 4. Unsigned necklace. Papier-mâché pears and apples in shades of red and yellow, 1920s, $250.00.

Plate 5. Chanel necklace. Floret links with raspberry, amethyst, and emerald glass beads and baroque pearls, separated by green glass beads and pearls, unsigned, marked *Made in France,* white metal, 1930s, $1150.00.

Plate 6. Hobé necklace and earrings set. Foliate pendants of unfoiled pink, blue, citrine, and white dentelles in twisted curlicues of brass wire, jeweled chain and clasp, 1930s, $150.00–$200.00 the set.

Plate 7. Left to right, top to bottom. Unsigned bracelet. Clear, hinged Bakelite bangle with red and black diagonal stripes, carved, 1930s, $175.00.

Unsigned bracelet. Cream-colored Bakelite bangle, heavily carved, 1930s, $225.00.

Unsigned bracelet. Butterscotch carved bangle with rising sun motif, 1930s, $275.00.

Unsigned bracelet. Green carved rope twist Bakelite bangle, 1930s. $75.00–$100.00.

Unsigned pin. Red carved Bakelite horse with brass trim, 1930s, $225.00.

Unsigned clip. Bakelite, geometric design in red, yellow, blue, green, orange, and cream, 1930s, $125.00.

Unsigned earrings. Butterscotch geometric, faceted Bakelite, 1930s, $30.00–$45.00.

Unsigned pin. Red Bakelite cherries with a Bakelite chain, 1930s, $175.00–$195.00.

Unsigned pin. Bakelite Buddha temple, red with brass Buddha and trim, 1930s, $295.00.

Plate 8. Top to bottom, left to right. Jo Copeland dress clips. Pair of Art Deco clips, shield shape with oval, blue rhinestones and white, triangular rhinestones, unsigned, white metal, 1930s, $175.00–$225.00 the pair.

Jo Copeland dress ornaments. Pair of sew-on bows with large blue center cabochons, round, white, pavé-set rhinestones, white metal, unsigned, 1930s, $75.00–$100.00 the pair.

Jo Copeland necklace. Art Deco pendant of blue glass beads, channel-set white rhinestones, necklace has blue glass beads, white rhinestone rondelles, rhinestone barrel clasp, unsigned, 1930s, $225.00–$275.00.

Jo Copeland dress clip. Art Deco fan-shape clip with large red cabochons, round, white, pavé-set rhinestones, unsigned, white metal, 1930s, $125.00–$175.00.

Jo Copeland dress clip. Flower and leaf motif, square, red glass beads, round, white, pavé-set rhinestones, unsigned, gold-plated, 1930s, $125.00–$175.00.

Plate 9. Top to bottom. Miriam Haskell necklace and bracelet set. Double-strand choker, freshwater pearls and pink glass beads in a circle and star pattern, matching bracelet, circa 1940s, $750.00–$950.00 the set.

Miriam Haskell necklace. Hand-formed pink glass leaves by Madame Gripoix with seed pearl clusters on a gold-plated chain, circa 1930s, $800.00–$1000.00.

Plate 10. Left to right, top to bottom. Marcel Boucher pin. Red enameled strawberries, green stem, yellow and white flower, marked *MB*, silver-plated, circa 1940s, $75.00–$125.00.

Marcel Boucher pin. Red enameled chili peppers with iridescent green leaves, round, white, pavé-set rhinestones on insides of the leaves, marked *Des.Pat'd, MB*, silver-plated, 1940s, $225.00–$300.00.

Marcel Boucher pin. Orange iridescent enameled pineapple with iridescent green leaves, round, white, pavé-set rhinestones on insides of the leaves, marked *Des. Pat'd., MB*, silver-plated, 1940s, $275.00–$350.00.

Marcel Boucher pin. Mexican with a sombrero and serape, iridescent enameled red, yellow, blue, and green, trimmed with round, white, pavé-set rhinestones, marked *Pat. Pend., MB, ZZ*, 1940s, $225.00–$300.00.

Plate 11. Coro necklace, bracelet, and earrings. Iridescent pink cabochon and faceted rhinestones in foliate settings, pear-shape pendants on the necklace and earrings, silver-plated, circa 1940s, $275.00–$350.00 the set.

Plate 12. Top to bottom. R. DeRosa pin. Basket of flowers, clear-faceted crystal basket, red glass beads with rhinestone tips, sapphire and emerald rhinestone flowers, round, white, pavé-set rhinestones in the leaves, gold-plated, 1940s, $400.00–$500.00.

Eisenberg Original pin. Basket with multicolored unfoiled rhinestone flowers, round, white rhinestone trim, 1940s, $1400.00.

Plate 13. Left to right. Unsigned pin. Red and black enameled lobster,

1940s, $175.00.

Unsigned pin. Crab with a pink, carved faux rose quartz body, turquoise glass beads, red enamel feet, gold-plated, circa 1940s, $650.00.

Unsigned pin. Red and black enameled lobster, round, white rhinestone trim, "tremblant" claws, gold-plated, 1940s, $175.00.

Plate 14. HAR bracelet and earrings set. Dragon motif, green enamel on textured, gold-plated metal, iridescent stones, matching earrings, 1950s, $550.00 the set.

Plate 15. Top to bottom. Renoir pin and earrings set. Leaf with blue enameled design, matching earrings, copper, 1950s, $155.00 the set.

Renoir necklace. Geometric design, square, red enameled pendants with triangular centers, copper, 1950s, $145.00.

Renoir necklace. Green enameled, oval, pellet-shaped pendants on a flat chain, copper, 1950s, $135.00.

Renoir bracelet. Multicolored, speckled, enameled rectangular links with square copper links in-between, 1950s, $125.00.

Plate 16. Miriam Haskell pins. Glass beads, rhinestones, and seed pearls in floral motifs, gold-plated, circa 1950s, $250.00–$600.00.

Plate 17. Unsigned necklace. Round links with red rhinestone baguettes in-between, a large floral pendant with sapphire and ruby marquis rhinestones, pear-shape ruby rhinestones, and white round and baguette rhinestones, gold-plated, circa 1950s, $700.00.

Plate 18. Top to bottom. Trifari pin. Crown, large, red cabochons, green, red, and white round rhinestones and white baguettes, gold-plated sterling silver, circa 1940s, $250.00.

Unsigned pin. Crown, round, white, pavé-set rhinestones with large yellow, red and green rhinestones, silver-plated, circa 1950s, $150.00.

Mazer pin. Large sword, round, white, pavé-set rhinestones, green, red, yellow, and blue rhinestone accents, silver-plated above the hilt and at the base, gold-plated in the center section, with dog faces on the sides of the hilt, circa 1950s, $375.00.

Unsigned pin. Crown with moonstones and red and white rhinestones, gold-plated, circa 1950s, $275.00.

Plate 19. Schreiner necklace/pin. Large blue rhinestones with dark pink centers on a neckband of smaller blue rhinestones; detachable floral pendant/pin, marked *Schreiner New York,* silver-plated, 1950s, $750.00–$1000.00.

Plate 20. Kenneth Jay Lane necklace. Green melon-cut glass beads, white rhinestone rondelles, round, white, pavé-set rhinestones; three ornaments with faux emerald and ruby cabochons and large green melon-cut glass centers, gold-plated, 1960s, $1500.00.

Plate 21. Lanvin bracelet and necklace set. Abstract floral, multicolored, enameled pendant on a snake chain with a double "L" signature tag on the catch. Matching hinged bangle, gold-plated, marked *Lanvin Paris,* 1960s, $110.00 the set.

Plate 22. Top to bottom, left to right. Mimi di N earrings. Copper paillettes with small gold beads, gold-plated tops, 1960s, $165.00.

Christian Dior earrings. Hoops, pink enameled flowers with dark pink rhinestone centers, green rhinestone flowers with dark pink rhinestone centers, matching cluster tops, gold-plated, 1967, $195.00.

Unsigned earrings. Two-tone pink plastic bubbles hanging from a filigree stamping, set with green and turquoise stones; tiny turquoise stones on the stem, green rhinestone tops, 1960s, $225.00.

Plate 23. Unsigned necklace and earrings set. Roman-style collar with large, faceted, prong-set green, yellow, and amethyst rhinestones on disks, suspended from a hammered herringbone chain, matching disk earrings, matte gold-plated, 1960s, $650.00–$800.00 the set.

Plate 24. Miriam Haskell necklace and earrings set. Three large blue and green glass bead floral clusters with blue and green glass bead tassels, on three strands of blue and green glass beads, matching cluster earrings, gold-plated, circa 1960s, $1500.00–$2000.00.

Plate 25. Top to bottom. Schiaparelli earrings. Moonstone centers, then a row of iridescent blue rhinestones, with a pink rhinestone outer ring; tops are made of the same rhinestones; the backs are large faux turquoises, giving the wearer two different designs, back and front, marked *Pat. No. 156452,* silver-plated, 1960s, $625.00.

Schiaparelli bracelet and earrings set. "Crab" shapes with turquoise glass stones, iridescent blue rhinestone accents, gold-plated, 1960s, $750.00 the set.

Plate 26. Kenneth Jay Lane necklace. Five strands of small baroque pearls with carved faux jade beads, faux coral beads, and jet glass spacers. The clasp is a black enamel oval with a large carved piece of faux jade, marked *K.J.L.,* gold-plated, circa 1970s, $200.00–$250.00.

Plate 27. Top to bottom, left to right. Unsigned pin. "Toi-Moi," gold-plated, 1970s, $10.00–$20.00.

Unsigned pin. Male torso, painted hair, eyes, mouth, and bathing suit, molded plastic, 1970s, $10.00–$20.00.

Unsigned necklace. Pigs on a square pendant, tubular chain, gold-plated with copper pigs, 1970s, $30.00–$50.00.

Unsigned pin. Blue bird, rainbow, and pot o'gold, enamel on gold plate, 1970s, $5.00–$10.00.

Unsigned pin. "True Love" in enameled red hearts, enameled yellow flower and green leaves, gold-plated, marked *Taiwan*, 1970s, $5.00–$10.00.

Ron Kuriloff for Green Tree pin. Devil/clown in vivid enameled colors, silver-plated, 1970s, $15.00–$25.00.

Unsigned pin. Broken, red plastic heart, gold-plated "break," 1970s, $10.00–$15.00.

Unsigned pin. Red metal lips, gold-plated, 1970s, $5.00–$15.00.

Plate 28. Wendy Gell bracelet. Cuff with a seashell and porcelain nude and flower, heavily decorated with Austrian crystals, sterling silver, 1970s, $2500.00.

Plate 29. Wendy Gell cuff. "Roger Rabbit" characters, © The Walt Disney Co., 1980s, about $770.00.

The Twenties

Madame Gripoix necklace. *Photo by Kenneth Chen, jewelry courtesy of the Costume Collection, Museum of the City of New York.*

Unsigned Art Deco necklaces. *Photo by Kenneth Chen, jewelry courtesy of Terry Rodgers, NYC.*

2

Left-Unsigned pins and bracelets. *Photo by Kenneth Chen, jewelry courtesy of Terry Rodgers, NYC.*

Right-Unsigned papier-mâché necklace. *Photo by Kenneth Chen, jewelry courtesy of Charles France.*

3

4

5

6

Left-Chanel necklace. *Photo by Kenneth Chen, jewelry courtesy of Muriel Karasik Gallery, NYC.*

Right-Hobé necklace and earrings set. *Photo by Kenneth Chen, jewelry courtesy of Charles France.*

Unsigned Bakelite jewelry. *Photo by Kenneth Chen, jewelry courtesy of The Good, the Bad and the Ugly, NYC, Only Yesterday, Hudson, NY, Charles France, and from the author's collection.*

Jo Copeland clips and necklace. *Photo by Kenneth Chen, jewelry courtesy of Raymond Cuminale.*

7

8

Marcel Boucher enameled pins. *Photo by Kenneth Chen, jewelry courtesy of Judith Bumberg.*

10

9

Miriam Haskell freshwater pearl necklace and bracelet set and leaf motif necklace. *Courtesy of Miriam Haskell.*

Coro necklace, bracelet, and earrings set. *Photo by Kenneth Chen, jewelry courtesy of Mr. and Mrs. Frank Corio.*

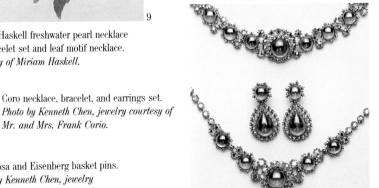

R. DeRosa and Eisenberg basket pins. *Photo by Kenneth Chen, jewelry courtesy of Charles France and Norman Crider Antiques, NYC.*

12

11

Unsigned figural pins. *Photo by Kenneth Chen, jewelry courtesy of Norman Crider Antiques, NYC.*

13

HAR dragon bracelet and earrings set. *Photo by Kenneth Chen, jewelry courtesy of The Good, the Bad and the Ugly, NYC.*

Renoir copper pin and earrings set, necklaces, and bracelet. *Photo by Kenneth Chen, jewelry courtesy of Route 66 Antiques, Chatham, N.Y.*

14

15

Miriam Haskell jeweled pins. *Photo by Kenneth Chen, jewelry courtesy of Miriam Haskell.*

16

Unsigned floral motif necklace. *Photo by Kenneth Chen, jewelry courtesy of Norman Crider Antiques, NYC.*

17

18

Trifari and unsigned crown pins, Mazer sword pin. *Photo by Kenneth Chen, jewelry courtesy of Norman Crider Antiques, NYC.*

19

Schreiner rhinestone necklace/pin. *Photo by Kenneth Chen, jewelry courtesy of Charles France.*

Kenneth Jay Lane pendant necklace. *Photo by Kenneth Chen, jewelry courtesy of Norman Crider Antiques, NYC.*

Lanvin enamel bracelet and necklace set. *Photo by Kenneth Chen, jewelry courtesy of Terry Rodgers, NYC.*

20

21

Mimi di N, Christian Dior, and unsigned drop earrings. *Photo by Kenneth Chen, jewelry courtesy of Muriel Karasik Gallery, NYC.*

22

23

24

Unsigned "Roman" necklace and earrings set. *Photo by Kenneth Chen, jewelry courtesy of Charles France.*

25

Miriam Haskell floral necklace and earrings set. *Photo by Kenneth Chen, jewelry courtesy of Miriam Haskell.*

Schiaparelli pendant "front and back" earrings and faux turquoise bracelet and earrings set. *Photo by Kenneth Chen, jewelry courtesy of Muriel Karasik Gallery, NYC.*

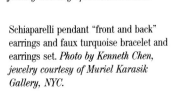

26

Kenneth Jay Lane pearl necklace. *Photo by Kenneth Chen, jewelry courtesy of Charles France.*

27

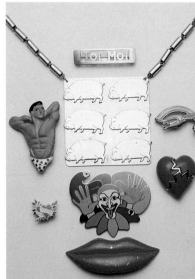

Unsigned pig necklace, figural pins, and a Ron Kuriloff devil pin. *Photo by Kenneth Chen, jewelry courtesy of Only Yesterday, Hudson, NY.*

28

Wendy Gell cuff bracelet. *Photo by Hadley Manings, jewelry courtesy of Wendy Gell.*

29

Wendy Gell "Roger Rabbit" bracelet. ©*Disney/Amblin. Photo by Hadley Manings, jewelry courtesy of Wendy Gell.*

Unsigned mesh-rope lariat necklace and tassel earrings, Volupté necklace and earrings set. *Photo by Kenneth Chen, jewelry courtesy of Patty Madden Miller and from the author's collection.*

Left to Right.

Unsigned Earrings. Mesh rope paisley shapes with chain tassels, gold-plated brass, late 1940s. *$45.00–$65.00*

Unsigned Necklace. Triple-strand mesh rope lariat, fastened with snap under rosette, gold-plated brass, late 1940s. *$60.00–$75.00*

Volupté Necklace and Earrings Set. Double-strand mesh rope choker, topaz-faceted, prong-set rhinestones, matching earrings, gold-plated brass, unsigned, late 1940s. *$85.00–$110.00 the set*

Unsigned military pins and "Rosie the Riveter." *Photo by Kenneth Chen, jewelry courtesy of Only Yesterday, Hudson, NY.*

Top to Bottom, Left to Right.

Unsigned Pin. Army cap with U.S. insignia enameled red, white, and blue, over gun, gold-plated metal, 1940s. *$15.00–$30.00*

Unsigned Pin. Dancing sailor, gold-plated.   *$15.00–$25.00*

Unsigned Pin. Soldier carrying rifle in a round frame, white metal, 1940s.
                                                                 $10.00–$20.00

Unsigned Pin. Marching soldier with rifle, gold-plated, 1940s.
                                                                 $15.00–$25.00

Unsigned Pin. Airplane on green plastic in oval frame, gold-plated, 1940s.
                                                                 $15.00–$25.00

Unsigned Pin. "Rosie the Riveter," green, white, and maroon ceramic,
1940s.   *$15.00–$30.00*

Unsigned multicolor plastic figural pins. *Photo by Kenneth Chen, jewelry courtesy of Only Yesterday, Hudson, NY.*

Unsigned Pins. Multicolored plastic animals, 1940s. *$15.00–$30.00 each*

Unsigned "monster" pins. *Illustration by Pam Smith, jewelry from the author's collection and courtesy of Only Yesterday, Hudson, NY.*

Left to Right.

Unsigned Pin. Cornucopia with round white rhinestone florets, green rhinestone at the base of the horn, gold-plated, 1940s.   *$25.00–$50.00*

Unsigned Pin. Pierced bow, two-tone metal, gold-plated, 1940s.
$45.00–$65.00

Unsigned Pin. Huge flower with round white pavé-set rhinestones, gold-plated, 1940s.   *$35.00–$55.00*

Unsigned bow and Truart flower pin. *Illustration by Pam Smith, jewelry from the author's collection and courtesy of Only Yesterday, Hudson, NY.*

Left to Right.

Unsigned Pin. Bow, pink-gold-plated, 1940s. $35.00–$55.00

Tru Art Pin. Swirled flower, blue cabochon centers in the bud and the flower, pink-gold-plated sterling silver, 1940s. $50.00–$75.00

. . . MORE FORTIES

Ciner Pin. Cartier-style blackamoor, black enameled face, turquoise stones on the breastplate and turban, small red rhinestone necklace and large red rhinestone in the turban and dangling from the breastplate, white baguette trim, gold-plated, circa 1940s. $200.00–$300.00

Coro Pin. Duettes with a pair of bell-shape flowers, round and emerald-cut white rhinestones, green enameled leaves, marked *Pat. No. 1798867*, silver-plated, 1940s. $200.00–$250.00

Coro Pin. Duettes with a pair of birds, white rhinestone bodies, blue enameled wings, a yellow and black beak, and pink, blue, yellow, red, and maroon flowers on a green branch, marked *Pat. No. 1798867*, silver-plated, 1940s. $250.00–$295.00

Coro Earrings. Birds with white rhinestone bodies, pink and blue enameled combs and wings, blue flowers, green leaves, unsigned, marked *Pat. 196765*, white metal, 1940s. $35.00–$50.00

Coro and Coro Craft Pins. Various Duettes with the following subjects: horses on horseshoes, pink painted cockatoos, painted owls, large frogs with green rhinestone bodies, rhinestone roses with green enameled leaves, birds with cherries, king and queen with rhinestone-and-pearl crowns and green rhinestone eyes, turtles with green rhinestone backs and small white rhinestone trim, Bugs Bunny, angels with a green rhinestone for May (manufactured with other birthstones), pink painted birds, beetles, one with white rhinestones, one with blue, and bees with matching earrings, some white metal, some sterling silver, circa 1940s. $125.00–$400.00

Coro Necklace. Snake chain with central bow, small round and baguette rhinestones, small pearls, gold-plated, 1940s. $125.00

Coro Pins. Chatelaine, woman in a 1940s outfit with a feather in the hat, connected by a chain to a dog, silver-plated, 1940s. $25.00–$40.00

Coro Pin. Man in the moon, round white pavé-set rhinestone trim, green marquis, prong-set rhinestone feet and hat, red rhinestone face, round red enameled heart, sterling silver, 1940s. $200.00–$275.00

Coro Craft Pin. Leaf motif with six sprays of jet glass and white rhinestones, small textured leaves, pink-gold-plated sterling silver, 1940s. $65.00–$95.00

Coro Craft Pin. Orchid with purple and yellow enameled leaves, three purple rhinestone baguettes in the center, round white pavé-set rhinestone accents on the petals, sterling silver, 1940s. $125.00–$175.00

Eisenberg Clip. Multicolored rhinestone spray, ribbon at the top with a large central pink rhinestone and round white pavé-set rhinestone trim, red, blue, purple, amber, and pink oval and emerald-cut rhinestones in the spray with small round rhinestones set between them, sterling silver, 1940s. $750.00–$1150.00

Eisenberg Pin. Cancan dancer, pierced ribbon skirt, round white pavé-set rhinestone hat, green enameled bodice and flesh-colored face, sterling silver, 1940s. $400.00–$500.00

Eisenberg Original Clip. Grapes with large round white pavé-set rhinestone leaves and stems, red enameled centers in leaves, pot metal, circa 1940s. $500.00–$600.00

Eisenberg Original Clip. Flower on a stem with pear-shape pink unfoiled rhinestone petals with a round pink central rhinestone, pink rhinestone buds at the tips of stems, gold-plated, 1940s.   *$750.00–$1000.00*

Eisenberg Original Clip. Four flowers on stems with multicolored pear-shape rhinestones and round white pavé-set rhinestones on the leaves, gold-plated sterling silver, 1940s.   *$750.00–$1000.00*

Eisenberg Original Clip. Art Deco style with a large oval dark-amethyst rhinestone, three rows of prong and pavé-set white rhinestones at the top and at the pointed bottom of the stone, 1940s.   *$375.00–$450.00*

Hattie Carnegie Clip. Floral design with a large green oval rhinestone surrounded by yellow marquis rhinestones, topped with a large amber emerald-cut rhinestone, three stems are tipped with small white prong-set rhinestones, sterling silver, 1940s.   *$175.00–$250.00*

Hobé Pin and Earrings Set. "Hungarian"-style enameling on a flower with a large purple square-cut central stone with turquoise and white enamel petals, blue cabochons and seed pearls in an oval frame around the center, antique-gold-plated, circa 1940s.   *$250.00–$350.00*

Hobé Pin. Large rose with carved leaves, sapphire prong-set dentelle accents, marked *Hobé* in a triangle, sterling silver, circa 1940s.
$150.00–$225.00

Jomaz Pin and Earrings Set. Fluted, stylized leaf with a floral spray of round white pavé-set rhinestones, matching smaller earrings, gold-plated, 1940s.   *$100.00–$150.00 the set*

Joseff-Hollywood Pin and Earrings Set. Pin is a hand holding a bouquet of six flowers with round white rhinestones, matching earrings are leaves with two rhinestone flowers, antique-gold-plated, circa 1940s.
$700.00–$950.00 the set

Korda Pin. "Thief of Bagdad" over large yellow crystal ball, marked *Korda 113 Thief of Bagdad* (from the film), white metal, 1940.   *$65.00–$85.00*

Kreisler Bracelet. Links with swirl centerpiece of yellow prong-set rhinestones, round white pavé-set and small red marquis rhinestone trim, marked *Kreisler Quality USA Pat. Pend.* in a circle, gold-plated, 1940s.
$250.00–$325.00

Mazer Pin and Earrings Set. Large circle with scalloped edges, white rhinestones, three tassels with pear-shape rhinestones at the tips, earrings are stylized bows with round white pavé-set rhinestone trim, marked *M.*, gold-plated.   *$115.00–$150.00 the set*

Mazer Clip. Leaf with round white pavé-set rhinestones in the center of the leaf and on the stem, sterling silver, 1940s.   *$125.00–$150.00*

Napier Necklace, Bracelet, and Earrings Set. Geometric-pattern links, matching earrings, sterling silver, 1940s.   *$600.00–$900.00 the set*

Nettie Rosenstein Pin. Flower with pink rose-quartz petals, green enameled leaves, gold-plated sterling silver, 1940s.   *$175.00–$250.00*

R. DeRosa Clip. Large turquoise and coral stones in an abstract design, with tiny white rhinestones in between, gold-plated sterling silver, 1940s.
$450.00–$600.00

Reja Pin and Earrings Set. Jack-in-the-box, round white pavé-set rhinestone gloved hands and accents, oval pink rhinestones in the collar, gold-plated sterling silver, circa 1940s.   *$275.00–$350.00 the set*

Robert Pin/Pendant. Cluster of pink, green, yellow, red, and amethyst round and marquis prong-set rhinestones with a large pear-shape amethyst rhinestone center, trimmed with gold-plated rope, circa 1940s.
$175.00–$250.00

Schreiner Pin and Earrings Set. Floral cluster with topaz rhinestones, turquoise marquis rhinestone flower clusters, sapphire marquis rhinestone trim, matching earrings with two flower clusters of topaz rhinestones, turquoise petals, gold-plated, circa 1940s.   *$175.00–$250.00 the set*

Schreiner Pin and Earrings Set. Floral cluster with three large oval pink rhinestones in the center, pear-shape and oval red and white rhinestone accents, matching earrings, gold-plated, 1940s.   *$175.00–$250.00 the set*

Trifari Pin. Eagle with a large blue central rhinestone, red and white baguettes on the wings, round white pavé-set rhinestone trim, a red rhinestone eye, gold-plated, 1943.   *$150.00–$225.00*

Trifari Pins. Donkey and elephant with pink rhinestone eyes, green marquis rhinestone donkey ears, green baguettes on the elephant's saddle, donkey marked *Copr. Pat. Pend,* gold-plated, 1948. *$50.00–$100.00 each*

Trifari Clip. Grasshopper with emerald and sapphire prong-set rhinestones, round white pavé-set accents, gold-plated, circa 1940s.
$50.00–$75.00

Trifari Pin and Earrings Set. Scallop shell with round white pavé-set rhinestones and baguettes, pearl center, matching smaller earrings, silver-plated, 1940s.   *$275.00–$350.00 the set*

Unsigned Pin. Floral swirl, blue pear-shape rhinestones on the bud spray, edged with round white pavé-set rhinestones, pink-gold-plated sterling silver, 1940s. $75.00–$135.00

Unsigned Pin. Flowers on a stalk with metal leaves, round yellow rhinestone flowers, round white pavé-set rhinestone trim, gold-plated, 1940s.
$50.00–$95.00

Unsigned Pin. Large abstract flower, round white pavé-set rhinestone leaves, gold-plated, 1940s. $35.00–$75.00

Unsigned Pin. Floral swirl, oval red rhinestone blossoms on a round white pavé-set rhinestone stalk, metal abstract leaves, pink-gold-plated sterling silver, 1940s. $75.00–$135.00

Unsigned Pin. Profile of a woman with round red, green, blue, and pink rhinestones in her hair, white metal, circa 1940s. $125.00–$150.00

Unsigned Pin. Cornucopia, green enamel with round white pavé-set rhinestone trim, large pearl "fruit," white metal, late 1940s. $50.00–$75.00

Unsigned Bracelet. Serpent links, green cabochons, gold-plated, 1940s.
$50.00–$75.00

Unsigned Bracelet. Links of square-cut sapphire rhinestones, sterling silver, 1940s. $85.00–$125.00

Unsigned Bracelet. Hinged cuff with a large bunch of grapes, silver-plated, 1940s. $40.00–$75.00

Unsigned Clips. Pair of floral clusters, tiny coral glass beads on thin wire in the center, small and large pearl clusters and small leafy branches at the base, gold-plated, 1940s. $80.00–$120.00

Unsigned Pin and Earrings Set. Overlapping heart design, large central oval amethyst rhinestone, spray of small square-cut white rhinestones, matching earrings, sterling silver, 1940s. $275.00–$375.00 *the set*

Unsigned Clip. Bird's head with round white pavé-set rhinestones, large aquamarine rhinestone in the beak, gold-plated, 1940s. $175.00–$250.00

Unsigned Pin. Flower with a large blue rhinestone blossom, round white pavé-set rhinestone trim, sterling silver, 1940s. $250.00–$375.00

Unsigned Pin. Palm tree with round white pavé-set rhinestones, white metal, 1940s. $20.00–$40.00

Unsigned Pin. Bow, covered with round white pavé-set rhinestones, white baguettes at the tips, white metal, 1940s. $75.00–$125.00

Unsigned Necklace. Victorian revival, small-link chain with an ornate floral pendant set with small and large oval blue rhinestones, five long drops, each with a large oval blue rhinestone, small oval blue rhinestone on the clasp, brass, circa 1940s. $90.00–$125.00

Mamie Eisenhower's Inaugural Jewels, 1953 (top) and 1957, created for her by Trifari. Mrs. Eisenhower was the first wife of a president to wear costume jewelry. Alfred Philippe, the company's chief designer, used "Orientique" pearls and barrel baguette rhinestones to create a triple-strand choker and matching earrings. Three sets were made, one for Mrs. Eisenhower, one for the Smithsonian, and one for Trifari's archives. In answer to Mrs. Eisenhower's request in 1957, another set was designed with a triple strand of graduated pearls with small rondelles, a matching bracelet, and cluster earrings. The necklace had nine pear-shaped drops. *Photo courtesy of Trifari.*

THE FIFTIES

The fabulous Fifties! While teenagers are wearing dungarees and their fathers' shirts and dancing to the new craze, rock and roll, their mothers are trying out the chemise, the unfitted look, and Yves St. Laurent's "trapeze." Coats look like cocoons, suits are unstructured, and the *bateau* (boat) neckline is featured on everything.

Skirts are slimmer, everyone's wearing casual dresses with pushup sleeves, and Balenciaga is showing the "semi-fit," which is close to the body in front and easy and straight in the back. The sheath dress is topped with a high Empire-line bolero, and for a different look, several bouffant crinolines are worn under short, full skirts that pair up with man-tailored shirts and wide, wide cinch belts. Crinolines are kept stiff with sugar and water. Some high schools put a limit on the number of crinolines worn to classes due to congestion in narrow hallways.

The trendy "beatniks" are wearing black leotard tights under black sweaters and skirts or tweed jumpers. Large overshirts go over tapered pants that stop mid-calf as "toreadors" or end just at the ankle. Little round-toed flat "ballerinas" complete the look.

The chemise is a natural to pair up with ropes up to 120 inches long, bibs, and lariats. Scatter pins in twos or threes dress up the simple lines and are worn everywhere, even on the hemline. Dog collars sparkle on bare necks. Matching pins and earrings sets are ornate; some have moving parts. Pins are noticeably bigger and more vibrantly set with multicolored stones; they are worn high on the bodice to accent the rising waist and hemline.

Colorful bracelets are worn in multiples with pushup sleeves. Rings of all types are popular. Beads range from the monochromatic in 1957 to vivid shades in 1958 that come in all textures, including facets, baroque pearls, and brushed gold.

Round necklines take huge, bulky, light necklaces worn on the bare neck. Some drop down to an Empire waistline and end with a large showy pendant that is often a detachable pin. Bib necklaces look best with the *bateau* neckline. Earrings are designed to continue the upswept look. Some fanciful ones look like wings poised for flight. Large rhinestone earrings are popular for evening. Giant button earrings go well with chokers; stringbean or shower styles complement longer necklaces or chains. Peacock, jet, and chalk white are used in combination or alone.

Watches have shapes inspired by space exploration. Some look like flying saucers or feature asymmetrical cases. Shorter sleeves stimulate manufacturers to produce fashion watchbands and wide silver- and gold-plated mesh bracelets.

There is a scarab revival, and in 1957 Angelo del Sesto of the Van Dell Company of Providence presents Mrs. Eisenhower with a scarab belt, matching bracelet, and two pairs of matching earrings.

By 1955 plastics are molded, compressed, extruded, combined with rhinestones, pearlized, made into chains, and popped apart to form different length beads, as desired by the wearer. Lucite, polystyrene, acetate, nylon, vinyl, and catalin are used for various effects that range from iridescence to chalky opaqueness. Clear plastic bracelets and earrings sets are embedded with metallic glitter squares, crescents and stars, real seashells and starfish, and tiny dried flowers. Plastics imitate faceted and cabochon jewels or are made to look like metal and pearls. Jewelry made of plastic is inexpensive to manufacture and easy to assemble with glue.

Metals used for costume jewelry are primarily brass, copper, copper-zinc alloys, bronze, tin, tin-base alloys, aluminum, nickel, and stainless steel. Gold, silver, rhodium, nickel, and chromium are electroplated onto the base metals for various effects. Costume jewelry manufacturing becomes a successful union of craftsmanship, mass-production techniques, and innovative materials.

In 1958, during the Korean "emergency," aluminum is used extensively in the jewelry trade, taking the place of traditional jewelry materials that are in short supply. "Alumilite" by Alcoa is featured in an exhibit at Macy's, showing gold-finished bracelets that accompany the newest sleeveless fashions. A thirty-five-strand aluminum necklace is featured in an advertisement.

In the fall of 1958 an article in *American Jewelry Manufacturers* suggests that all shades of amethyst will be important in jewelry that emphasizes the bust, neck, and head, newly prominent because of the high-waisted dresses. The author suggests shorter, more ornate necklaces, pins in the center of the dress, large Directoire pieces, groups of smaller pins, and important earrings. Chokers, beads, and pearls are attractive on suits, which are once again in style.

Advertisements in 1958 show a necklace and earring set by Trifari with gold-speckled carved beads, a textured gold bangle bracelet with pointed ends, a large flower pin by Trifari, and "frankly fake copies of real gems." Tassel pins, an "antique" look by Benedikt, Greek crosses with large stones by Van S Authentics, Sandor enameled moon and stars, and pins by Lisner with iridescent stones are advertised in fashion magazines. Other Fifties companies whose creations are collectible today are HAR, B.S.K., Kramer, Marvella, Robert Zentall, ART, Regency, Florenza, Bartek, DeNicola, Sarah Coventry, Weiss, Schreiner, Accessocraft, and Renoir/Matisse and Rebajes copper jewelry.

In France innovative costume jewelry designers are using bamboo, seashells, melon pits, nuts, tortoise shells, ivory, and plastic. Half of their output is sold to the United States. It's still not mass-produced there and is closely connected to the high-fashion dressmaking industry. Each year there is a collection shown in the spring and in the fall. The jewelry is not considered "cheap" but luxurious, integrated with the costumes of the great French couturiers.

In Paris shorter skirts, suits with longer jackets, the barrel silhouette, dolman and three-quarter sleeves, and hats that cover the ears all need a new look in jewelry. For evening, hemlines are moving downward; low necklines and strapless backs are shown. Ropes and sautoirs 90 inches long are caught at the hip with a large brooch. In Italy earrings 4 to 6 inches long balance the short skirts and show even under the newest hats. Pins often have dangles and are worn vertically on hats.

In the United States the fashion focus shifts from the Twenties to the Thirties in feeling. The sheath dress goes to the slim-hemmed, tapered look, similar to the chemise. Waistlines are coming back, with feminine peplums, tucking and draping at the hipline. Softer fabrics cut on the bias, standaway collars, capes, and capelets are in restrained colors such as black, gray, beige, plum, and cranberry. Colorful pins are used to brighten suits and capes. Ropes drape over tapered sheaths and open collars. Chokers in varied materials sit high on the neck. Rhinestone necklaces and jeweled bibs complement elegant evening wear.

Everyone loves "character" jewelry. Two weeks after Sputnik is launched, Coro has a Sputnik bracelet on store counters. Mano also creates a Sputnik bracelet, and another company quickly manufactures a satellite charm bracelet. Disney characters and Zorro bracelets are made by Dexter, Coro puts out a Ten Commandments bracelet, Mano creates Liberace's piano and candelabra earrings and for Leru, Barclay produces an "Around the

World in Eighty Days" bracelet. The movies have a very strong influence on fashion.

At the U.S. World Trade Fair in 1958, Switzerland, Italy, and Israel exhibit an array of costume jewelry. Japan shows cultured pearls, and Czechoslovakia displays an enticing assortment of synthetic stones. Since the end of World War II there has been huge growth and expansion in the costume jewelry industry. There has been a redistribution of national income and a decline in popularity of fine jewelry partly because of high purchase taxes. Once again people are spending money, and there is an expansion in both the amount and variety of consumer goods available.

World War II ended half a decade ago, and people now have enough leisure time to concern themselves with philosophical questions. Espresso and Existentialism are the new partners in coffeehouses all over Europe and the United States. Camus, Sartre, Malraux, and Simone de Beauvoir are widely read. Colette casts Leslie Caron as her Gigi, and with her luminescent dark eyes she is the perfect gamine.

The "ballerina look" is worn by many types of women. Chanel reopens her salon in 1954 and introduces a new collection of easy suits and an uncorseted body. Yves St. Laurent creates the "trapeze," Givenchy the "A-line" and the "sack dress," and Dior shows the A- and H-lines in 1955. The woman's counterpart to the man in the gray flannel suit is the cashmere twin sweater set over a tweed skirt worn with a simple string of pearls and a gold circle, or "virgin" pin as the teenagers call it. For casual wear it's a madras skirt or Bermuda shorts with a simple round-collared blouse. The cocktail dress is worn in the evening, and red ballet slippers are a frivolous note to a conservative look. Marlon Brando and motorcycle fans wear T-shirts and black leather jackets. Increased leisure time and the casual suburban life with occasional dress-up evenings lead to a search for the new and the different, giving women the freedom to wear costume jewelry for its own beauty.

Ciner enamel choker necklace. *Photo by Kenneth Chen, jewelry courtesy of Charles France.*

Ciner Necklace. Scalloped choker of royal blue enamel with turquoise glass prong-set stones, gold-plated, 1950s.   *$150.00–$200.00*

Coro Craft crown pin and earrings set. *Photo by Kenneth Chen, jewelry courtesy of Charles France.*

Coro Craft Pin and Earrings Set. Crowns with invisibly set pink rhinestones, white baguettes and tiny white bezel-set rhinestones, gold-plated, 1950s.   *$125.00–$175.00 the set*

Coro Craft sterling silver proscenium pins. *Photo by Kenneth Chen, jewelry courtesy of Charles France.*

Coro Craft Pins. On the left, a group of musicians and on the right a pair of ballerinas, turquoise, white, and red rhinestone trim, gold-plated sterling silver, 1950s.   *$400.00–$500.00 each*

Eisenberg rhinestone pin. *Photo by Kenneth Chen, jewelry courtesy of Beverly Birks, New York.*

Eisenberg Pin. Abstract design with large round white prong-set rhinestones and small round white pavé-set rhinestones set in three geometric shapes, rhodium-plated, 1950s.   *$200.00–$250.00*

Eugene rhinestone-and-pearl earrings, Pioneer Indian-inspired rhinestone necklace, unsigned floral rhinestone necklaces. *Photo by Kenneth Chen, jewelry from the author's collection.*

Top to Bottom.

Eugene Earrings. Floral clusters of seed pearls strung on wire, round and marquis white rhinestones, silver-plated, 1950s.　　　*$55.00–$75.00*

Pioneer Necklace. Indian-inspired choker of round white rhinestones and seed pearls multilayered, unsigned, silver-plated, 1950s.

$150.00–$175.00

Unsigned Necklace. Ornate choker, pink metal rosebuds with white rhinestone centers, filigree bows with pink ceramic flower centers, large amethyst rhinestones, green metal leaves, small pink round and pear-shape rhinestones on gold-plated chain with a double strand of baroque pearls leading to the hook clasp, 1950s.　　　*$165.00–$195.00*

Unsigned Necklace. Floral pendants with turquoise rhinestones, opaque turquoise and glass beads, textured leaves, on a double strand of turquoise crystal beads, coral glass spacers, and opaque turquoise and black glass beads, gold-plated filigree stampings, 1950s.　　　*$160.00–$190.00*

HAR Buddha pin and Napier charm bracelet. *Photo by Kenneth Chen, jewelry courtesy of Norman Crider Antiques, New York, and The Napier Co.*

Top to Bottom.

HAR Pin. Smiling Buddha with two chunks of faux jade and accents of iridescent rhinestones, antique-gold-plated, 1950s.   *$95.00*

Napier Bracelet. Oriental charms of plastic and metal, multicolored beads, antique-gold-plated, 1950s.   *$300.00–$400.00*

Hobé rhinestone necklace, bracelet, and earrings set. *Photo by Kenneth Chen, jewelry courtesy of Terry Rodgers, New York.*

Hobé Bracelet, Necklace, and Earrings Set. Link bracelet with a double row of round prong-set white, yellow, and brown rhinestones separated by gold-plated links, similar design on the choker and matching earrings, 1950s.
                    $160.00 the set

Hobé textured necklace, bracelet, and earrings set. *Photo by Kenneth Chen, jewelry courtesy of Charles France.*

Hobé Necklace, Bracelet, and Earrings Set. Heavily textured surface, disk-shaped pendants with large green cabochons, white rhinestone accents, the bracelet links repeat the same design, the earring tops have the same design and their pendants have round white pavé-set rhinestones, 1950s.

$250.00–$300.00 the set

Hobé abstract necklace, bracelet, pin, and earrings set. *Photo by Kenneth Chen, jewelry courtesy of Jóia, New York.*

Hobé Necklace, Bracelet, Pin, and Earrings Set. Hinged cuff with an abstract design of gold crescent stones, peach oval iridescent cabochons and round green prong-set rhinestone accents. The pin continues the same design as the cuff, with matching earrings. The choker has links of the same design on green rhinestone chain, gold-plated, 1950s.   *$1200.00 the set*

Hollycraft multicolor rhinestone pin and earrings. *Photo by Kenneth Chen, jewelry courtesy of Terry Rodgers, New York.*

Top to Bottom.

Hollycraft Pin. Bow with round, marquis, square-cut, and baguette rhinestones in pastel shades of pink, blue, yellow, and green, marked *Copr. 1955,* gold-plated.   *$85.00*

Hollycraft Earrings. Floral cluster with oval drops, round and oval rhinestones in pastel shades of pink, blue, yellow, and green, marked *Copr. 1950,* gold-plated.   *$50.00*

Jomaz "exotic" necklace, bracelet, and earrings set. *Photo by Kenneth Chen, jewelry courtesy of Charles France.*

Jomaz Necklace, Bracelet, and Earrings Set. Choker with shield-shape links of large faux Burma ruby prong-set rhinestones, small square-cut faux sapphires and round white rhinestone accents. The bracelet is a hinged cuff with matching red and blue rhinestones, earrings are florets with matching stones; all the pieces are brushed-gold-plated, 1950s.

$1200.00–$1500.00 the set

Joseff-Hollywood pearl drop earrings, worn by Grace Kelly. *Photo courtesy of Joan Castle Joseff.*

Joseff-Hollywood Earrings, Worn by Grace Kelly. Pearl-centered floral pendants with pearl and chain drops, gold-plated, circa 1950s.

$250.00–$350.00

Joseff-Hollywood seashell necklace, bracelet, and earrings set, worn by Pier Angeli.
Photo courtesy of Joan Castle Joseff.

Joseff-Hollywood Necklace, Bracelet, and Earrings Set, Worn by Pier Angeli. Scallop shells and dragon pendant on a twisted-link chain, matching bracelet and drop earrings, gold-plated, circa 1950s.

$750.00–$1000.00 the set

Miriam Haskell floral pearl-and-rhinestone necklace and earrings set. *Photo by Kenneth Chen, original photo courtesy of Miriam Haskell.*

Miriam Haskell Necklace and Earrings Set. Baroque pearl and chain cross-over necklace with a pair of foliate pearl and rhinestone pendants, matching earrings, circa 1950s.   *$750.00–$950.00 the set*

Miriam Haskell floral pearl earrings. *Photo by Kenneth Chen, jewelry courtesy of Miriam Haskell.*

Miriam Haskell Earrings. Floral motifs, baroque pearls, seed pearls, gold-plated, circa 1950s.   *$75.00–$150.00*

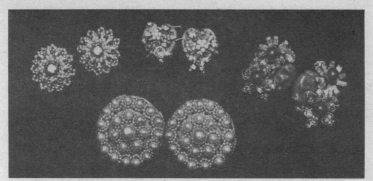

Miriam Haskell pearl-and-rhinestone earrings. *Photo by Kenneth Chen, jewelry courtesy of Miriam Haskell.*

Miriam Haskell Earrings. Floral motifs with seed pearls, baroque pearls, glass beads, white baguettes, circa 1950s. $75.00–$150.00

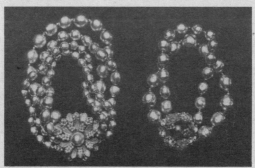

Miriam Haskell pearl bracelets with floral clasps. *Photo by Kenneth Chen, jewelry courtesy of Miriam Haskell.*

Left to Right.

Miriam Haskell Bracelet. Four graduated strands of baroque pearls, floral clasp of seed pearls between leaves with a large center pearl, gold-plated, circa 1950s. $225.00–$325.00

Miriam Haskell Bracelet. Two graduated strands of baroque pearls, floral clasp with a raspberry-color cabochon center, pale green glass beads and pink stones surrounded by round white rhinestones, gold-plated, circa 1950s. $195.00–$275.00

Miriam Haskell seed pearl pins. *Photo by Kenneth Chen, jewelry courtesy of Miriam Haskell.*

Miriam Haskell Pins. Ornate floral motifs with seed pearls, baroque pearls, and rhinestones on brass wire, gold-plated filigree stampings, 1950s.
$250.00–$475.00

Miriam Haskell pearl necklaces with pearl clasps. *Photo by Kenneth Chen, jewelry courtesy of Miriam Haskell.*

Left to Right.

Miriam Haskell Necklace. Single strand of graduated baroque pearls, floral clasp with seed pearls and a larger center pearl, gold-plated, circa 1950s.
$225.00–$350.00

Miriam Haskell Necklace. Double strand of medium and large baroque pearls, floral clasp with rows of seed pearls with innermost circle on stalks, larger center pearl, gold-plated, circa 1950s. $300.00–$450.00

Miriam Haskell Necklace. Double strand of small and medium baroque pearls, floral clasp with unfoiled blue and green stones, a tiny baroque pearl cluster, and rhinestone flowers with pink bead centers, silver-plated, circa 1950s. $300.00–$450.00

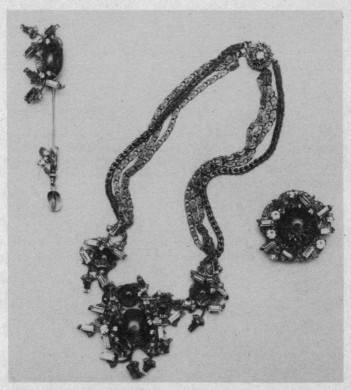

Miriam Haskell rhinestone necklace, pin, and stickpin set. *Photo by Kenneth Chen, jewelry courtesy of Miriam Haskell.*

Miriam Haskell Necklace, Pin, and Stickpin Set. Topaz cabochons, white baguettes in a modernistic design suspended from four strands of hammered "S" chains, floral clasp, matching pin and stickpin, 1950s.

$575.00–$650.00 the set

Miriam Haskell glass-seashell necklace. *Photo by Kenneth Chen, jewelry courtesy of Charles France.*

Miriam Haskell Necklace. White glass-seashell choker with multicolored beads, circa 1950s.   *$150.00–$200.00*

Miriam Haskell bead-and-rhinestone flower pin. *Photo by Kenneth Chen, jewelry courtesy of Beverly Birks, New York.*

Miriam Haskell Pin. Flower with jet bugle beads and round white rhinestones, textured-gold-plated, circa 1950s.   *$200.00–$250.00*

Miriam Haskell pendant pearl necklace. *Photo by Kenneth Chen, jewelry courtesy of Beverly Birks, New York.*

Miriam Haskell Necklace. Single-strand baroque pearls with gold spacers, pearl floral pendant with twin pearl drops suspended on pearls, circa 1950s.   *$200.00–$250.00*

Miriam Haskell floral rhinestone necklace and pin set. *Photo by Kenneth Chen, jewelry courtesy of Norman Crider Antiques, New York.*

Miriam Haskell Necklace and Earrings Set. Flowers with round and marquis red and white prong-set rhinestones, a large flower pendant, flower clasp and a matching pin, pewter-silver-plated, 1950s.   *$1500.00*

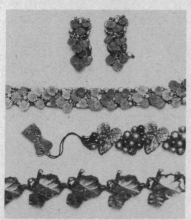

Miriam Haskell bracelet and earrings set, Schiaparelli bracelet, and an unsigned bracelet, all with leaf motifs. *Photo by Kenneth Chen, jewelry courtesy of Muriel Karasik Gallery, New York.*

Top to Bottom.

Miriam Haskell Bracelet and Earrings Set. Flat, textured, overlapping leaves with baroque pearls and white rhinestones, gold-plated, circa 1950s.
                                                    $625.00 the set

Schiaparelli Bracelet with Original Hang Tag. Iridescent gray rhinestones on leaf links, separated by clusters of gray and black pearls with iridescent rhinestones, silver-plated, 1950s.   *$350.00*

Unsigned Bracelet. Frosted glass topaz-color leaves linked with textured "branches," tipped by rhinestones, gold-plated, 1950s.   *$150.00*

Napier earrings on the cover of *Movies*, 1950s, with Marilyn Monroe photographed wearing one of the pairs. *Photo of the cover and earrings by Kenneth Chen, original photo courtesy of The Napier Co.*

Left to Right.

Napier Earrings. Upswept design, topaz pear-shape and round rhinestones on twisted wire, gold-plated, marked *Napier Pat. Pend.*, 1950s.

$65.00–$85.00

Napier Earrings. Drops with pale green marquis rhinestones, gold-plated, marked *Napier Pat. Pend.*, 1950s.   *$65.00–$85.00*

Napier Earrings. Birdcage drops with crystal glass beads, gold-plated, marked *Napier Pat. Pend.*, 1950s. (Marilyn Monroe is wearing an identical pair in the photograph.)   *$100.00–$150.00*

Napier leaf-motif bracelet, pin, and earrings set. *Photo courtesy of The Napier Co.*

Napier Bracelet, Pin, and Earrings Set. Leaf motif, silver-plated, 1950s.
                                    $325.00–$450.00 the set

Pauline Trigère floral rhinestone neck-lace. *Photo by Kenneth Chen, jewelry courtesy of Pauline Trigère.*

Pauline Trigère Necklace. Bib, multiple flowers with blue, aqua, and ame-thyst cabochon petals and round white rhinestone centers in gold-plated twisted wire, unsigned, 1951.   *$800.00–$1000.00*

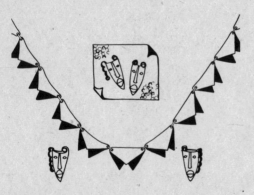

Rebajes copper pin and ear-rings set, Matisse copper-and-enamel necklace. *Illustration by Pam Smith, jewelry courtesy of Only Yesterday, Hudson, NY.*

Top to Bottom.

Rebajes Pin and Earrings Set. Male and female masks, matching earrings, copper, 1950s.   *$75.00–$100.00 the set*

Matisse Necklace. Geometric triangular design, copper and enameled green and black speckled links, 1950s.   *$95.00–$125.00*

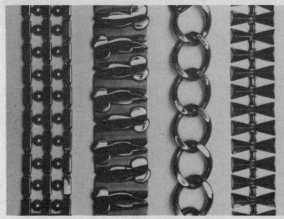

Renoir copper link bracelets. *Photo by Kenneth Chen, jewelry courtesy of Route 66 Antiques, Chatham, NY.*

Left to Right.

Renoir Bracelet. Triple strand, bar links with ball separators, copper, 1950s. *$95.00*

Renoir Bracelet. Leaf-shape links, copper, 1950s. *$130.00*

Renoir Bracelet. Chain links, copper, 1950s. *$105.00*

Renoir Bracelet. "Bow tie" links, copper, 1950s. *$75.00*

Robert rhinestone pin. *Photo by Kenneth Chen, jewelry courtesy of Beverly Birks, New York.*

Robert Pin. Palette with light blue and pink round prong-set rhinestones in twisted wire, green glazed leaves with multicolored marquis and round rhinestones in the centers of florettes, marked *Fashion Craft Robert*, gold-plated, 1950s. *$200.00–$250.00*

Schreiner, Hollycraft, and HAR sets. *Photo by Jessica Michael, jewelry courtesy of Tania Santé's Classic Collectables, Miami.*

Top to Bottom.

Schreiner, New York, Pin/Pendant and Earrings Set. Floral cluster convertible pin/pendant and matching earrings with unfoiled citrine and amber prong-set rhinestones, 1950s.   *$260.00 the set*

Hollycraft Bracelet and Earrings Set. Multicolored pastel round and baguette prong-set rhinestones, gold-plated, 1955.   *$300.00 the set*

HAR Pin and Earrings Set. Smiling Buddhas with ivory plastic faces and jade-color stones, antique-gold-plated, 1950s.   *$180.00 the set*

Schreiner rhinestone pin. *Photo by Kenneth Chen, jewelry courtesy of Charles France.*

Schreiner Pin. Large flower pin with pink and blue prong-set rhinestones, large central blue rhinestone with a dark pink center, marked *Schreiner New York*, silver-plated, 1950s.   *$400.00*

Selro and unsigned figural bracelet and earrings sets. *Photo by Kenneth Chen, jewelry from the author's collection.*

Top to Bottom.

Selro Bracelet and Earrings Set. Carved coral plastic faces, green cabochons and amethyst-faceted bezel-set rhinestones in foliate settings, matching earrings, textured-gold-plated, 1950s.

$250.00–$300.00 the set

Unsigned Necklace (not shown), Bracelet, and Earrings Set. Blackamoors alternating with red plastic marquis stones in rope frames, pearl and rhinestone accents, matching blackamoor earrings, silver-plated, 1950s.

$135.00–$150.00 the set

Tortolani twist bracelet. *Photo by Kenneth Chen, jewelry courtesy of Beverly Birks, New York.*

Tortolani Bracelet. Twist hinged cuff, overlapping cactus leaves, pewter-silver-plated, 1950s.   *$125.00–$175.00*

Advertisement for Trifari "Clair de Lune" necklace, bracelet, and earrings set in *Harper's Bazaar*, February 1950. *Photo of ad by Kenneth Chen, ad courtesy of Trifari.*

Trifari Necklace, Bracelet, and Earrings Set. "Clair de Lune" simulated moonstones, faux rubies and diamonds in a choker on a twist chain, matching hinged cuff bracelet and earrings, 1950.   *$500.00–$750.00 the set*

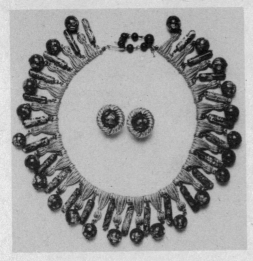

Trifari Egyptian-style necklace and earrings set. *Photo by Kenneth Chen, jewelry courtesy of Charles France.*

Trifari Necklace and Earrings Set. Egyptian-style choker with blue and red Venetian glass drops, matching earrings with a single glass bead in a frame, textured-gold-plated, 1950s.   *$250.00–$325.00 the set*

Unsigned triple-strand crystal-bead and rhinestone choker. *Photo by Kenneth Chen, jewelry courtesy of Charles France.*

Unsigned Necklace. Triple-strand choker, green crystal beads with white rhinestone rondelles and white crystal bead drops, 1950s.

$200.00–$250.00

Unsigned Lucite pins, earrings, and pendant. *Photo by Kenneth Chen, jewelry courtesy of Charles France.*

Unsigned Pins, Earrings, and a Pendant. Clear Lucite with carved or embedded designs, 1950s.   *$45.00–$55.00*

Unsigned "glitter" bracelets and earrings. *Photo by Kenneth Chen, jewelry courtesy of Norman Crider Antiques, New York.*

Top to Bottom.

Unsigned Bracelet and Earrings Set. Red background, gold crescents and bars, glitter embedded in clear Lucite links, matching earrings, gold-plated, 1950s.   *$100.00 the set*

Unsigned Bracelet. Black background with white mother-of-pearl glitter imbedded in Lucite links, silver-plated, 1950s.   *$75.00*

Unsigned Earrings. Disks with a black background with white mother-of-pearl glitter embedded in Lucite, 1950s.   *$90.00*

Unsigned plastic-and-rhinestone bracelet and earrings set. *Photo by Kenneth Chen, jewelry courtesy of Charles France.*

Unsigned Bracelet and Earrings Set. Cherry pink plastic with round white rhinestones in diagonal stripes, matching earrings, 1950s.

$225.00–$275.00 the set

Unsigned geometric cuff bracelet. *Photo by Kenneth Chen, jewelry courtesy of Charles France.*

Unsigned Bracelet. Hinged cuff with a geometric horizontal and vertical design, matte-gold-plated, 1950s. *$65.00–$100.00*

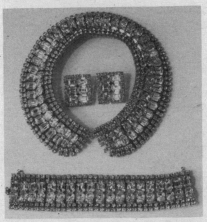

Unsigned rhinestone collar necklace, bracelet, and earrings set. *Photo by Jessica Michael, jewelry courtesy of Tania Santé's Classic Collectables, Miami.*

Unsigned Necklace, Bracelet, and Earrings Set. Large white square-cut, prong-set rhinestone collar, edged with a double row of round white prong-set rhinestones, matching wide bracelet and square earrings, rhodium-plated, 1950s. *$800.00 the set*

Unsigned and Florenza pin and earrings sets. *Photo by Kenneth Chen, jewelry courtesy of Terry Rodgers, New York.*

Left to Right.

Unsigned Pin and Earrings Set. Abstract design of pink, raspberry, and red round and marquis rhinestones, matching pinwheel earrings with pink center rhinestones, 1950s.   *$58.00 the set*

Florenza Pin and Earrings Set. Pinwheel shape with a large blue faceted center rhinestone surrounded by iridescent pear-shape cabochons and oval foil-backed cabochons, matching earrings, silver-plated, 1950s.

$75.00 the set

Unsigned Pin and Earrings Set. Swirled cluster of red and iridescent marquis and round rhinestones, matching earrings, 1950s.   *$55.00 the set*

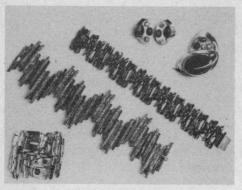

Unsigned modernistic pin, bracelets, and pin and earrings set. *Photo by Kenneth Chen, jewelry from the author's collection and courtesy of Terry Rodgers, New York.*

Left to Right.

Unsigned Pin. Abstract "modern art" design, multicolored cabochons, gold-plated, 1950s.   *$25.00–$45.00*

Unsigned Bracelet. Textured "pickets" alternating with blue and green enamel, gold-plated, 1950s. *$135.00–$175.00*

Unsigned Bracelet. Abstract, shadowed, "sculptural" design, marked *835*, silver, 1950s. *$210.00–$250.00*

Unsigned Pin and Earrings Set. Modernistic swirled motif, textured and smooth, coral, jet, and gold rhinestones, 1950s. *$45.00 the set*

Unsigned mesh necklace and earrings set, Monet earrings and charm bracelet. *Photo by Kenneth Chen, jewelry from the author's collection and courtesy of Monet.*

Top to Bottom.

Unsigned Necklace and Earrings Set. Mesh neckband with geometric pendant, matching earrings, gold-plated, 1950s. *$40.00–$60.00 the set*

Monet Earrings. Buttons, gold-plated, 1950s. *$25.00–$45.00*

Monet Bracelet. Charm bracelet with a French poodle in a frame, gold-plated, 1950s. *$35.00–$55.00*

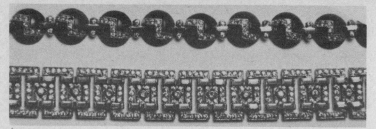

Unsigned Art Deco–design bracelets. *Photo by Kenneth Chen, jewelry courtesy of Charles France and Clare Feldman.*

Top to Bottom.

Unsigned Bracelet. Art Deco design, red and blue enamel circle links with a geometric pattern formed by round white pavé-set rhinestones, silver-plated, circa 1930s.   *$100.00–$150.00*

Unsigned Bracelet. Art Deco revival design, round white pavé-set rhinestones and white baguettes in a geometric pattern of square links, silver-plated, 1950s.   *$75.00–$95.00*

. . . MORE FIFTIES

Bartek Necklace. Choker, circle links with a carved concentric circle pattern, rectangular spacers with three carved channels, gold-plated, 1950s.
$50.00–$75.00

Chanel Clip. Cluster of red, blue, and green glass beads with rhinestone tips and pearls, made by Madame Gripoix, marked *Made in France,* gold-plated, 1950s.   *$350.00–$500.00*

Coro Pin. Blackamoor with a black enamel face, red lips, pearl drop earrings, and a red rhinestone in the turban, gold-plated, circa 1950s.
$25.00–$45.00

Hattie Carnegie Necklace and Bracelet Set. Turquoise and garnet rhinestone links, chain drop ball of turquoise and garnet rhinestones, matching double-row choker with turquoise rhinestones, gold-plated, 1950s.
$175.00–$225.00 the set

Hobé Necklace and Earrings Set. Egyptian-style collar with green plastic beads alternating with pearl drops from a herringbone chain, matching earrings are flowers with a large green central plastic stone and tiny white rhinestones on the petals, gold-plated, 1950s.   *$100.00–$125.00 the set*

Hollycraft Pins. Pair of shield-shape small scatter pins, pale oval amethyst central rhinestones, surrounded by multicolored pastel stones, gold-plated, marked *Copr. 1950.*   *$25.00–$45.00 the pair*

Hollycraft Pin. Horizontal oval with a large central amethyst rhinestone, surrounded by pink, green, lilac, and pale yellow rhinestones, gold-plated, 1951.   *$125.00–$175.00*

Hollycraft Earrings. Vertical oval with an oval amethyst central rhinestone, surrounded by pink, blue, and green rhinestones, gold-plated, 1950.
$75.00–$100.00

Karu Pin. Baroque revival pins connected with multiple strands of chain, green intaglio rhinestones, marked *Karu Fifth Avenue,* gold-plated, circa 1950s.   *$125.00–$160.00*

Miriam Haskell Necklace, Pin, and Earrings Set. Three feather links on a rope chain, seed pearls, small round white rhinestone trim with a pearl and rhinestone clasp, matching feather pin and earrings, gold-plated, circa 1950s.   *$550.00–$650.00 the set*

Miriam Haskell Bracelet. Four large oval orange glass disks, separated by three tiny corrugated balls, ornate filigree caps and clasp, gold-plated brass, circa 1950s.   *$75.00–$125.00*

Miriam Haskell Earrings. Round filigree stamping with a cascade of clear stippled blue glass beads suspended on a brass chain, gold-plated, circa 1950s.   *$45.00–$65.00*

Kramer Pin. Abstract design, large purple and light pink rhinestones, circa 1950s.   *$35.00–$48.00*

Monet Pin. Large puffed bow, sterling silver, 1950s.   *$100.00–$150.00*

Panetta Earrings. Long bow with round white pavé-set rhinestones ending in a round pearl drop, gold-plated, circa 1950s.   *$35.00–$45.00*

Pennino Pin. Floral spray of marquis-shape white rhinestones and white baguettes, rhodium-plated, 1950s.   *$85.00–$120.00*

Rebajes Pin. Rectangle with three flowers in a diagonal strip, copper, 1950s.   *$55.00–$85.00*

Rebajes Pin. Two leaves with a coiled stem, copper, 1950s.
$35.00–$65.00

Reja Pin. Abstract leaf with round white pavé-set rhinestone stems, large white prong-set rhinestones on the leaf with small white rhinestone accents, silver-plated, circa 1950s.   *$45.00–$65.00*

Robert Pin. Large circle with various kinds of faceted and bezel-set pink stones, marked *Original by Robert,* gold-plated, circa 1950s.

$90.00–$125.00

Sarah Coventry Earrings. Button style, clear Lucite with multicolored embedded diamond-shape glitter, white background with black criss-cross lines, gold-plated, marked *Sarah Cov,* 1950s. $25.00–$40.00

Schiaparelli Bracelet. "Ribbon" links with large pink and green iridescent rhinestone centers, gold-plated, 1950s. $125.00–$175.00

Schiaparelli Pin. Pea pod, green textured enamel with seven pearl "peas," gold-plated, 1950s. $125.00–$175.00

Schiaparelli Pin. Gold and white iridescent rhinestones in a cluster, gold-plated, 1950s. $125.00–$150.00

Schiaparelli Pin. Flower with blue cabochons surrounded by marquis iridescent blue rhinestone leaves, gold-plated, 1950s. $125.00–$175.00

Schiaparelli Pin and Earrings Set. Iridescent carved glass roses, branches accented with marquis white and iridescent dark pink rhinestones, gold-plated, matching smaller earrings, 1950s. $225.00–$275.00 the set

Schiaparelli Pin and Earrings Set. Oval black rhinestones surrounded by green and blue iridescent rhinestones in a cluster, matching smaller earrings, gold-plated, 1950s. $250.00–$295.00 the set

Trifari Pins. Lucite, with crystal "bellies": hummingbird with white rhinestones on the wings and tail, red rhinestone eyes; frog with large green cabochon eyes, white rhinestones on the legs and mouth; bird with white rhinestones on the wings, throat, and tail, red rhinestone eyes; spider with white rhinestones on the legs and head; sailfish with white rhinestones on the head and tail, large red cabochon eyes; all brushed-gold-plated, 1950s.

$125.00–$175.00 each

Trifari Pin. Flower with an emerald cabochon center surrounded by white marquis rhinestones, circa 1950s. $35.00–$45.00

Trifari Pin. Flower, with large pear-shape white rhinestone petals, white rhinestone baguette stems, gold-plated, 1950s. $75.00–$100.00

Trifari Pin. Dancing cowboy with a white rhinestone face, small rhinestone accents, silver-plated, 1950s. $40.00–$60.00

Trifari Necklace. Snake chain choker, leaf and branch design center motif, pear-shape emerald rhinestones, gold-plated, 1950s. $75.00–$125.00

Unsigned Pin. Maltese cross in purple, green, blue rhinestones, gold-plated, 1950s. $25.00–$38.00

Unsigned Pin. Abstract floral design with a large red square-cut central rhinestone with round pink and red rhinestones at one side and at the bottom, gold-plated, 1950s. $35.00–$45.00

Unsigned Necklace and Earrings Set. Triple strands of alternating thin green glass beads and crystal barrel beads with pink centers, gold spacers, floral clasp and matching earrings with the same pink and green beads, marked *Made in Italy,* gold-plated, circa 1950s. $195.00–$225.00

Unsigned Necklace. Double strand of mixed glass and plastic beads in black, aurora borealis, marbleized gray, black, and gray, and clusters of tiny black, gray, and white beads, black glass spacers, silver-plated hook closure with a tiny violin-shape drop, 1950s. $50.00–$65.00

Unsigned Bracelet. Lucite open bangle with embedded square gold glitter, 1950s. $25.00–$35.00

Unsigned Necklace. Lucite pendant on a heavy chain with a gold-color background, embedded with pearls and gold glitter, gold-plated, 1950s. $120.00–$135.00

Unsigned Bracelet. Hinged twist cuff with diagonal points, clear Lucite with embedded silver glitter, 1950s. $35.00–$45.00

Unsigned Pins. A pair of hands with cuffs holding a round crown-set mirror, marked *Made in France,* gold-plated, 1950s. $50.00–$75.00

Unsigned Pin. Flower on a hammered crescent shape, copper, 1950s. $20.00–$45.00

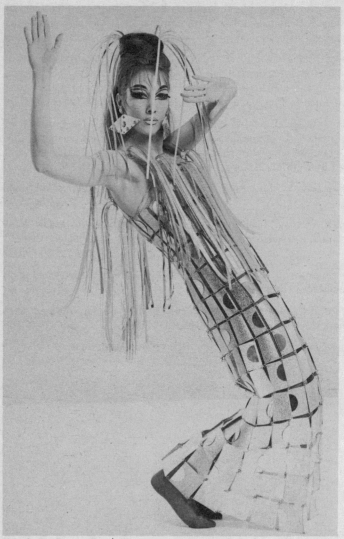

Valérie Camille as she appeared on Television Française wearing a custom-designed dress and earrings by Paco Rabanne. *Photo by Nogrady, courtesy of Valérie Camille.*

THE SIXTIES

In the Swinging Sixties clothing and accessories take on a whole new social importance. The seeds of the sexual revolution have been planted and blossom into full flower with the advent of "the Pill." There's a new body awareness, and tight-fitting, hip-hugging bell-bottom dungarees are worn with an exposed midriff and a tiny top. Bralessness is rampant, and the ultimate style that shocks the conservative older generation is Rudi Gernreich's topless bathing suit. For those women who insist on some coverage Rudi invents the "no-bra" bra, the forerunner of today's unconstructed styles. For the truly modest, Band-Aids are used to cover the nipples in Rudi's figure-revealing knit designs. Pantyhose replace the more cumbersome garter belt and stockings, and *Hair* debuts on Broadway, exposing both men and women in the first display of nudity on the legitimate stage.

Meanwhile, mothers of the braless and barefoot young women are wearing the wildly patterned, beautifully colored, ubiquitous Pucci dresses and their copies. They become the first clothing that is a status symbol. Young matrons affect the "Jackie Kennedy look," and Lilly Pulitzer wallpapers the horsey set with huge pastel and neon floral patterns for men and women. In 1964 Courrèges shows a "space age" geometric look with a white helmet, white sculptural tunic, and white boots that catch on like crazy. Women of all ages wear the majorette lookalikes, and they are knocked off by nearly every shoe manufacturer.

The "London Look" spreads to the United States, and everyone wants to wear what the English "birds" do. Mary Quant, Zandra Rhodes, Thea Porter,

185

and Jean Muir lead the group of English designers who find an audience
in the United States. Mini-skirts and tights are the foremost sellers in the
boutiques of Chelsea. Going shopping for clothes becomes a form of enter-
tainment that both sexes enjoy. London boutiques Biba, Bus Stop, and Just
Looking have their American counterpart on Madison Avenue at a chrome
and Lucite store called Paraphernalia. Its next-door neighbor is the Vidal
Sassoon hair salon, with imported young English hairdressers giving everyone short, shiny, geometric cuts.

In Paris women are wearing minis, the "baby doll" look, Yves St. Laurent's retro Forties look, and Paco Rabanne's dresses made from metal or
plastic disks linked together with rings and worn over flesh-colored body
stockings. Boots are worn with everything; patterned stockings cover the
part of the leg exposed by the mini. For evening, silver dresses, silver lamé
shoes and stockings, and glittery materials and brocades add a touch of
glamour.

Everywhere men and women are experimenting with costumey outfits—caftans; antique dresses; floral and embroidered shirts; Indian head-
bands and beads; studded, patched, and embroidered denim; military
surplus uniforms; and fantasy creations from the harem to outer space.

African and ethnic motifs, psychedelia, and signs of the zodiac permeate
clothing and jewelry. Hallucinogenic drugs stimulate music, art, and fashions in wild patterns and colors. The most adventurous fashion leaders
substitute body paint for clothing and wear paper dresses and jumpsuits.
Models are the new celebrities of the Sixties, with "The Shrimp" (Jean
Shrimpton), Twiggy, and Verushka leading the pack.

Costume jewelry ranges from Kenneth Jay Lane's fabulous fakes and
Chanel-inspired jewels to the massive Lucite dome rings; tiered, mobile
earrings; and belts made of electronic templates and silver chain by Harri-
son and Garrison.

Advertisements in the fashion magazines show Lisner painted flower
pins, a Brania sunburst pin of mock turquoise and gold, a DeNicola medallion pin with a gold coin center, Giovanni roses, mesh jewelry by Wells,
Kramer revivals of Victorian pins, Adele Simpson necklaces, and Weiss
rhinestone pins. Corocraft, Krementz, Vendome space pins with large colored rhinestones, Bergère rhinestone pins, Chanel, Danecraft perfume pins,
François enameled flowers, a Hattie Carnegie faux coral and rhinestone pin,
and a textured gold choker for Carnegie Originals are also advertised.

Newspaper ads highlight Nettie Rosenstein, Joseph Mazer, Robert Originals, Panetta, Castlecliff, Joseph Warner intaglios, Mimi di N, Capri,
Napier's Egyptian look, Laguna for beads, a Marcel Boucher faux turquoise
and gold pin, replicas of antique European jewelry, and Albert Weiss's
"Cleopatra Collection" with faux turquoise stones and tassels. Sandor Gold-

berger, Judith McCann, Scaasi earrings, a Miriam Haskell pin and collar of gold-plated metal and jet beads, Van S Authentics, a Berger dog collar, jewelry by Shannon Rodgers for Jerry Silverman for Vendome, and a white collar and bib by Vogue are in other ads.

Today the most collectible Sixties costume jewelry is some of the prettiest—Kenneth Jay Lane's oversize earrings, animal bracelets, and bold pins; Mimi di N's enameled bracelets and striking pendants; Hattie Carnegie's rhinestone pin and earring sets; Miriam Haskell's pearl sets; and jewelry by Schiaparelli, Mazer, and Boucher.

Boucher rhinestone flower pin. *Photo by Kenneth Chen, jewelry courtesy of Beverly Birks, New York.*

Boucher Pin and Earrings Set (earrings not pictured). Multilayered flower with alternating rows of round white pavé-set rhinestones and dark blue faux sapphire cabochons, marked *7732P,* silver-plated, 1960s.

$250.00–$350.00 the set

Boucher rhinestone pin and earrings set. *Photo by Kenneth Chen, jewelry courtesy of Charles France.*

Boucher Pin and Earrings Set. Round white prong-set rhinestones with white baguettes and large red faceted "rubies" in a geometric criss-cross design, marked *7950P,* matching smaller earrings, silver-plated, 1960s. (This set was also made in the following colors: sapphire and white; sapphire and ruby; topaz, amber, and emerald; topaz and sapphire; topaz, amber, and ruby.)

$200.00–$250.00 the set

Brania black and hematite bead pin and earring set. *Photo by Kenneth Chen, jewelry courtesy of Jóia, New York.*

Brania Pin and Earrings Set. Black and hematite glass teardrop beads with round white and amber rhinestone accents on black wires, matching earrings, black setting, 1960s.   *$250.00 the set*

Butler & Wilson rhinestone hand pin and unsigned rhinestone spider pin. *Photo by Kenneth Chen, jewelry courtesy of Charles France.*

Left to Right.

Butler & Wilson Pin. Hand with round white prong-set rhinestones, jet pear-shape rhinestone fingernails and bracelet, gunmetal-plated, circa 1960s.   *$100.00–$150.00*

Unsigned Pin. Spider with round white prong-set rhinestones, black enamel setting, circa 1960s.   *$100.00–$150.00*

Chanel drop earrings and Schiaparelli tassel necklace. *Photo by Kenneth Chen, jewelry courtesy of Muriel Karasik Gallery, New York.*

Top to Bottom.

Chanel Earrings. Emerald glass pendants surrounded by red glass beads and white rhinestone rondelles, tops of round prong-set emerald rhinestones, white metal, unsigned, 1960s.   *$1200.00*

Schiaparelli Necklace. Ruby glass pendants surrounded by red glass beads and white rhinestone rondelles, silver-plated chain, 1960s.   *$725.00*

Note: The earrings are attributed to Chanel, made by Madame Gripoix, in the Sotheby's catalog for the auction of the Diana Vreeland Collection of Fashion Jewelry on October 21, 1987. Note, however, the similarity between them and the necklace made by Schiaparelli. The earrings sold for $550.00 at the auction.

Christian Dior rhinestone floral necklace. *Photo by Kenneth Chen, jewelry courtesy of Muriel Karasik Gallery, New York.*

Christian Dior Necklace. Abstract floral collar with sapphire blue and white marquis-shape prong-set rhinestones, silver-plated, marked *Chr. Dior Germany*, 1965.   *$1200.00*

Ciner enamel strawberry pin and Kramer enamel schnauzer dog pin. *Photo by Kenneth Chen, jewelry courtesy of Charles France.*

Left to Right.

Ciner Pin. Red enameled strawberries with round white pavé-set rhinestones on gold-plated textured branches, 1960s.   *$250.00–$300.00*

Kramer Pin. Schnauzer dog with two shades of red enameled body; round white pavé-set rhinestone trim, gold-plated, 1960s.   *$250.00–$300.00*

Hattie Carnegie rhinestone bow pin. *Photo by Kenneth Chen, jewelry courtesy of Norman Crider Antiques, New York.*

Hattie Carnegie Pin. Large bow with emerald green faceted glass beads, round white prong-set rhinestones, white rhinestone pendants, 1960s.

$450.00

Jomaz, Mimi di N, and Trifari Maltese cross pins. *Photo by Kenneth Chen, jewelry courtesy of Muriel Karasik Gallery, New York.*

Left to Right, Top to Bottom.

Jomaz Pin. Maltese cross, pink opal cabochon stones, ruby and white rhinestones, gold-plated, 1960s. $750.00

Jomaz Pin. Maltese cross with faux rubies in the center with a green cabochon, white pavé-set rhinestones, gold-plated, 1960s. $575.00

Mimi di N Pin/Pendant. Double Maltese cross with turquoise glass beads, blue cabochons, and a large central aqua stone with green swirls, round white pavé-set rhinestones; a ring at the top converts it to a pendant, gold-plated, 1960s.   *$575.00*

Jomaz Pin. Maltese cross with cabochon rubies, round white pavé-set rhinestones, gold-plated, 1960s.   *$675.00*

Trifari Pin. Maltese cross with emerald cabochon stones, round white pavé-set rhinestones, gold-plated, 1960s.   *$425.00*

Jomaz Pin. Maltese cross with central turquoise cabochon stones, faux lapis lazulis, round white pavé-set rhinestones, gold-plated, 1960s.

    $650.00

Jomaz enamel dragon pin and earrings set, Trifari "Ming" dragon pin, and Ciner fish pin. *Photo by Kenneth Chen, jewelry courtesy of Muriel Karasik Gallery, New York; Trifari; and Norman Crider Antiques, New York.*

Top to Bottom.

Jomaz Pin and Earrings Set. Dragon pin with green and gray enameled body, round white pavé-set rhinestones on the head, body and tail with green prong-set cabochons. Matching tail earrings with green cabochons and gray and green enamel, gold-plated, 1960s.   *$700.00 the set*

Trifari Pin. Ming dragon with baroque pearl center, red enameled body, round white pavé-set rhinestone trim with a tiny green stone on the head, gold-plated, 1965. $250.00–$300.00

Ciner Pin. Fish with blue and green enameled fins, round white pavé-set rhinestones on the body, green stone eye, gold-plated, 1960s. $375.00

Kenneth Jay Lane enamel cuff bracelet with a jeweled Maltese cross and a "headlight" necklace. *Photo by Kenneth Chen, jewelry courtesy of Kenneth Jay Lane.*

Kenneth Jay Lane Necklace. "Headlight" design with large oval and oblong faux diamonds, set in black enameled metal, 1960s (still being manufactured). *Currently about $188.00*

Note: A duplicate of this necklace, along with a matching bracelet and earrings, was sold at the Diana Vreeland Collection of Fashion Jewelry auction at Sotheby's, October 1987, for $1045.00.

Kenneth Jay Lane Bracelet. Hinged cuff, black enamel with a gold-plated Maltese cross (inspired by Chanel), cabochon and faceted multicolored rhinestones, marked Kenneth Lane, 1960s (still being manufactured). *Currently about $113.00*

Note: Similar bracelets were sold at the same Sotheby's auction for $1100.00–$1430.00.

Kenneth Jay Lane faux-coral earrings and enamel figural pins. *Photo by Kenneth Chen, jewelry from the author's collection and courtesy of Only Yesterday, Hudson, NY, and Charles France.*

Top to Bottom, Left to Right.

Kenneth Jay Lane Earrings. Large coral cabochon center stone, surrounded by round white rhinestones and coral cabochons, gold-plated, marked *K.J.L.*, 1960s.   *$50.00–$75.00*

Kenneth Jay Lane Pin. Cupid with a bow and arrows, orange enameled torso, round white pavé-set rhinestone trim, gold-plated, marked *K.J.L.*, circa 1960s.   *$175.00–$225.00*

Kenneth Jay Lane Pin. Lizard with reversible belly, round white pavé-set rhinestones, green cabochon eyes and at top of the head, belly reverses to turquoise glass beads, gold-plated, marked *K.J.L.*, circa 1960s.

$175.00–$225.00

Kenneth Jay Lane Pin. Reindeer, round white pavé- and bezel-set rhinestone and green cabochon accents, pearl drop from jeweled neckpiece, textured gold-plated with silver-plated horns and leaves on the neckpiece, marked *K.J.L.*, circa 1960s. $175.00–$225.00

Kenneth Jay Lane Pin. Sea goddess playing a lyre, round white pavé-set rhinestone body, white enameled legs, gold-plated, marked *K.J.L.*, circa 1960s. $175.00–$225.00

Kenneth Jay Lane Pin. Two-headed unicorn, cream enamel body, green cabochon eyes, white rhinestone trim, gold-plated, marked *K.J.L.*, 1960s. $125.00–$175.00

Kenneth Jay Lane Pin. Walrus, gray enameled body, white enameled tusks, large central glass coral cabochon, green rhinestone eye, white rhinestone trim, gold-plated, marked *K.J.L.*, circa 1960s. $175.00–$225.00

Kenneth Jay Lane Pin. Fish with round white pavé-set rhinestone scales and a green cabochon eye, gold-plated, marked *K.J.L.*, circa 1960s. $125.00–$175.00

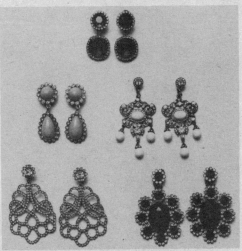

Kenneth Jay Lane rhinestone drop earrings. *Photo by Kenneth Chen, jewelry courtesy of Charles France.*

Top to Bottom, Left to Right.

Kenneth Jay Lane Earrings. Round red faceted rhinestone drops circled by round white prong-set rhinestones with matching smaller tops, marked *K.J.L.*, silver-plated, 1960s. $200.00–$225.00

Kenneth Jay Lane Earrings. Round and pear-shape plastic turquoise stone drops, circled with white bezel-set rhinestones, marked *K.J.L.*, gold-plated, 1960s.   *$200.00–$225.00*

Kenneth Jay Lane Earrings. Ornate girandole pendants with white plastic center stones and bead drops, trimmed with white, bezel- and pavé-set rhinestones, marked *K.J.L.*, gold-plated, circa 1970s.   *$200.00–$225.00*

Kenneth Jay Lane Earrings. Large drop medallion with round white rhinestones, marked *K.J.L.*, dark plated metal, 1960s.   *$200.00–$225.00*

Kenneth Jay Lane Earrings. Large floral drops with a red faceted center rhinestone surrounded by florets, each with a red rhinestone center and white prong-set rhinestone petals, marked *K.J.L.*, gunmetal-plated, 1960s.
                                                         $200.00–$225.00

Kenneth Jay Lane oversize gypsy hoop earrings with white and jet rhinestones. *Photo courtesy of Kenneth Jay Lane.*

Kenneth Jay Lane Earrings. Oversize Gypsy hoops, round white prong-set rhinestones and large prong-set jet stone centers, 1967.
                                                         $150.00–$200.00

Kenneth Jay Lane geometric gladiator cuff bracelets. *Photo courtesy of Kenneth Jay Lane.*

Kenneth Jay Lane Bracelets. A pair of "gladiator" cuffs, geometric spiked design, gold-plated, 1966.   *$150.00–$225.00 each*

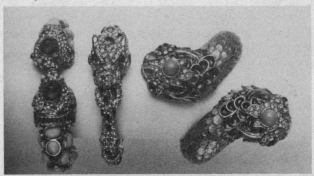

Kenneth Jay Lane animal bracelets. *Photo by Kenneth Chen, jewelry courtesy of Charles France.*

Left to Right.

Kenneth Jay Lane Bracelet. Hinged bangle with a pair of dragon heads, large turquoise bezel-set cabochons, enameled tongues and teeth, white baguettes on the collars, small turquoise bead eyes, sapphire domed cabochon at the top of each head, gold-plated, marked *K.J.L.,* 1960s.

$750.00

Kenneth Jay Lane Bracelet. Hinged bangle, panther with tail in mouth, round white pavé-set rhinestones with tiny "spots" of green enamel, small green cabochon eyes, marked *K.J.L.*, 1960s.   *$750.00*

Kenneth Jay Lane Bracelet. Hinged open-twist bangle, double serpent heads, golden scales, blue enameled scales near the heads, round white pavé-set rhinestone heads, small green cabochon eyes, large coral bezel-set cabochons at the top of each head with yellow enamel on each face, gold-plated, marked *K.J.L.*, 1960s.   *$750.00*

Lanvin abstract floral enamel bracelet and necklace. *Photo by Kenneth Chen, jewelry courtesy of Terry Rodgers, New York.*

Lanvin Bracelet and Necklace Set. Abstract floral, multicolored, enameled pendant on a snake chain with a double "L" signature tag on the catch. Matching hinged bangle, gold-plated, marked *Lanvin Paris*, 1960s.
                                        $110.00 the set

Lanvin hoop earrings, DeNicola enamel-and-rhinestone horoscope pins. *Photo by Kenneth Chen, jewelry courtesy of Charles France.*

Top to Bottom.

Lanvin Earrings. Large hoops with tiny green rhinestones in snail shell tops, marked *Lanvin Paris*, gold-plated, 1960s.   *$150.00–$200.00*

DeNicola Pins. Part of a horoscope series. Aries has a green plastic head, green enameled horns, an orange enameled body with round white pavé-set rhinestone trim, gold-plated. Pisces has carved coral plastic bodies, green enameled heads and tails with round white pavé-set rhinestone trim, gold-plated, 1960s. $100.00–$125.00 each

Mimi di N filigree ball necklace. *Photo by Kenneth Chen, jewelry courtesy of Mimi di N.*

Mimi di N Necklace. Double row of large round white prong-set rhinestones edged with small gold filigree balls, with medium and large gold filigree ball drops, 1967–68. $400.00–$550.00

Mimi di N rhinestone chandelier earrings. *Photo by Kenneth Chen, jewelry courtesy of Mimi di N.*

Mimi di N Earrings. Rhinestone chandeliers, round white prong-set rhinestones with pear-shape rhinestone drops, gold-plated, 1968–69. $250.00–$300.00

Mimi di N multistrand pearl-and-bead necklace. *Photo by Kenneth Chen, jewelry courtesy of Mimi di N.*

Mimi di N Necklace. Eight strands of pearls, spiral tube beads over plastic, French handmade emerald glass beads and small white prong-set rhinestone balls with an ornate criss-cross clasp of round white pavé-set rhinestones and an emerald cabochon rhinestone, 1965.   *$450.00–$550.00*

Mimi di N structural pin. *Photo by Kenneth Chen, jewelry courtesy of Mimi di N.*

Mimi di N Pin. Structural metal loops with a blue Lucite center, textured-bronze-plated, unsigned, 1960s.   *$175.00–$225.00*

Mimi di N corrugated cross pin. *Photo by Kenneth Chen, jewelry courtesy of Mimi di N.*

Mimi di N Pin. Corrugated cross with Swarovski round white prong-set rhinestones, silver-plated brass,   *$75.00–$125.00*

Mimi di N heart pin. *Photo by Kenneth Chen, jewelry courtesy of Charles France.*

Mimi di N Pin. Red cabochon heart with round white prong-set rhinestones in a spray, gold-plated, 1960s. $150.00–$200.00

Miriam Haskell turquoise bead and pearl necklace, bracelet, pin, and earrings set. *Photo by Kenneth Chen, jewelry from the author's collection.*

Top to Bottom.

Miriam Haskell Pin, Necklace, Earrings, and Bracelet Set. Floral pin with small turquoise glass beads on brass wire, wrapped around gold-plated circles and turquoise pear-shape glass stone petals with a round white rhinestone center and white rhinestone trim. The double-strand baroque pearl necklace has gold spacers and a floral clasp of turquoise pear-shape glass stones with a round white rhinestone center. Earrings have the same gold-plated leaf with white rhinestone and turquoise beaded motif as the pin. Bracelet has turquoise beads wrapped around a flexible gold band with a floral clasp of tiny white rhinestones in gold-plated filigree, with a center turquoise glass bead, two pendants, one the same as the earring design, the other similar to the clasp on the pearls, 1960s. $800.00–$950.00 the set

Napier, Hattie Carnegie, DeNicola, Boucher, ART, and Mimi di N pins. *Photo by Kenneth Chen, jewelry courtesy of The Napier Co. and Terry Rodgers, New York.*

Top to Bottom, Left to Right.

Napier Pin. Camel with multicolored glass beads over a blue rhinestone ball, with purple rhinestones at the bottom of the saddle, a red bead hanging from the bridle, gold-plated, 1960s.   *$125.00–$175.00*

Hattie Carnegie Pin. Tree with blue and turquoise glass bead "fruit," gray rhinestones in the branches, gold-plated, 1960s.   *$30.00*

DeNicola Pin. Three intertwined snakes with green stone eyes, gold-plated, 1960s.   *$38.00*

Boucher Pin. Bees and a honeycomb with round white pavé-set rhinestones on the wings, marked *9160P*, gold-plated, 1960s.   *$60.00*

ART Pin. Peacock with a black enameled body, blue, black, and brown tail feathers, white rhinestones in the body, gold-plated, 1960s.   *$48.00*

Mimi di N Pin. Smiling fish with a pearl in the mouth, green enameled body, green stone eye, round pink pavé-set rhinestones in the head, gold-plated, 1960s.   *$45.00*

Napier Pin. Donkey with a cart filled with multicolored glass beads, gold-plated, 1960s.   *$125.00–$175.00*

Napier figural scatter pins and unsigned rosette pin and earrings set. *Photo by Kenneth Chen, jewelry courtesy of The Napier Co. and Mr. and Mrs. Frank Corio.*

Left to Right, Top to Bottom.

Napier Pins. Hummingbird, bee, and butterfly scatter pins, round white pavé-set rhinestone trim, red rhinestone eyes, the hummingbird and bee are gold-plated, the butterfly is silver-plated, 1960s.   *$60.00–$85.00 each*

Unsigned Pin and Earrings Set. Gold-plated flower with smaller matching earrings, 1950s.   *$35.00–$50.00 the set*

Napier rhinestone chandelier earrings. *Photo by Kenneth Chen, jewelry courtesy of Cindy Shulga, The Napier Co.*

Napier Earrings. Rhinestone chandeliers, crown-shape tops with white baguettes and round white prong-set rhinestones, drops with white baguettes and round white rhinestone fringe, silver-plated, 1960s.

$250.00–$400.00

Nettie Rosenstein portrait necklace and earrings set. *Photo by Kenneth Chen, jewelry courtesy of Norman Crider Antiques, New York.*

Nettie Rosenstein Necklace and Earrings Set. Ornate revival design, woman's portrait on a pendant, circled with round white rhinestones in a foliate frame with Maltese crosses on a drop and on the matching earrings, twisted rope chain, gold-plated, 1960s.   *$750.00 the set*

Nettie Rosenstein bull pin. *Photo by Kenneth Chen, jewelry courtesy of Charles France.*

Nettie Rosenstein Pins. Three bulls, large black, large and small white (not pictured), ornate floral neckpieces with white rhinestones and turquoise or red cabochons, gold-plated, 1960s.   *$1400.00 the set*

Pauline Trigère jet rhinestone collars. *Photo by Kenneth Chen, jewelry courtesy of Pauline Trigère.*

Top to Bottom.

Pauline Trigère Necklace. Dog collar with six strands of large square prong-set jet rhinestones, unsigned, dark plated metal, 1960s. *$300.00*

Pauline Trigère Necklace. Collar, large marquis and round prong-set rhinestones with black teardrop-shape beads, unsigned, gold-plated, 1960s. *$500.00*

Pauline Trigère rhinestone collar. *Photo by Kenneth Chen, jewelry courtesy of Pauline Trigère.*

Pauline Trigère Necklace. Collar with large emerald and topaz round prong-set rhinestones on a twisted snake chain, unsigned, gold-plated, 1962. *$500.00*

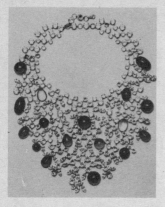

Pauline Trigère bib necklace. *Photo by Kenneth Chen, jewelry courtesy of Pauline Trigère.*

Pauline Trigère Necklace. Bib with large round and marquis white prong-set rhinestones with multicolored cabochons, unsigned, 1963.   *$500.00*

Pauline Trigère cover for *Harper's Bazaar*, November 1962, with a six-strand rhinestone collar. *Photo of cover and jewelry by Kenneth Chen, original cover and jewelry courtesy of Pauline Trigère.*

Pauline Trigère Necklace Photographed on a Harper's Bazaar *Cover Showing a Pauline Trigère Evening Dress.* Dog collar with six strands of large round white prong-set rhinestones with ruby drops, dark plated metal, unsigned, 1960s.   *$500.00*

Pauline Trigère enamel bib necklace. *Photo by Kenneth Chen, jewelry courtesy of Beverly Birks, New York.*

Pauline Trigère Necklace. Bib with large white enameled, textured plates suspended from a chain, brass rings, gold-plated, 1962.   *$650.00*

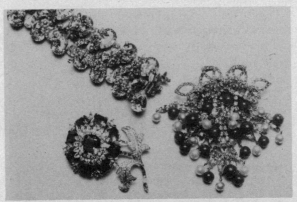

Robert rhinestone bracelet, Jomaz rhinestone pin, and Hattie Carnegie rhinestone-and-pearl cascade pin. *Photo by Kenneth Chen, jewelry courtesy of Charles France.*

Left to Right, Top to Bottom.

Robert Bracelet. Large pear-shape, white prong-set rhinestones in a double row, with seed pearl florets with white rhinestone centers between the rows, on gold-plated link chain, marked *Original by Robert,* circa 1960s.
$675.00–$750.00

Jomaz Pin. Flower with central blue faceted rhinestone, white marquis rhinestones, green faceted rhinestone petals, white baguettes on the stem and white pavé-set rhinestone leaves, silver-plated, 1960s.

$500.00–$600.00

Hattie Carnegie Pin. White prong-set rhinestone bows with a cascade of green glass beads, pearls, and white rhinestones, 1960s.

$250.00–$300.00

Roger Jean Pierre rhinestone necklace. *Photo by Kenneth Chen, jewelry courtesy of the Costume Collection, Museum of the City of New York.*

Roger Jean Pierre Necklace. Graduated crest-shape links with convex, faceted, citron-colored rhinestone centers circled by round white rhinestones and white baguettes, circa 1960s. $600.00–$750.00

Schiaparelli rhinestone bracelet and earrings set. *Photo by Kenneth Chen, jewelry courtesy of Muriel Karasik Gallery, New York.*

Schiaparelli Bracelet and Earrings Set. Clear emerald and jet kite-shape, faceted prong-set rhinestone link bracelet, with round, iridescent, blue faceted rhinestones at edges and between links, silver-plated, marked *Pat. No. 156452,* matching earrings, 1960s. $950.00 the set

Stanley Hagler pin, pendant necklaces, and earrings. *Photo by Kenneth Chen, jewelry courtesy of Terry Rodgers, New York.*

Top to Bottom.

Stanley Hagler Pin. Large purple agate stone in a bamboo frame with tiny pink beads and purple stones, gold-plated, 1960s. $75.00

Stanley Hagler Necklace. Single pendant with two side pieces made of black glass with gold swirls in bamboo frames on a double chain, gold-plated, unsigned, 1960s. $65.00

Stanley Hagler Necklace. Lucite cube beads, gold beads, baroque pearls, crystal beads with Art Nouveau pendant, gold-plated, unsigned, 1960s.
$75.00

Stanley Hagler Earrings. Large Lucite "lightbulb" drops in a gold- and copper-plated holder, suspended on white rhinestone rondelles, unsigned, 1960s. $85.00

SERPENTINE... beautiful twists of imagination in the colors of the current mood: turquoise, coral, black, black-and-white, or chalk white. New long necklace 25.00, Choker (not shown) 15.00, Bracelet 7.50, with disc 12.50. Earrings 7.50. Prices plus tax.

Advertisement for Trifari turquoise "Serpentine" necklace, bracelet, and earrings set in *Harper's Bazaar*, March 1961. *Photo of ad by Kenneth Chen, original ad courtesy of Trifari.*

Trifari Necklace, Bracelet, and Earrings Set. Round turquoise beads in a twisted "Serpentine" long necklace, double-strand bracelet with a pendant disk, matching disk earrings, gold plated setting, 1961. (Also manufactured with a choker necklace and made in coral, black, black and white, and white.)   *$225.00–$350.00 the set*

Advertisement for Trifari white enamel and coral cabochon bracelets, pin, and earrings set in *Vogue*, March 1968. *Photo of ad by Kenneth Chen, original ad courtesy of Trifari.*

Trifari Bracelets, Pin, and Earrings. Indian-inspired "L'Orient" white enamel "scales," coral cabochons with green rhinestone trim in a link bracket, snake twist cuff bracelet, pin and matching earrings, gold-plated, 1968.   *$350.00–$450.00 the set*

Trifari faux diamond and emerald floral necklace, bracelet, and earrings set. *Photo by Kenneth Chen, jewelry courtesy of Charles France.*

Trifari Necklace, Bracelet, and Earrings Set. Marquis, prong-set faux diamonds, with round, faceted, prong-set faux emeralds in a flower motif, matching flower earrings, 1960s.   *$1000.00–$1250.00*

Trifari enamel and faux-carved-jade swan and dragon pins. *Photo by Jessica Michael, jewelry courtesy of Tania Santé's Classic Collectables, Miami.*

Left to Right.

Trifari Pin. Large swan with orange enameled feathers, a carved glass jade body and white pavé-set rhinestone trim, gold-plated, 1960s.   *$300.00*

Trifari Pin. Large dragon with orange enameled body, a large carved glass jade center and white pavé-set rhinestone trim, 1960s.   *$500.00*

Unsigned four-strand pearl tassel necklace, rhinestone pendant earrings, and multiple circle earrings. *Photo by Jessica Michael, jewelry courtesy of Tania Santé's Classic Collectables, Miami.*

Top to Bottom.

Unsigned Necklace. Four-strand pearl tassel necklace, round white pavé-set rhinestones and white baguettes form a double paisley-shape clasp, elongated pearl drops at the base, 1960s. $125.00

Unsigned Earrings. Pendants with round white rhinestone swirls, black plated metal, 1960s. $50.00

Unsigned Earrings. Round white prong-set rhinestones in multiple circles, gold-plated, 1960s. $5C 00

Unsigned rhinestone "star" necklace. *Photo by Kenneth Chen, jewelry courtesy of the Costume Collection, Museum of the City of New York. (Gift of Mrs. Wilda Symonds to the museum.)*

Unsigned Necklace. Collar with blue, amethyst, and green marquis and round prong-set rhinestones in tracery-linked points, black enameled setting, circa 1960s. $500.00–$650.00

Unsigned rhinestone-and-pearl "over the wrist" bracelet. *Photo by Kenneth Chen, jewelry courtesy of the Costume Collection, Museum of the City of New York. (Gift of Mrs. Wilda Symonds to the museum.)*

Unsigned Bracelet. Indian-inspired, raised and branched links encircling the wrist and extending over the hand to the knuckle, round and marquis white rhinestones and three teardrop faux pearls in a black enameled setting, 1965. $275.00–$350.00

Note: A photo of this bracelet appeared in *Vogue,* August 15, 1965.

Unsigned floral rhinestone necklace and bracelet. *Photo by Kenneth Chen, jewelry courtesy of the Costume Collection, Museum of the City of New York. (Gift of Mrs. Wilda Symonds to the museum.)*

Left to Right.

Unsigned Necklace. Linked pastel pavé-set rhinestones in foliate tendrils with square-cut iridescent-pastel rhinestone centers, graduated with central multistone shape, 1960s. $1500.00–$1750.00

Unsigned Bracelet. Periwinkle, turquoise, and light blue round and pear-shape prong-set rhinestones, three-dimensionally linked in floral shapes, marked Austria, 1960s. $250.00–$300.00

Unsigned "Maharajah" rhinestone necklace and earrings set. *Photo by Kenneth Chen, jewelry courtesy of the Costume Collection, Museum of the City of New York. (Gift of Mrs. Wilda Symonds to the museum.)*

Unsigned Necklace and Earrings Set. Linked leaf-shape pendants with round white pavé-set rhinestones and emerald-cut red rhinestone centers, with additional connecting white rhinestones, matching smaller earrings, silver-plated, 1960s.   *$1200.00–$1500.00 the set*

Unsigned and Scaasi rhinestone earrings. *Photo by Kenneth Chen, jewelry courtesy of the Costume Collection, Museum of the City of New York. (The Scaasi earrings were a gift of Mrs. Wilda Symonds to the museum.)*

Left to Right, Top to Bottom.

Unsigned Earrings. Large "over the ear" square-cut and round white rhinestone coils with a rhinestone spray, silver-plated, 1960s.

$75.00–$125.00

Unsigned Earrings. Starburst with round and pear-shape white rhinestones, 1960s.   *$50.00–$75.00*

Scaasi Earrings. Large linked marquis rhinestones with oversize red pear-shape drops, 1960.   **$125.00–$175.00**

Note: The Scaasi earrings appeared on the cover of *Vogue,* November 15, 1960, as "glittery Christmas-tree earrings."

Unsigned crystal basket earrings and unsigned rhinestone pendant necklace, and "over the ear" earrings set. *Photo by Jessica Michael, jewelry courtesy of Tania Santé's Classic Collectables, Miami.*

Top to Bottom.

Unsigned Earrings. Crystal baskets suspended from rhinestone chains, black-plated metal, 1960s.   **$100.00**

Unsigned Necklace and Earrings Set. Large pear-shape rhinestone double pendant on a rhinestone chain, matching "over the ear" earrings, black-plated metal, 1960s.   **$180.00 the set**

... MORE SIXTIES

Boucher Pin. Shell with aquamarine and cream enamel, gold-plated trim, signed, 1960. $35.00–$50.00

Christian Dior Pin. Stylized Maltese cross with red and green cabochons and round white rhinestones, four pearls in the center with tiny green rhinestones, bordered by round green cabochons and oval purple rhinestones, gold-plated, marked *Chr. Dior 69 Germany.* $200.00–$250.00

Jomaz Pin. Owl, cream-colored enamel back and head, round white pavé-set rhinestone eyes with black enameled centers, gold-plated, circa 1960s.
$45.00–$75.00

Kenneth Jay Lane Necklace. Mesh dog collar, marked *K.J.L.*, gold-plated, circa 1960s. $25.00–$45.00

Kenneth Jay Lane Earrings. Buttons with plastic turquoise (or coral) stones and round white prong-set rhinestones, marked *K.J.L.*, pewter-plated, 1960s. $200.00–$275.00

Kenneth Jay Lane Bracelet. Hinged bracelet with a ram's head, round white pavé-set rhinestones, green rhinestone eyes, marked *K.J.L.*, gold-plated, 1960s. $350.00–$500.00

Kenneth Jay Lane Bracelet. Hinged bracelet, white and black enamel, ram's head with curled horns, white rhinestone ring in the mouth, marked *K.J.L.*, gold-plated, 1960s. $375.00–$500.00

Note: A similar bracelet sold for $495.00 at Sotheby's auction of the Diana Vreeland Collection of Fashion Jewelry in 1987.

Kenneth Jay Lane Bracelet. Hinged bracelet, black and white enamel, crossover zebra heads with green rhinestone eyes, marked *K.J.L.*, gold-plated, 1960s. $150.00–$275.00

Note: A pair of similar bracelets sold for $550.00 at Sotheby's auction of the Diana Vreeland Collection of Fashion Jewelry in 1987.

Kenneth Jay Lane Pin/Pendant. Maltese cross with pale faux coral pear-shape cabochons and gold-plated corrugated sections, round white pavé-set rhinestones in between, marked *K.J.L.*, 1960s. $60.00–$100.00

Mimi di N Pin. Sunburst with a green cabochon center, spray of small round white rhinestones, gold-plated, 1960s. *$60.00–$75.00*

Mimi di N Bracelet. Hinged twist bangle, blue and green enameled diamond-pattern snake, round white pavé-set rhinestones on the head and tail, green chabochon eyes, gold-plated, 1960s. *$125.00–$175.00*

Monet Bracelet. Curved geometric double links, gold-plated, circa 1960s. *$35.00–$50.00*

Robert Bracelet. Hinged bangle with alternating azure blue and white enamel sections, divided by a raised gold-plated channel design, marked *Original by Robert,* circa 1960s. *$35.00–$60.00*

Trifari Pin and Earrings Set. Leaf motif, tiny round pavé-set white rhinestones, gold-plated, 1960s. *$75.00–$100.00 the set*

Trifari Pin. Indian-inspired lattice design, white enamel with turquoise cabochons and tiny sapphire rhinestones, 1960s. *$125.00–$150.00*

Trifari Pins. Three seahorses with red rhinestone eyes, four birds in flight with red rhinestone eyes, four butterflies in flight with red rhinestone eyes, three angelfish (two large, one small) with red rhinestone eyes, brushed-gold-plated, 1965. *$50.00–$75.00 each*

Trifari Necklace, Bracelet, and Earrings Set. Choker of an alternating brushed and polished gold-plated diamond pattern, matching wide linked bracelet and hoop earrings, 1960s. *$125.00–$150.00 the set*

Trifari Earrings. Red, white, and blue enameled pinwheels, gold-plated, 1967. *$25.00–$50.00*

Trifari Pins. Clam with turquoise enamel, orange seaweed, set-in pearls, oyster with orange enamel, green seaweed, pearls, seahorse with brown enamel, blue seaweed, pearls, and a green rhinestone eye, gold-plated, 1968. *$20.00–$40.00*

Trifari Pin. "Ming" turtle, red enamel with a baroque pearl center, green rhinestones on the tail, feet, and neck, gold-plated, 1965. *$250.00–$350.00*

Trifari Pin. Green enameled fleur-de-lis, gold-plated, 1960s. *$25.00–$50.00*

Trifari Pin. Red, white, and blue enameled eagle, gold-plated, 1960s. *$35.00–$55.00*

Unsigned Necklace. Lucite goldfish bowl with goldfish, gold-plated link chain, 1960s. *$125.00–$150.00*

Unsigned Necklace. Long chain made up of peace symbols, gold-plated, late 1960s.   *$15.00–$25.00*

Unsigned Bracelet and Earrings Set. Links with multistrand green glass beads, gold spacers, geometric crystal beads, rope clasp, matching earrings, gold-plated, 1960s.   *$125.00–$150.00 the set*

Unsigned Bracelet. Hinged bangle, green enamel with a plastic jade ram's head with carved plastic coral horns, round white rhinestone eyes, gold-plated, 1960s.   *$150.00–$195.00*

Unsigned Bracelet. Hinged twist bangle, brown and black diamond-pattern snake, round white bezel-set rhinestone accents and eyes, gold-plated, 1960s.   *$125.00–$150.00*

Unsigned Pin. Large painted daisy, pink and navy petals, a turquoise center and green stem and leaves, metal, 1960s.   *$10.00–$15.00*

Unsigned Pin and Earrings Set. Small painted daisy with green petals, a navy blue center and green leaves, gold-plated, 1960s.   *$10.00–$15.00*

Unsigned Earrings. Small painted daises with red petals and a yellow textured center, gold-plated, 1960s.   *$5.00–$8.00*

Unsigned Earrings. Drop balls, salmon-colored sequins with clear glass bead centers, suspended on a white chain, 1960s.   *$5.00–$10.00*

Kenneth Jay Lane's "hammered" neck rings, studded cuffs, and faux jade earrings, 1970. *Photo courtesy of Kenneth Jay Lane.*

THE SEVENTIES

The Seventies are a short chapter in the annals of costume jewelry. Manufacturers in Providence shrug their shoulders, designers in New York mutter something about chains, and women we interview can't exactly remember what they wore around their necks except love beads, peace symbols, puka shells, and huge medallions.

Space exploration; discos; flower children; women returning to the office with new status as lawyers, corporate vice presidents, and heads of their own companies; the end of the Vietnam non-war; unisex; and most important, the "do your own thing" credo—all greatly influence fashion and costume jewelry. The height of something or other is reached with men's chest wigs being advertised for those who are embarrassed about their hairless chest, now that they wear their shirts open to show off their gold chains.

For a while there's a fashion-is-dead movement when long floral skirts, vests, and imported caftans from Pakistan and India seem to take over the fashion scene. The midi skirt in 1970 gives way to the micro-mini in 1972, only to be transformed to a softer silhouette and lower hemline by 1975. Designer Mary McFadden bases her dress designs on historical periods or cultural phenomena, with accessories in hammered shapes, disks, and abstract designs in golden tones. She shows them draped across the shoulder or as one huge pendant. Zandra Rhodes's prints are freewheeling and spirited, with the shape of the dress inspired by the fabric. She parodies the street punks with a "conceptual chic" collection.

In the late Seventies, Laura Ashley emerges with a flourish, showing a country gentlewoman look that taps into a longing for the simpler life, while Yves St. Laurent's woman is wearing a man's tuxedo and other women are borrowing their lovers' Nehru suits. Catherine Deneuve's man-tailored style typifies the menswear look for women.

At the office, women discover the feminine counterpart to the male executive's "uniform" and wear two- or three-piece conservative skirt suits with full silk bowties at their throats, leaving no room for necklaces or pins; earrings are tiny, almost invisible studs or classic pearl buttons. Bracelets are gold bangles, usually worn singly, and watches are the size of men's.

Away from the office, anything goes, with skirt lengths varying from maxi to midi and some mini leftovers. Hot pants are worn by the young and the thin and by some who are neither. Anklets, once considered trashy, are shown with the new, sexy, feminine clothing styles. "Looks" are ethnic, peasant, cowboy, hippy, Gypsy, arty, and others created innovatively by their wearers. The "Rich Gypsy" look originates with Millicent Rogers's wardrobe exhibit at the American Women of Style show at the Metropolitan Museum of Art in New York. At popular discos such as Studio 54 and at art openings at the hip Jewish Museum in New York City, one sees every major style at once, including people who come with their bodies painted "Yves Klein blue" in honor of his exhibit. Women are working on developing their bodies and show them off with bare shoulders, bare arms, bare backs, see-through dresses with or without body stockings underneath, and skinny dresses that hug the body.

Romantic necklines are even prettier adorned with beaded chokers and jewelled bibs. Longer necklaces with rhinestones and carved beads are in proportion for leggy jumpsuits. Gimmicky designs flow from Paris. Yves St. Laurent shows a "Can-Can" bride and "Carmen" outfits with cinched waists and huge blousons. The African tribal look, Moroccan caftan styles, fanny wrappers, see-through fabrics, wrapped ankles, plunging necklines front and back, and gold lamé dresses with gold trim and gold jewelry are popular.

John Travolta heats up everyone with "Saturday Night Fever," and *tout le monde* goes disco dancing after midnight. Jewelry and pocketbooks are scaled down to fit the nightlife. Unobtrusive accessories that don't interfere with dancing complement wild and crazy disco outfits. Earrings become very important and are shown bulky, hammered, textured, in the shape of drops, hoops, door knockers, buttons, and elaborate pendants. Bracelets get lost in long sleeves made of floaty fabrics, but large rings make a big comeback. Necklaces are dog collars, chokers, wooden beads, macramé bibs, ethnic amulets, and large, heavy medallions. For evening, big "headlight" crystals, long pendants, dressy dog collars, and gold beads are worn. In the mid-Seventies, neck rings with suspended ornaments and crescent-shape necklaces are made by all the big manufacturers. Once again, initials and zodiacs are everywhere—answering the favorite California question, "What's your sign?" In 1977, a pyramid pendant is sold with an accompanying booklet extolling its mysterious powers. In 1979 King Tut travels across the country, sparking yet another Egyptian revival in jewelry.

Ripped black stockings, bruised-looking eye makeup, rainbow-hued hair, and other-worldly music is what's hot at the punk Mudd Club in New York. Bicycle chains, safety pins, and pointed studs on leather collars that are usually worn by killer dogs pass for jewelry on all sexes.

We see very little Seventies jewelry from the major companies at current flea markets and antiques shows. By chance last week, we saw the Erwin Pearl necklace shown in the photograph on the next page, but usually we see closeouts of inexpensive jewelry from mass manufacturers. It would probably be an excellent time to start collecting Seventies jewelry now because very few dealers and collectors are.

WENDY GELL, A SEVENTIES' INNOVATOR

WENDY GELL
©DISNEY CO *Wendy Gell* WENDY GELL

In 1975, a young New York songwriter named Wendy Gell creates her first "wristy" when she glues together some bits and pieces she finds in remnant bins on Canal Street. Rhinestones, plastic palm trees and flamingos are artistically arranged on an expandable copper bracelet and presented to a friend for his birthday. He loves it so much he goes into the "wristy" business with her. They show their first samples in a wooden wine case and are a huge success.

Through the Seventies and on into the Eighties, Wendy Gell's designs are on the cover of *Vogue* and in thousands of editorials in magazines all over the world. She says she's inspired by a wide range of stimuli—the artist Georgia O'Keefe, King Tut's exhibit, a vacation trip to Mexico.

Today Wendy creates collectible sequined Disney characters (© Disney), a jewelled "Roger Rabbit" (© Disney/Amblin) and friends, Wizard of Oz jewelry (© MGM/Turner), and masks from "The Phantom of the Opera" (© Really Useful Group). She produces four lines of jewelry each year, in addition to the special pieces she does for fashion shows for Bill Blass, Oscar de la Renta, and Louis Dell'Olio. There are a thousand styles of earrings in the line, because the company specializes in a "different" look. Chain stores often buy dozens of one style, but put just one of each style in a store. Many of the fabulous large cuff bracelets are one-of-a-kind or produced in small groups of multiples. Wendy's pieces are collected by Marisa Berenson, who shows them in her book, Liza Minelli, Elizabeth Taylor, Elton John, and the late Liberace.

Collectors of Wendy Gell jewelry can tell the older pieces by the glue around the edge of the cuff, which yellows with age. The early signature is made by an electric pen, or may be signed "Wristies by Wendy TM," and is replaced in 1986 by an oval disk which is soldered into the piece. Detail bead work gets finer in the more recent pieces. If a collector wants a piece dated or validated, send a polaroid to Wendy Gell Jewelry, Inc., 37 West 37th Street, 11th Floor, New York, NY 10018.

Erwin Pearl molten "gold" abstract necklace. *Photo by Kenneth Chen, jewelry courtesy of Erwin Pearl.*

Erwin Pearl Necklace. Heavy molten gold-plated abstract pendant with sculptural links, 1970s.   *$75.00–$125.00*

Eva Graham leaf necklace. *Photo by Kenneth Chen, jewelry courtesy of Charles France.*

Eva Graham Necklace. Choker of overlapping textured leaves with corrugated spacers, gold-plated, 1970s.   *$90.00–$125.00*

Mimi di N cutout pendant necklace. *Photo by Kenneth Chen, jewelry courtesy of Mimi di N.*

Mimi di N Necklace. Brass cutout pendant on a gold chain with a carved black bone and gold coin center, unsigned, 1970.   *$175.00–$225.00*

Mimi di N shell-design necklace. *Photo by Kenneth Chen, jewelry courtesy of Mimi di N.*

Mimi di N Necklace. Seashell pendants on a seashell link chain, with blue glass lapis-lazuli stones, cast-gold-plated metal, signed Mimi di N, 1972.
$250.00–$300.00

Napier two-tone metal necklace and bracelets, Pierre Cardin metal necklace (center). *Photo by Kenneth Chen, jewelry courtesy of The Napier Co. and Sloane Miller.*

Top to Bottom.

Napier Bracelet. Open cuff, two-tone gold- and silver-plated textured and smooth metal, 1970s.   *$75.00–$100.00*

Pierre Cardin Necklace. Double pendant, black and silver metal on a silver chain, marked *Pierre Cardin Made in France,* circa 1970s.

                                              $50.00–$75.00

Napier Necklace. Pendant, two-tone silver and gold metal on a snake chain, 1970s.   *$50.00–$75.00*

Napier Bracelet. Two-tone metal in links, 1970s.   *$50.00–$75.00*

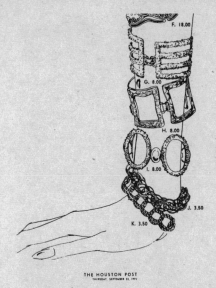

Advertisement for Napier link bracelets in *The Houston Post*, September 23, 1971. *Original ad courtesy of The Napier Co.*

Napier Bracelets. Various-shaped link bracelets in polished, textured, and hammered finishes, gold-plated, 1971. $25.00–$50.00

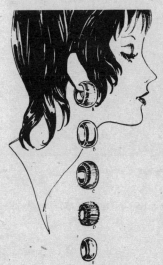

Advertisement for Napier "wedding band" earrings in *The Washington Daily*, September 29, 1971. *Original ad courtesy of The Napier Co.*

Napier Earrings. "Wedding band" hoop earrings, textured, polished, fluted, silver- and gold-plated, 1971. $15.00–$35.00

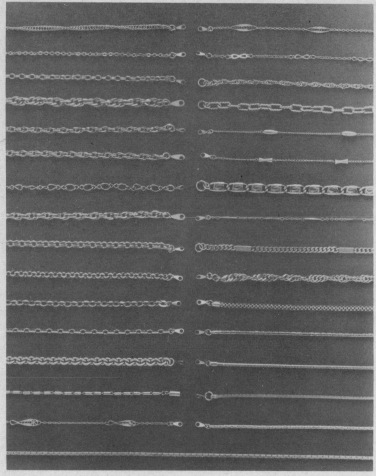

Trifari chain necklaces. *Photo courtesy of Trifari.*

Trifari Necklaces. Various chains, gold- or silver-plated.　*$15.00–$35.00*

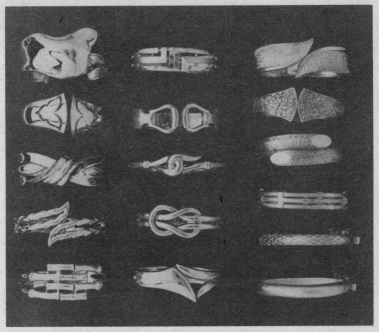

Trifari metal bracelets. *Photo courtesy of Trifari.*

Trifari Bracelets. Bangles, hinged cuffs, open cuffs, twists, gold- or silver-plated, 1970s. $20.00–$65.00

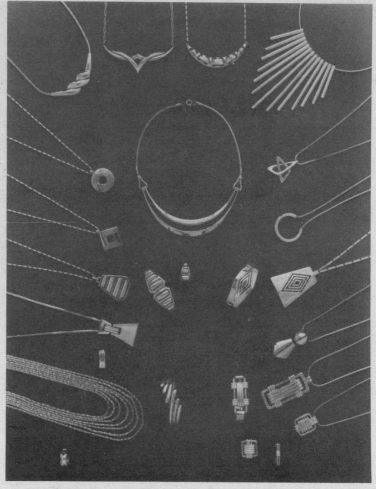

. Trifari necklaces, bracelets, and set. *Photo courtesy of Trifari.*

Trifari Necklaces, Bracelets, and Rings. Pendants, chains, neck rings, gold- or silver-plated, 1970s.   *$20.00–$45.00*

. . . MORE SEVENTIES

DeNicola Pin. Curved branches, central turquoise heart, gold-plated, circa 1970s. $20.00–$40.00

Kenneth Jay Lane Bracelet. Hinged cuff with an allover "X" pattern, marked *K.J.L.*, gold-plated, circa 1970s. $25.00–$50.00

Polcini Pin. Winston Churchill, gold-plated, 1970s. $15.00–$25.00

Polcini Pin. Art Deco revival, golfer with allover, round, white, pavé-set rhinestones, pearl "golfball," 1970s. $20.00–$35.00

Unsigned Pin. Lips, red sparkly plastic, $5.00–$15.00

Unsigned Pin/Pendant. Forties revival, large profile of a woman with tendrils of hair on a semicircular frame, pink enameled flower in her hair, gold-plated with a silver-plated face, 1970s. $20.00–$40.00

Madonna, the entertainer who rocked the fashion world in the 1980s, is shown here at the 1984 MTV Awards. *Photo by Robin Platzer, courtesy of Warner Bros. Records.*

THE EIGHTIES

The Eighties—the peak of the self, the "me" generation, health clubs and oat bran, designer chocolates, Reaganomics, total freedom in dress, hemlines that are fine wherever they land, Madonna's global fashion influence, Barbara Bush's pearls, and the old "mirror, mirror" question now being "Who is the thinnest of them all?"—answered by Tom Wolfe's social X rays and Nancy Reagan, the reigning Queen of Thin.

Costume jewelry is practically a religion, with devotees numbering among the millions. Accessories shows overflow huge convention halls, women don't even bother to use the excuse of traveling to wear it with ball gowns, and people are collecting vintage costume jewelry with a vengeance, waiting in line hours before estate sales begin. Copies of copies are sold on street corners for the price of a magazine. Every major fashion designer has a line of costume jewelry that accessorizes each season's line. Materials reflect the experimental days of the Twenties and Thirties, with designers using plastics, metals, wood, shells, cork, coins, papier-mâché, glass, leather, and all kinds of combinations.

Women wear multiples of everything. Earrings are worn in a series along the outer edge of pierced ears, bracelets are worn in clusters, and groups of necklaces combine old, new, real, and costume. Diane Smith, senior fashion editor at *Glamour,* collects multiple strands of beads in every color to fill in a collar or a neckline. She thinks it's great to mix everything—chains, gold lockets, and costume jewelry that give the look heft and importance. Diane says that the simple way we dress today requires elegant, glamorous jewelry. The basic double-breasted dark evening suit needs the most spectacular piece to dress it up—it should be basic but big, important basic.

Diane notes that today's woman wants to be able to wear something over and over and not tire of it. She can't be bothered with fussy or fragile jewelry. She wants jewelry that can be relied on all the time.

In the fall of 1985, Donna Karan, a leading designer of contemporary clothing, starts her own line of designer jewelry. As Donna sees it, "Jewelry is important because it gives a woman a chance to express her individuality. It allows a woman to achieve her own fashion personality."

The look of Donna's jewelry is inspired by the drape and silhouette of the fabrics she uses in her collections. There is nothing stiff about the jewelry, it is comfortable to wear and has movement like the clothing Donna designs. Pieces go from the softness and fluidity of beads and chain mesh to unique hard-edge pieces that become signature sculptural work. The cast pieces are 24K gold-plated brass with semi-precious stones.

Donna loves jewelry that makes noise. She believes that in the way a woman has a scent, she also has a sound that is uniquely hers. Since Donna's jewelry is inspired by her clothing designs and is an integral part of the collection, it is housed alongside the clothing in the in-store Donna Karan Boutiques, so that women can appreciate the total look.

Artists as well as clothing designers are turning to jewelry design as an outlet for their creative energies. In 1986 Maria Snyder, a young, former Yves St. Laurent model who had studied art in Paris and received a master's degree in art history, starts her own costume jewelry company.

> I'm a born sculptor. I see jewelry as an extension of sculpture. I use plastic that I mold with my hands. I never draw my designs; I sculpt them in plastic or clay. I also cast white metal and resin and use freeform plastics. The pieces are plated in 24K gold or gold leafed by hand.
>
> I entered jewelry making so innocently; I knew nothing about the industry. I made my first bracelets over my own wrist, and they didn't fit anyone else. Some things I do are truly experimental. I just say to myself, "Wouldn't it be fun to try that!" I've designed jewelry for Giorgio di Sant'Angelo, Geoffrey Beene, Carolina Herrera, and Isabel Toledo for their fashion shows. My rings are worn by Jody Watley on her album cover, and the model Paulina is wearing my earrings in the Estée Lauder ads. My jewelry is in fifty or sixty stores. I love to design, and I love working with different materials. The important thing for me is the grace of the line.

Maria's jewelry and sculptures have been exhibited in art galleries in New York and Florida. The direction her work is taking is an important one in the designs of the Eighties—bold, well-crafted, and innovative, with an excellent use of materials that satisfies form, function, and design.

Artisan jewelry, replicas of precious jewelry, "theme" jewelry such as Miriam Haskell's "Phantom of the Opera" line and Wendy Gell's Disney characters are the outstanding design motifs in the late Eighties. Candy Pratts Price, senior fashion director for accessories and shoes at *Vogue*, believes that estate jewelry is coming back into fashion because of today's value-consciousness. She thinks costume jewelry that copies estate collections will be popular in the future, in the way that so many manufacturers are influenced by the Duchess of Windsor's jewelry.

Street jewelry that gets its rough edges refined continues to find its way into the mainstream of design. Crystals, once the province of the New Age, are now designed by Tina Chow and Yves St. Laurent and sold at real jewelry prices. Rhinestones, once bought at secondhand stores by teenagers and used to dress up black leather jackets, are revived. New marcasite jewelry is imported from the Far East and is bought up by people who never saw it the first time around. Variations of heavy Byzantine and Renaissance jewelry encrusted with deep-colored rhinestones, enameled Sixties revivals of animal bracelets, ethnic and tribal creations, coin necklaces, charm bracelets, and glittery rhinestone pieces are made by hundreds of manufacturers.

Using the measuring stick of what collectors look for in vintage jewelry—quality of workmanship, design, and materials—we are attempting to make some predictions of what will be valuable in the year 2000. We haven't seen everyone's work. We've chosen a few designers who've come to our attention through the media, from suggestions of fashion editors, and from our own knowledge of what has survived from the past and is interesting to contemporary collectors.

The big names—Trifari, Napier, Monet, Miriam Haskell, Christian Dior, Kenneth Jay Lane, Yves St. Laurent, and Chanel—are joined by relative newcomers Robert Lee Morris, Carolee, Jay Feinberg, Frances Patiky Stein, Herve Van Der Straeten, Eric Beamon, Steve Vaubel, Donna Karan, Maria Snyder, Wendy Gell, and Erwin Pearl. Companies such as Ciner, Panetta, Mimi di N, Hobé, and Joseff-Hollywood continue to make high-quality costume jewelry. The best advice from all of the experts we've asked to make predictions about collecting contemporary costume jewelry (with an eye to future investment) is to buy what you love, look for well-made pieces, and take care of them properly.

Carole Daner geometric crystal earrings. *Photo by Nicholas Politis, jewelry courtesy of Carole Daner.*

Carole Daner Earrings. Red, jet, and crystal Austrian pavé-set rhinestones in a geometric pattern, 1980s.   *About $225.00*

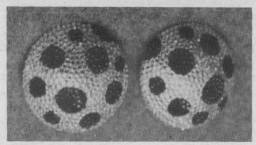

Carole Daner polka dot crystal earrings. *Photo by Nicholas Politis, jewelry courtesy of Carole Daner.*

Carole Daner Earrings. Jet and crystal Austrian pavé-set rhinestones in a polka dot pattern, 1980s.   *About $235.00*

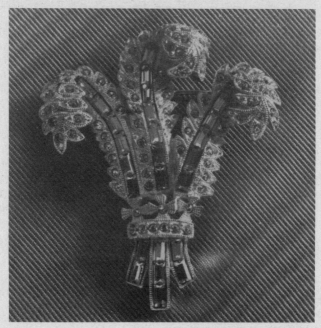

Carolee feather pin. *Photo courtesy of Carolee Designs.*

Carolee Pin. Feathers with round and baguette white rhinestones, from "The Estate Collection," inspired by the Duchess of Windsor's jewelry, silver-plated, 1987.   *About $95.00*

Carolee flamingo pin. *Photo courtesy of Carolee Designs.*

Carolee Pin. Flamingo with red, green, and blue channel-set rhinestones in the tail feathers, round white pavé-set rhinestones on the head, neck, and body and a round blue rhinestone eye, from "The Estate Collection," inspired by the Duchess of Windsor's jewelry, gold-plated, 1987.

About $75.00

Carolee heart pin. *Photo courtesy of Carolee Designs.*

Carolee Pin. Heart shape with a green enameled double-entwined "W" and "E" monogram, round red rhinestones in the crown, round white pavé-set rhinestones, and red enamel "X"s at the base, signifying the 20th anniversary of the Duke and Duchess of Windsor, from "The Estate Collection," inspired by the Duchess of Windsor's jewelry, gold-plated, 1987.

About $95.00

Carolee pearl-and-crystal necklaces and pearl earrings. *Photo courtesy of Carolee Designs.*

Carolee Necklaces and a Pair of Earrings. A group of pearl and crystal necklaces with gold coins, gold-plated, Spring 1989.

About $55.00–$125.00

Pearl button earrings, gold rope frames, Spring 1989.   *About $55.00*

Christian Dior parrot pins. *Photo courtesy of Christian Dior Bijoux, Grosse Jewels.*

Christian Dior Pin. Male parrot, multicolored enamel in blue, green, red, and gold, pavé-set crystals, ruby cabochon eye, 18K-gold-plated, Spring 1989.   *About $100.00*

Christian Dior Pin. Female parrot, 18K-gold-plated metal and pavé-set crystals, emerald cabochon eye, Spring 1989.   *About $75.00*

Christian Dior pearl-and-sea-creature necklace. *Photo courtesy of Christian Dior Bijoux, Grosse Jewels.*

Christian Dior Necklace. Thirty-inch strand of handmade baroque and seed pearls with handcrafted sea creatures, 18K-gold-plated, Spring 1989.   *About $490.00*

Donna Karan charm bracelet. *Photo by Arnell, courtesy of Donna Karan, New York.*

Donna Karan Bracelet. Charm bracelet with large disks of rose quartz set in 24K-gold-plated metal, suspended from chain links, Spring 1989.

About $375.00

Donna Karan necklaces. *Photo by Arnell, courtesy of Donna Karan, New York.*

Top to Bottom.

Donna Karan Necklaces. "Agate caviar" beads, rose quartz and gold-plated clusters, Spring 1989.   *About $300.00*
    Opalescent charm necklace, with rose quartz beads, gold-dipped, Spring 1989.   *About $595.00*

Eric Beamon charm necklace. *Photo by Kenneth Chen, jewelry courtesy of Showroom Seven, New York.*

Eric Beamon Necklace. Chunks of faux turquoise and amber "charms" suspended from chain links, silver-plated, 1989.   *About $326.00*

Frances Patiky Stein rhinestone necklace, bracelets, and earrings. *Photo courtesy of Frances Patiky Stein, Paris.*

Frances Patiky Stein Necklace, Bracelets, and Earrings. "Maharajah necklace" of chunks of white rhinestones set in gold on a cord of black silk.

About $712.00

Cuffs of white rhinestones and white and ruby rhinestones.

About $350.00–$450.00

Earrings with white rhinestones set in gold.   *About $162.00–$350.00*

Note: All jewelry is from the 1989 collection and is set in handmade, hammered 18K-gold-washed brass.

Herve Van Der Straeten necklace and pin. *Photo by Kenneth Chen, jewelry courtesy of Showroom Seven, New York.*

Herve Van Der Straeten Necklace. Geometric-design choker with triangular tiered pendants, gold-plated, 1989.   *About $264.00*

Herve Van Der Straeten Pin. Sun with a center of clear aqua glass, gold-plated, 1989.   *About $500.00*

Leslie Correll necklace and earrings. *Photo by Kenneth Chen, jewelry courtesy of Basil & Co., New York.*

Leslie Correll Necklace. Collar of spiked red horn, 24K-gold-plated abstract shapes, 1989.   *About $162.00*

Leslie Correll Earrings. Abstract curlicue shapes in polished and textured gold plate, 1989.   *About $50.00*

Maria Snyder necklaces. *Photo by Kenneth Chen, jewelry courtesy of Maria Snyder, New York.*

Top to Bottom.

Maria Snyder Necklace. Surrealistic face with red enameled lips, a black eye with a hematite cabochon pupil, and a blonde lock of hair, gold-plated cast metal, late 1980s.   *About $162.00*

Maria Snyder Necklace. Round links with large dark purple rhinestones, small sculpted links, gold-plated cast metal, 1980s.   *About $220.00*

Maria Snyder Necklace. Cast black plastic with round and pear-shape white rhinestones on jet braided cord, 1980s.   *About $300.00*

Maria Snyder pendant necklace. *Photo by Kenneth Chen, jewelry courtesy of Maria Snyder, New York.*

Maria Snyder Necklace. Oval links with large orange rhinestone centers, two large oval pendants, sculpted chain links, gold-plated cast metal, 1980s.   *About $325.00*

Mimi di N pearl necklace and earrings set. *Photo by Kenneth Chen, jewelry courtesy of Mimi di N.*

Mimi di N Necklace and Earrings Set. Three strands of simulated pearls with rhinestone rondelle spacers and a black enamel and round white pavé-set rhinestone wreath-shaped clasp, signed Mimi di N, 1983. The earrings are a smaller version of the clasp with a pearl center.

About $150.00

Note: This design was originally produced in 1965. In 1987 a version of it with pink stone beads that belonged to Diana Vreeland was auctioned at Sotheby's in New York for $880.00.

Miriam Haskell pendant earrings. *Photo by Bert Stern, courtesy of Self, copyright © 1987 by The Conde Nast Publications Inc.*

Miriam Haskell Earrings. Fan-shape tops with elongated pendants, antique Russian gold-plated brass, late 1980s.   *About $25.00*

Monet link necklace and earrings set. *Photo courtesy of Monet.*

Monet Necklace and Earrings Set. Bold square metal links, silver-plated with accents of gold, 1989. Necklace.   *About $115.00*
    Earrings.   *About $35.00*

Monet enamel necklace, bracelets, and earrings set. *Photo courtesy of Monet.*

Monet Necklace, Bracelets, and Earrings Set. Black and white circles on a gold-plated metal link chain, matching bracelet and earrings (also available in navy and white or black and white on silver), 1989. Necklace.

	About $55.00
Bracelets.	*About $50.00 each*
Earrings.	*About $18.00–$20.00*

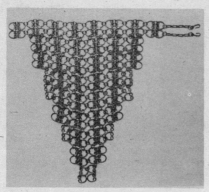

Pauline Trigère chain-link necklace. *Photo by Kenneth Chen, jewelry courtesy of Pauline Trigère.*

Pauline Trigère Necklace. Bib of gold-plated interlocking chain links, unsigned. (This necklace was originally produced in the 1970s and reissued in 1989.)   *$300.00*

Robert Lee Morris gong necklace. *Photo by Donald Waller, courtesy of Robert Lee Morris.*

Robert Lee Morris Necklace. Long graduated "gong" necklace, 1989.
Nonprecious metal. *$650.00*
  Plated brass. *$800.00*
  Sterling silver. *$1200.00*

Robert Lee Morris fertility goddess bracelet and necklace. *Photo by Donald Waller, courtesy of Robert Lee Morris.*

Robert Lee Morris Bracelet and Necklace. "Fertility goddess" charms suspended from chain links, 1989. Bracelet in nonprecious metal. *$550.00*
  Plated brass. *$600.00*
  Sterling silver. *$875.00*
  Necklace in nonprecious metal. *$1000.00*
  Plated brass. *$1200.00*
  Sterling silver. *$1650.00*

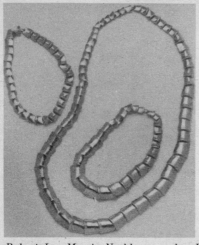

Robert Lee Morris snakescale necklaces and belt/necklace. *Photo by Donald Waller, courtesy of Robert Lee Morris.*

Robert Lee Morris Necklaces and a Belt/Necklace. "Snakescale" links, 1989. Two smaller necklaces, nonprecious metal.   *$550.00*
   Plated brass.   *$650.00*
   Sterling silver.   *$850.00*
   Largest belt/necklace, non-precious metal.   *$1100.00*
   Plated brass.   *$1200.00*
   Sterling silver.   *$1800.00*

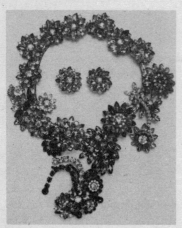

Robert Sorrell rhinestone necklace/pin and earrings set. *Photo by Kenneth Chen, jewelry courtesy of Basil & Co., New York.*

Robert Sorrell Necklace/Pin and Earrings Set. Large, multicolored pastel marquis rhinestone florets on a cobra link chain, detachable pin, matching pale blue rhinestone earrings, silver-plated, 1989.

About $800.00 the set

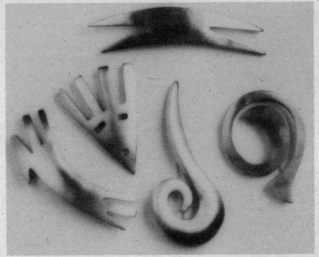

Steve Vaubel abstract pins. *Photo by Chris Johnson, jewelry courtesy of Steve Vaubel.*

Steve Vaubel Pins. Abstract shapes, 18K-gold-plated brass, 1989.
About $300.00–$350.00 each

Steve Vaubel charm necklace. *Photo by Chris Johnson, jewelry courtesy of Steve Vaubel.*

Steve Vaubel Necklace. Abstract charms on round chain links, 18K-gold-plated brass, 1989.
About $1240.00

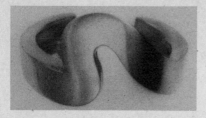

Steve Vaubel snake bracelet. *Photo by Chris Johnson, jewelry courtesy of Steve Vaubel.*

Steve Vaubel Bracelet. "Snake" open cuff, 18K-gold-plated brass, 1989.
About $280.00

Theresa Dahl papier-mâché earrings, Bev Overton Buddha pin. *Photo by Kenneth Chen, jewelry courtesy of Basil & Co., New York.*

Top to Bottom.

Theresa Dahl Earrings. Coil tops, curlicue pendants in a classical design with tubular agate drops, gold-plated papier-mâché, 1989.
About $62.00

Bev Overton Pin. Three Buddhas, two in faux jade, one in faux ivory, suspended from a bar pin with a large green rhinestone set in pink, gold-plated metal, brass dangles, 1989.   *About $87.00*

Yves St. Laurent charm necklace and earrings. *Photo courtesy of Yves St. Laurent.*

Yves St. Laurent Necklace and Various-size Earrings. "Games" motif charms suspended from chain links, with aces, diamonds, clubs, and hearts in yellow, blue, violet, red, green, rose, and gold, 1989. Necklace.

About $310.00

Earrings.   *About $50.00–$80.00 depending on size*

Yves St. Laurent Rock Crystal necklace, bracelet, and earrings. *Photo courtesy of Yves St. Laurent.*

Yves St. Laurent Necklace, Stickpin, and Earrings. Crystals wrapped in gold-plated wire, 1989. Necklace.   *About $620.00*
    Stickpin.   *About $150.00*
    Earrings.   *About $180.00*

Yves St. Laurent Bracelet and Earrings. Gold-plated chunk crystals, 1989. Bracelet.   *About $215.00*
    Earrings.   *About $65.00*

3

Resources

DEALERS WHO SPECIALIZE IN COSTUME JEWELRY*

California

Antique World
1335 Ventura Boulevard
Sherman Oaks, CA 91423
(818)789-0817

Piccolo Pete's
13814 Ventura Boulevard
Sherman Oaks, CA 91423
(818)990-5421

Off the Wall
7325 Melrose Avenue
Los Angeles, CA 90046
(213)930-1185

Country Pine & Design
1318 Montana Avenue
Santa Monica, CA 90403
(213)451-0317

Connie Parente's Accessories
Los Angeles, CA
(213)650-6882
(by appointment)

The Haight Ashbury
1500 Haight Street
San Francisco, CA 94117
(415)621-2136

Daisy's Antiques & Collectibles
131 W. Chapman Avenue
Orange, CA 92666
(714)633-6475

Patsy Comer's Antiques
7445 Reseda Boulevard
Reseda, CA 91335
(818)342-2210

*Dealers who would like to be included in this listing for future editions should write
to the author c/o House of Collectibles, 201 East 50th Street, New York, NY 10022.

Century Antiqes
1552 E. Colorado Street
Glendale, CA 91205
(818)244-9992

Connecticut

Ann Maries Vintage Boutique
1569 Chapel Street
New Haven, CT 06516
(203)787-1734

Irena Urdang's Detour
92 Main Street
Deep River, CT 06417
(203)526-9797

Rubber Dumbo
c/o Essex Old Saybrook Antique
   Center
(Attention Judy Gansuindt)
985 Middlesex Turnpike
Old Saybrook, CT 06475
(203)388-0689

The Discerning Eye
Southbury Antiques Center
750 Main Street
Southbury, CT 06488
(203)262-6313

Florida

Terri's Treasures
743 Lincoln Road
Miami Beach, FL 33139
(305)534-3322

Deco Dermots
1436 NE 163rd Street
North Miami Beach, FL 33162
(305)940-1587

Tania Santé's Classic Collectables
6556 Bird Road
Miami, FL 33155
(305)662-4975

Miami Twice
6576 Southwest 40th Street
(Bird Road)
Miami, FL 33155
(305)666-0127

Illinois

Studio V
672 N. Dearborn
Chicago, IL 60610
(312)440-1937

Flashy Trash
3524 N. Halsted
Chicago, IL 60657
(312)327-6900

Strange Cargo
3438 N. Clark
Chicago, IL 60657
(312)327-8090

The Brokerage
3448 N. Halsted
Chicago, IL 60657
(312)248-1644

Martha Torno & Rick Wright
2155 W. Highland Avenue #2W
Chicago, IL 60659
(312)465-2449
(by appointment)

Steve Starr Studio
2654 N. Clark Street
Chicago, IL 60614
(312)525-6530

Louisiana

Blackamoor
324 Chartres
New Orleans, LA 70116
(504)523-7786

Decatur Street Market
1101 Decatur Street
New Orleans, LA 70116
(504)522-0140

Monamia Antiques
1200 Decatur Street
New Orleans, LA 70116
(504)525-8686

Maine

Orphan Annie's
96 Court Street
Auburn, ME 04210
(207)782-0638

Maryland

The Antique Station
U.S. Route 15 at Motter Avenue
Exit 194, Thomas Johnson Drive
Fredrick, MD 21701
(301)695-0888

Massachusetts

Remembrances of Things Past
376 Commercial Street
Provincetown, MA 02657
(508)487-9443
(by appointment, weekends)

Sadie Green
319 Main Street
Southbridge, MA 01550
(508)765-9209

Michigan

R.F. Willis Gallery
2 Jefferson S.E.
P.O. Box 2931
Grand Rapids, MI 49501
(616)235-0990
(616)456-8400

Minnesota

Antique Jewels
Riverplace
43 S.E. Main Street
Minneapolis, MN 55414
(612)379-1660

New Jersey

Bridge Street Antiques
15 Bridge Street
Lambertville, NJ 08530
(609)397-9890

New York

Lucy Silverstein
308 S. Liberty Street
Endicott, NY 13760
(607)748-5626

Sally McEnteer
R.D. 2, Box 138
Oswego, NY 13827

Clarence Courtyard Co-op Antiques
10255 Main Street
Clarence, NY 14031
(716)759-7080

Norman Crider Antiques
Trump Tower
725 Fifth Avenue
New York, NY 10022
(212)832-6958

Jackie's Place
Route 20
Bouckville, NY 13310
(315)893-7457

Only Yesterday
608 Warren Street
Hudson, NY 12534
(518)828-6824

Beverly Birks
1215 Fifth Avenue #12C
New York, NY 10029
(212)722-3263

Mood Indigo
181 Prince Street
New York, NY 10012
(212)254-1176

Matthew Burkholz
Route 66 Antiques
21 Hudson Avenue
Chatham, NY 12037
(518)392-4777
(Friday–Monday, or by
   appointment)

Muriel Karasik Gallery
1094 Madison Avenue
New York, NY 10028
(212)535-7851

Muriel Karasik Gallery
124 Main Street
Westhampton, NY 11978
(516)288-1372
(closed during winter)

Terry Rodgers
Manhattan Art and Antiques Center
Shop 30
1050 Second Avenue
New York, NY 10022
(212)758-3164

Rita Sacks
Limited Additions
Manhattan Art and Antiques Center
1050 Second Avenue
New York, NY 10022
(212)421-8132

Ad Infinitum, Inc.
Nancy Goldsmith
(212)696-0831
(by appointment)

The Good, the Bad and the Ugly
143 East 13th Street
New York, NY 10003
(212)228-2838

Partners in Time
66 Jobs Lane
Southampton, NY 11968
(516)287-1143
(closed during winter)

The Little Shop of Antiques
230 East 80th Street
New York, NY 10028
(212)861-6656

Jóia
1151 Second Avenue
New York, NY 10022
(212)754-9017

Richard Utilla
244 East 60th Street
New York, NY 10022
(212)737-6673

Beverly Austrian
Irvington, NY
(914)591-8317
(by appointment)

Barbara Flood
Flood's Closet
New York, NY
(by appointment only)

Divine Idea
Charles France
New York, NY
(212)362-9243

Ohio

The Gatsby Collection
32770 Cannon Road
Solon, OH 44139
(216)248-2397
(by appointment)

Pennsylvania

Barbara Strand
Box 53
Neelyton, PA 17239
(Bakelite)

The Antique Market
333 Court Street
P.O. 788
Allentown, PA 18105
(215)437-9022

Carl Barto
2717 Long Farm Lane
Lancaster, PA 17601
(717)569-3536, (717)569-3505,
(215)484-4385

Candlelight Antiques & Collectibles
1110 Smithbridge Road
Glens Mills, PA 19382
(215)358-6053

Adams Antiques
Pennsylvania Turnpike,
  Exit 21, ½ mile north
  on Route 272
Denver, PA 17517
(215)267-8444
(215)267-4547

Heritage Antique Center
Pennsylvania Turnpike,
  Exit 21, one mile north
  on Route 272
Adamstown, PA 19501
(215)484-4646
(215)921-9529

Heritage Antique Center II
Pennsylvania Turnpike,
  Exit 21, two miles south
  on Route 272
Reamstown, PA 17567
(215)267-0888

Heidelberg Antiques
1550 Collier Avenue
Heidelberg, PA 15106
(412)429-9222

Rose Marie's Antiques
2136 Market Street
Camp Hill, PA 17011
(717)763-8998
(717)528-4441

Sassafrass Antiques
Silver Springs Flea Market
Carlisle Pike
Mechanicsburg, PA 17055
(717)652-7619
(Sundays)

Decades A.D.
615 South 6th Street
Philadelphia, PA 19147
(215)592-0256

Sue White
Psychedelics
R.D. 2
Box 1110
Holtwood, PA 17532
(717)284-4349

Vintage Touch
333 Montgomery Avenue
Bala Cynwyd, PA 19004
(215)667-2969

Clive H. Ensher
(215)878-4942
(by appointment)

Joseph Simms
(215)885-8399
(by appointment)

E. & J. Rothstein Antiques
611 N. High Street
West Chester, PA 19380
(215)696-1500

Collectibles by Rosemarie
Philadelphia, PA
(215)726-7452
(by appointment)

The Saturn Club
3426 Sansom Street
Philadelphia, PA 19104
(215)387-8981

Retro
244 South Street
Philadelphia, PA 19147
(215)922-5695

Texas

Past Perfect
3053 S. University Drive
Fort Worth, TX 76109
(817)926-4917

Women from Mars
Brothers from Venus
3414 Camp Bowie
Fort Worth, TX 76107
(817)877-0338

Virginia

The Antique Station
110 Possum Point Road
Dumfries, VA 22026
(703)221-7534

London

Cobra & Bellamy
149 Sloane Street
SW1 London, England

Pierre Le Frenais,
Antiquarius
131-141 Kings Road
SW3 London, England

John Jesse & Irina Laski
160 Kensington Church Street
W8 London, England

Acushia Hicks
Grays Antique Market
Davies Mews
W1 London, England

Van Peterson
117 Walton Street
SW3 London, England

Maria Merola
178 Walton Street
SW3 London, England

ANTIQUES MALLS AND MARTS WITH DEALERS WHO SPECIALIZE IN COSTUME JEWELRY*

California

Sherman Oaks Antique Mall
Sherman Oaks, CA 91403
(818)906-0338

Folsom Mercantile Exchange
724-26 Sutter Street
Folsom, CA
(916)985-2169

Newport Antique Mall
1957 Newport Boulevard
Costa Mesa, CA
(714)645-4272

Showcase Antiques
#417 Ginger Moro
13603 Ventura Boulevard
Sherman Oaks, CA
(818)905-5007

Anaheim Antique Plaza
#11 Patty's Paraphernalia
406 W. Vermont Avenue
Anaheim, CA
(714)774-3240

Connecticut

Old Library Antiques & Art Center
7 Post Road East
Westport, CT 06880
(203)227-4078

*Mall and Mart managers who would like to be included in this listing for future
editions should write to the author c/o House of Collectibles, 201 East 50th Street,
New York, NY 10022.

Maryland

Emmitsburg Antique Mall
1 Chesapeake Street
Emmitsburg, MD 21727
(301)447-6471

Beaver Creek Antique Market
Hagerstown, MD 21740
(301)739-8075

Mid-Atlantic Antiques Market
P.O. Box 701
Cambridge, MD 21613
(301)228-8858

New Jersey

Country Antiques Center
Route 38, Hainesport
Mt. Holly, NJ 08060
(609)261-1924

Ohio

The Springfield Antique Show
　and Flea Market
P.O. Box 2429
Springfield, OH 45501
(513)325-0053

Pennsylvania

Ardmart Antiques Mall
Landsdowne Avenue & State Road
Drexel Hill, PA 19026
(215)789-6622
(open Thursday–Sunday)

Famous Antique & Flea Market
Exit 6, off I-81
1495 Lincoln Way East
Chambersburg, PA 17201
(717)264-5916

Adamstown Markets
Box 107
Adamstown, PA 19501
(215)267-2177
(Sunday only)

Kutztown Markets
R.D. #1
Kutztown, PA 19530
(215)683-6848
(Saturday only)

ANTIQUES SHOW PROMOTERS

The following state-by-state listing of some of the major antiques show promoters and managers is meant to serve as a guide. At the time of publication, we were assured by each company that there would be dealers of quality vintage costume jewelry at the shows we featured. To be on the safe side, the reader should contact individual promoters to find out specific information about the shows as to dates, locations, and types of antiques being sold. Each promoter with an address and/or phone number is specified, with a list of their shows following the entry. Some promoters produce shows in and out of their home states, so they are listed under the appropriate states. We welcome additions to our listing for the next edition. To find promoters in your area that aren't listed in this section, please contact: Professional Show Managers Association, (203) 755-5278.

ARIZONA

Bustamante Enterprises
P.O. Box 637
Atwater, CA 95301
(209)358-3134
(702)827-8813 (Reno, Nevada)
(See California listings for information about this promoter)

Scottsdale
Scottsdale Activity Center
Scottsdale, AZ
(Shows twice yearly)

Fairgrounds Antique Market
214 S. 37th Street
Phoenix, AZ 85034
(800)678-9987
(Shows third weekend of each month)

Nedra Quick, Owner/Manager
Acorn Antique Guild Shows
P.O. Box 30040
Mesa, AZ 85275
(602)962-5503
(Largest show promoter in Arizona, with ten shows per year. Each show features a mix of collectibles, with 50% of the dealers exhibiting costume jewelry. The largest shows have 100 carefully selected quality dealers, with about 3,000 people in attendance)

Flagstaff Antique Show
Exhibit Building
Coconino Fairgrounds
Flagstaff, AZ
(Shows twice yearly)

Mesa Antique Show
Mesa Community Center
201 N. Center
Mesa, AZ
(Shows twice yearly)

Phoenix Antique Show
Arizona State Fairgrounds
1826 E. McDowell Road
Phoenix, AZ
(Annual February show)

Prescott Antique Show
Prescott Activity Center
824 E. Gurley Street
Prescott, AZ
(Annual August show)

Scottsdale Antique Show
Scottsdale Activity Center
11420 E. Shea Boulevard
Scottsdale, AZ
(Shows twice yearly)

Tucson Antique Show
Tucson Community Center
260 S. Church Street
Tucson, AZ
(Annual November show)

Wickenburg Antique Show
Wickenburg Community Center
120 N. Valentine Street
Wickenburg, AZ
(Annual January show)

Yuma Antique Show
Civic and Convention Center
1140 Desert Hills Drive
Yuma, AZ
(Annual February show)

CALIFORNIA

Bustamante Enterprises
P.O. Box 637
Atwater, CA
(209)358-3134
(702)827-8813 (Reno, Nevada)
(Twenty-six shows produced in ten cities yearly with a required code of
ethics for all dealers; all shows are called "Bustamante Enterprises Inc.
Antique Show & Sale" except Palm Springs)

Del Mar
Del Mar County Fairgrounds
Del Mar, CA
(Shows twice yearly)

Monterey
Monterey Civic Auditorium
Monterey, CA
(Shows twice yearly)

Palm Springs
Palm Springs Rotary Club Show
Palm Springs Convention
Center
Palm Springs, CA

Pasadena
Pasadena Center
400 E. Green Street
Pasadena, CA
(Shows four times yearly with
over 230 exhibitors; 10% of
dealers have costume jewelry)

Sacramento
Sacramento Convention Center
14th & J
Sacramento, CA
(Shows twice yearly)

San Diego
San Diego Convention Center
San Diego, CA

San Francisco
Brools Hall
Fulton & Hyde
San Francisco, CA
(Shows three times yearly)

Santa Clara
Great American Parkway
Santa Clara, CA
(Shows three times yearly)

Santa Monica
Santa Monica Civic Auditorium
Corner of Pico & Main
Santa Monica, CA
(Shows three times yearly)

Pomona Antique Market
P.O. Box 1116
Claremont, CA 91711-1116
(800)678-9987
(Shows last weekend of each month)

Sy Miller Productions
P.O. Box 967
Rancho Santa Fe, CA 92067
(619)436-3844
(Shows have 80–100 dealers, with most exhibiting some costume jewelry)

Anaheim Antique Show & Sale
Anaheim Exhibition Hall at
    Stadium
2000 State College
Anaheim, CA
(Shows three times yearly;
largest show in this group)

Bakersfield Prestigious Antique Show & Sale
Kern County Fairgrounds
1148 South P Street
Bakersfield, CA
(Shows three times yearly)

San Diego's Prestigious Antique Show & Sale
Scottish-Rite Center
1895 Camino del Rio South
San Diego, CA
(Shows four times yearly)

Santa Barbara Antique Show & Sale
Earl Warren Show Grounds
Las Positas, CA
(Shows three times yearly)

Santa Maria's Antique Show & Sale
Santa Maria Fairgrounds
Santa Maria, CA
(Shows three times yearly)

Ventura Antique Show & Sale
Ventura Fairgrounds
10 West Harbor Boulevard
Ventura, CA
(Shows three times yearly)

CONNECTICUT

Cord Shows Ltd.
23D Whipporwill Road
Armonk, NY 10504
(914)273-4667
(For information, leave a message on the answering machine)

Old Greenwich Civic Center
Old Greenwich, CT
(Held annually in December)

Morgenstein Enterprises
P.O. Box 6
New City, NY 10956
(914)634-9663

Hartford Civic Center Antique Show
Hartford, CT
(Show held yearly on Thanksgiving weekend; 150 exhibitors with 10
costume jewelry dealers)

Young Management Co.
P.O. Box 1538
Waterbury, CT 06721
(203)755-5278

Vintage Clothing, Estate & Costume Jewelry, &
Vintage Textiles Show & Sale
Stratford Armory
Armory Road & Route 108
Stratford, CT
(Largest show of its kind in the East with 4,000–5,000 attendees; all
dealers exhibit some costume jewelry, 10 show costume jewelry
exclusively; shows are held twice yearly)

FLORIDA

Lewis Baron
266 NE 70th Street
Miami, FL 33138
(305)754-4931

Baron Antique Show
Miami Beach Convention Center
Washington Avenue
Miami Beach, FL
(Largest show in the United States with 10,000–15,000 attendees;
exhibitors are screened to maintain quality, many costume jewelry
dealers in each show)

MASSACHUSETTS

J & J Promotions
Route 20
Brimfield, MA 01010
(413)245-3436
(508)597-8155
(Gordon Reid began the original "Brimfield" shows in Brimfield,
Massachusetts, in 1959. Now daughters Jill and Judy run the business
that has grown to one of the largest shows in the country, with
thousands of attendees. Call for directions, motels, and other
information.)

Antique Acres
Route 20
Brimfield, MA 01010

*J & J Promotions Antique &
Collectible Show*
Brimfield, MA
(800 exhibitors in May, 600 in
July, and 800 in September,
many of whom are costume
jewelry dealers)

NEVADA

Bustamante Enterprises
P.O. Box 637
Atwater, CA
(209)358-3134
(702)827-8813 (Reno)
(See California listings for information about this promoter)

Reno
Reno-Sparks Convention Center
4590 S. Virginia
Reno, NV
(Shows twice yearly)

NEW JERSEY

Brimfield Associates
P.O. Box 1800
Ocean City, NJ 08226
(800)526-2724

  Atlantic City
Atlantic City Convention Hall
Florida Avenue & Boardwalk
Atlantic City, NJ
(Held annually on the third weekend in March; "largest indoor
antique and collectible show in North America" with over 1,000
dealers from 45 states on seven and a half acres; 30–40% have
costume jewelry, and 50 dealers are in the Jewelry Galleria, a special
section adjacent to the main boardwalk)

50s Collectibles
Drawer G7
Long Valley, NJ 07853
(201)876-9100
(For information about shows, leave a message on the answering
machine)

Great American Antique Promotions
P.O. Box 4440
Cherry Hill, NJ 08034
(609)654-0003
(For information about shows, leave a message on the answering
machine)

  Brimfield in Jersey
Vincentown, NJ
(Shows held yearly in May [300 dealers] and September [250 dealers])

Morgenstein Enterprises
P.O. Box 6
New City, NY 10956
(914)634-9663

*Meadowlands Stadium Club
Antique Show*
East Rutherford, NJ
(Annual shows last weekend in
January and third weekend in
April; 110 exhibitors with 15
costume jewelry dealers)

New Jersey Antique Classic
Fairleigh Dickinson University
Hackensack, NJ
(Annual shows third weekend in
July; 160 exhibitors with 25
costume jewelry dealers;
indoors; air conditioned)

Raritan Center Antique Show
Raritan Center
Edison, NJ
(Shows twice yearly on first
weekends in March and October;
358 exhibitors with 75 costume
jewelry dealers)

Stella Shows
294 Harrington Avenue
Closter, NJ 07624
(201)768-2773
(20 years of promoting antique shows)

*Cold Spring Village Antique
Show*
Cape May, NJ
(Shows held yearly in July and
August; 60 exhibitors)

Garden State Antiques Fair
Garden State Expo Center
Somerset, NJ
(New annual show held in
August, with some costume
jewelry)

Labor Day Street Fair
Rutherford, NJ
(Annual September show with a
large amount of costume
jewelry)

Liberty Collectible Expo
Liberty State Park
Jersey City, NJ
(This show, along with the
Rothman Center show, has the
most costume jewelry of all the
Stella shows; held annually in
June and October)

Rothman Center
Fairleigh Dickinson University
Hackensack, NJ
(Annual April show)

*Waterloo Village Field Antique
Fair*
Stanhope, NJ
(Held annually in May and
September; some costume
jewelry)

NEW YORK

Cord Shows Limited
23D Whipporwill Road
Armonk, NY 10504
(914)273-4667
(For information, leave a message on the answering machine)

Gloria Rothstein Shows, Inc.
Box J
Highland Hills, NY 10930
(914)928-9494
(15 years of promoting antique shows)

Nyack Street Fair
Main Street
Nyack, NY
(Shows held three times yearly
in May, July, and October)

The Big Event
White Plains, NY
(150–160 dealers; shows four to
six times yearly in January,
March, June, September, and
December)

Morgenstein Enterprises
P.O. Box 6
New City, NY 10956
(914)634-9663
(17 years of promoting antique shows)

Collectors Expo
Rockland Community College
Suffern, NY
(Shows twice yearly on the first
weekend in November and
April; 250 exhibitors with 50
costume jewelry dealers showing
a tremendous amount of
jewelry)

The Big Bash
Fox Lane High School
Bedford/Mt. Kisco, NY
(Held annually on July 4th
weekend, outdoors rain or shine;
175 exhibitors with 35 costume
jewelry dealers)

Stella Shows
294 Harrington Avenue
Closter, NJ 07624
(201)768-2773
(20 years of promoting antique shows; call for a calendar of shows)

Manhattan Antiques & Collectibles Triple Pier Expo
"The Pier Show"
Hudson River Passenger Ship, Piers 88, 90, 92
12th Avenue from 48th Street to 55th Street
New York, NY
(600 exhibitors, with 250 dealers of costume jewelry mostly on Pier 88; show is held twice a year in February/March and November)

Strawberry Hill Shows
467 Clubhouse Road
Binghamton, NY 13903
(607)723-3332
(607)723-3606
(All shows have costume jewelry; call for more specific information)

Hudson Valley Mall Antique Show
Hudson Valley Mall
Kingston, NY
(Shows twice yearly in April and August)

Ithica Pyramid Mall Antique Show
Ithica Pyramid Mall
Ithica, NY
(Shows three times yearly in April, July, and November)

Oakdale Mall Antique Show
Oakdale Mall
Binghamton, NY
(Shows twice yearly in May and October)

PENNSYLVANIA

Cathy Chambers Antiques Shows & Sales
Box 1786
Allentown, PA 18105
(215)437-5534
(215)437-3486

Antiques Show & Sale
State Farm Show Building
Harrisburg, PA
(Annual show held the weekend before Thanksgiving; 300 exhibitors; 34-year-old show)

Greater Pittsburgh Antique Show & Sale
Expo Mart
Monroeville, PA
(Shows twice yearly in April/March and October; 100 exhibitors)

Nadia
P.O. Box 156
Flourtown, PA 19031
(Some jewelry-only shows)

> *Nadia Antique Collectible Show*
> Cape May Convention Hall
> Cape May, NJ
> (Shows three times yearly in
> July, August, and September;
> emphasis is on vintage clothing
> and jewelry)
>
> *Nadia Jewelry Show and Sale*
> Days Hotel
> Pennsylvania Turnpike, Exit 26
> Fort Washington, PA
> (Shows twice yearly in April
> and December; all jewelry, with
> 80 tables)

> *Nadia Jewelry Show and Sale*
> Holiday Inn
> Route 70, Sayre Avenue
> (Across from Garden State
> Racetrack)
> Cherry Hill, NJ
> (Annual show held in
> November; all jewelry, with 50
> tables)

VIRGINIA

Commonwealth Promotions
P.O. Box 7003
Charlottesville, VA 22906

> *Norfolk Winter Antiques Show*
> The Scope
> Norfolk, VA

Heritage Promotions
Expoland
Fishersville, VA
Raymond Stokes
(804)846-7452
(804)845-7878

GLOSSARY

Art Deco. Refers to the style of design that succeeded Art Nouveau in Europe in the Twenties and Thirties, which was exhibited at the Exposition Internationale des Arts Décoratifs et Industriels Modernes in Paris in 1925; geometric, streamlined, rectilinear interpretations of roses, garlands and baskets of flowers, fountains, deer, and nudes, followed by austere, Cubistic, "machine age" motifs.

Baguette. A narrow, rectangular-cut rhinestone usually used in conjunction with other rhinestones.

Bakelite. The name for phenolic resin (phenol formaldehyde) coined by Dr. Leo Baekeland in 1908; used in the Thirties for necklaces, bracelets, and pins, with popular motifs of animals, fruits and vegetables, flowers and leaves, oriental subjects, hearts, sporting themes, polka dots, and whimsical designs.

Baroque pearl. An irregularly shaped pearl.

Bezel setting. A setting that circles the entire stone with flanges soldered and folded over.

Bracelet.
  Bangle—a rigid, circular bracelet that slips over the hand.
  Charm—link bracelets with various charms suspended.
  Cuff—an oval or round bracelet with a hinge and clasp.
  Flexible—made of metal or mesh, set with rhinestones or pearls.
  Indian or gauntlet—a rigid oval with an opening at the underside of the wrist.

Spiral—a long span of rhinestones, metal, beads, or pearls that wraps around the wrist or upper arm.

Tab—a rigid bracelet with a suspended charm.

Brilliant. Usually refers to a round-shape rhinestone.

Brooch. An alternate name for pin, from the French *broche,* meaning a spit or skewer; often used when describing pins made before the Fifties.

Cabochon. A smooth, dome-shape stone without facets.

Cap. A tube or cone-shape cup closed at one end; holds a bead or pearl.

Carnelian (cornelian). A translucent, dull red quartz with a waxy finish; often used in Art Deco jewelry, seals, and intaglios.

Casting. Jewelry formed by the "lost wax" method; pouring a metal into a mold, usually rubber, that makes an impression when it hardens, producing a piece with weight and depth.

Celluloid. A name for the highly flammable composition cellulose nitrate, patented in 1869, called Xylonite in London. An early translucent plastic used for haircombs, bangles, and pins in the Twenties; imitated ivory, bone, tortoise shell, coral, and pearls.

Champlevé. Enamel fused over a metal base with colors that blend; sections are cut.

Channel setting. Rhinestones are placed in a channel cut into the metal, with the top edge of the channel bent over the stones to retain them.

Charms. Objects worn initially for their protective properties, attracting good luck or averting ill health; now worn to commemorate an event or as a fashion object.

Chatelaine. Formerly used to describe a chain attached to an ornamental brooch or hook worn at the waist, from which was suspended various objects useful to the wearer, such as keys, a watch, purse, or grooming items; later used to describe pins connected by a chain.

Choker. A short necklace, usually 15″ long, worn high on the neck; popular in the Fifties, revived in the Seventies with the addition of ornaments cascading to cover the chest.

Citrine. Yellow quartz that ranges from pale yellow to a reddish hue.

Clip. Ornamental pieces that attach to shoes, a dress or fur, held in place by spring pressure; may have teeth or two prongs.

Cloisonné. Enamel divided by sections of metal *(cloisons)* on a metal base.

Dentelles. Forerunner to rhinestones; unfoiled stones cut with 32 or 64 facets to create and reflect light.

Deposé. A word often found on the back of jewelry made in France, similar to a copyright or patent stamp.

Die-stamping. Dies are created from models made according to designers' drawings, then machines stamp out stampings of brass, sterling silver, or other metals which are then trimmed, soldered, polished, plated, and lacquered.

Dog collar. A broad necklace worn tightly around the neck; popular in the Sixties.

Earrings. Buttons, clusters, hoops, drops, pendants, chandeliers with spring clips, screw-backs, earwires, or posts.

Electroplating. A method of depositing a thin layer of precious metal on base metal using an electronic device.

Enamel. Colored glass or glaze fused onto a metal base; reached a height of artistry in the Forties and was revived in the Sixties.

Filigree. Twisted and soldered fine strands of wire in intricate, lacy patterns; often used as backings for earrings and pins.

Findings. Functional parts of jewelry.
    Closings—findings used to close parts of a piece of jewelry: catches, clasps, hooks, rings, springs.
    Fastenings—findings used to hold jewelry to clothing or the body: clips, clutches, pins.
    Joinings—findings that hold parts of jewelry together: bails, bezels, bolts, caps, cords, chains, eyes, head and eye pins, loops, jumpsprings, nuts, rivets, screws, stone settings, swivels, wires.

Foil. Reflective material put under a rhinestone to enhance its shine or color.

French strasse. A stone made of a cut crystal base and a manufactured upper section which is fused together electronically.

German silver. Term used to describe an alloy of nickel, zinc, and copper with no silver content; also called nickel silver.

Gold-filled. A "sandwich" of two thin slices of gold with another metal in between; jewelry is marked with the fraction of gold content and the initials "g.f."

Grisaille. Enamel with a monochromatic effect obtained by using dark and light colors of similar hue.

Gutta percha. A natural substance obtained from the bark of the Malayan palaquilm tree; used to make jewelry in the 1800s.

Hematite. A blue-black stone used for intaglio and beads.

Intaglio. An engraving cut into a stone; if the stone is pressed into a softer material, an image is produced in relief.

Japanned. The result of a process that blackens metal, originally used for mourning jewelry; later used to blacken a setting for decorative purposes.

Jet. Black lignite; used extensively in Victorian jewelry, originally worn to express mourning, now may refer to any black stone used in jewelry.

Lapis lazuli. An opaque silicate; dark blue with white dots, often simulated for costume jewelry.

Lavaliere. A drop with a single stone suspended from a chain, also called a *negligé.*

Locket. A pendant made in two parts that opens to reveal photographs, a lock of hair, or a charm.

Marcasite. White iron pyrite cut to look like diamonds, also available in "gold"; cut steel can be mistaken for marcasites, used extensively in the Twenties and Thirties, usually set in sterling silver in fanciful pins.

Millefiori. Glass rods of various colors fused and then sliced across to form cubes.

Moonstone. Bluish translucent stone; used in jewelry in the Thirties and Forties, often simulated.

Niello. Alloys of silver, copper, or lead with sulfur, producing a deep black color used to "shadow" a design.

Papier-mâché. A process patented in 1772, using layers of paper and glue placed in a mold and allowed to harden or dry in an oven; painted or plated when used in jewelry.

Parkesine. Early celluloid developed by Alexander Parkes in the 1840s; used in jewelry through the Twenties.

Parure. A matching set of jewelry consisting of a necklace, bracelet, pin, and earrings. A partial set, e.g., a bracelet and earrings, is a *demi-parure.*

Pavé. Small rhinestones set into metal without prongs; "nicked in" to metal beads using a special tool, secured with glue, or a combination of both, producing a "paved" effect.

Pendant. A movable ornament suspended from a chain or another part of the same ornament.

Plique à jour. Enamel over an open design, allowing the light to strike it from the back.

Repoussé. Using a hammer and punches to produce a design in reverse relief in metal.

Rock crystal. Clear quartz that is harder, colder, and has double the refraction of glass; often used in jewelry as beads or frosted in Art Deco pins.

Rondelles. Small, round jeweled beads, often used as spacers.

Sautoir. A long necklace made of pearls, beads, or chains, often ending in tassels; popular in the Twenties.

Scarf pin. A pin, often with tassels, used to secure a scarf.

Scatter pins. Small pins, usually birds, insects, or flowers worn in groups; popular in the Fifties.

Tassels. A pendant with free-hanging chains, pearls, or other ornaments; common in the Twenties, revived in the Fifties.

Tremblant. When a part of the jewelry is set on a spring, causing it to "nod" or "tremble"; often used in the Forties on pins of flowers, birds, and animals, from the French word for trembling, also called "nodders."

Wire drawing. A production method in which pencil-size rods of cast metal are pulled through draw plates of various dimensions and styles to meet functional and decorative requirements.

Zircon. A silicate of zirconium; transparent crystals in various colors.

BIBLIOGRAPHY

BOOKS

Batterberry, Michael and Ariane. *A Social History of Fashion.* New York: Holt, Rinehart & Winston, 1977.

Cartlidge, Barbara. *Twentieth Century Jewelry.* New York: Harry N. Abrams, Inc., 1985.

Davidow, Corinne and Dawes, Redington, Ginny. *The Bakelite Jewelry Book.* New York: Abbeville Press, 1988.

DiNoto, Andrea. *Art Plastic: Designed for Living.* New York: Abbeville Press, 1984.

Dolan, Maryanne. *Collecting Rhinestone Jewelry.* Alabama: Books Americana, Inc., 1984.

Duncan, Alistair (ed.). *Encyclopedia of Art Deco.* New York: E. P. Dutton, Quarto Publishing, 1988.

Ewing, Elizabeth. *History of 20th Century Fashion.* Totowa, NJ: Barnes & Noble, 1974, 1986.

Gold, Annalee. *75 Years of Fashion.* New York: Fairchild Publications, 1975.

Hall, Carolyn. *The Twenties in Vogue.* London: Octopus Books Ltd., 1983.

Hoffer, Ott. *Imitation Gemstones—Random Personal Reminiscences,* 1980.

Kelley, Lyngerda, Schiffer, Nancy. *Plastic Jewelry.* West Chester, PA: Schiffer Publishing Co., 1987.

Mason, Anita. *An Illustrated Dictionary of Jewellry.* New York: Harper & Row, 1974.

McClinton, Katharine Morrison. *Art Deco: A Guide for Collectors.* New York: Clarkson N. Potter, 1972.

Milbank, Caroline Rennolds. *Couture. The Great Designers.* New York: Stewart, Tabori & Chang, Inc., 1985.

Rose, Augustus F. *Jewelry Making and Design.* Worcester, MA: The Davis Press, Inc., 1949.

Sarett, Morton R. *The Jewelry in Your Life.* Chicago: Nelson-Hall, 1979.

Untracht, Oppi. *Jewelry Concepts and Technology.* New York: Doubleday & Co., 1982.

Warren, Geoffrey. *Fashion Accessories Since 1500.* New York: Drama Book Publishers, 1987.

PERIODICALS

"Bakelite Envy." *Connoisseur,* July 1985.

"Costume Jewelry: High Style at Low Cost." *Mass Bay Antiques,* September 1982.

Fried, Eunice. "Faux but Fabulous—Joseff: Jeweler to the Stars." *Almanac,* November/December 1988.

Klein, Mim. "Joseff of Hollywood." *Collectors Clocks and Jewelry,* Fall 1988.

Main, Eve. "Joseff, of Hollywood." *Modern Plastics,* September 1939.

"Star Fashions." *Movie Mirror,* December 1938.

AUCTION CATALOGS

Fine Antique and Modern Jewelry. New York: Phillips, January 22, 1985.

The Diana Vreeland Collection of Fashion Jewelry. New York: Sotheby's, October 21, 1987.

RECOMMENDED PERIODICALS FOR
ADDITIONAL READING

Accent Magazine
Accessories
American Jewelry Manufacturer
Ceramics Monthly
Craft Horizon
Design
Harpers Bazaar (back issues)

Hobbies
Jewelers Circular Keystone
Life (back issues)
Modern Plastics
Vanity Fair (back issues)
Vogue (back issues)

INDEX

The HOUSE OF COLLECTIBLES Series

☐ Please send me the following price guides—
☐ I would like the most current edition of the books listed below.

THE OFFICIAL PRICE GUIDES TO:

☐ 753-3	American Folk Art (ID) 1st Ed.	$14.95
☐ 784-3	Silver & Silverplate (ID) 6th Ed.	$12.95
☐ 513-1	Antique Clocks 3rd Ed.	10.95
☐ 091-1	Antique & Modern Dolls (ID) 4th Ed.	12.95
☐ 287-6	Antique & Modern Firearms 6th Ed.	11.95
☐ 792-4	Antique & Modern Teddy Bears 1st Ed.	10.95
☐ 805-X	Antiques & Collectibles (ID) 11th Ed.	12.95
☐ 289-2	Antique Jewelry 5th Ed.	11.95
☐ 362-7	Art Deco (ID) 1st Ed.	14.95
☐ 447-X	Arts and Crafts: American Decorative Arts, 1894–1923 (ID) 1st Ed.	12.95
☐ 539-5	Beer Cans & Collectibles 4th Ed.	7.95
☐ 521-2	Bottles Old & New 10th Ed.	10.95
☐ 532-8	Carnival Glass 2nd Ed.	10.95
☐ 295-7	Collectible Cameras 2nd Ed.	10.95
☐ 548-4	Collectibles of the '50s & '60s 1st Ed.	9.95
☐ 803-3	Collectible Toys (ID) 5th Ed.	10.95
☐ 531-X	Collector Cars 7th Ed.	12.95
☐ 538-7	Collector Handguns 4th Ed.	14.95
☐ 748-7	Collector Knives 9th Ed.	12.95
☐ 361-9	Collector Plates 5th Ed.	11.95
☐ 296-5	Collector Prints 7th Ed.	12.95
☐ 787-8	Costume Jewelry (ID) 1st Ed.	10.95
☐ 001-6	Depression Glass 2nd Ed.	9.95
☐ 589-1	Fine Art 1st Ed.	19.95
☐ 311-2	Glassware 3rd Ed.	10.95
☐ 243-4	Hummel Figurines & Plates 6th Ed.	10.95
☐ 523-9	Kitchen Collectibles 2nd Ed.	10.95
☐ 772-X	Lunch Box Collectibles 1st Ed.	9.95
☐ 080-6	Memorabilia of Elvis Presley and The Beatles 1st Ed.	10.95
☐ 291-4	Military Collectibles 5th Ed.	11.95
☐ 788-6	Movie Memorabilia (ID) 1st Ed.	9.95
☐ 525-5	Music Collectibles 6th Ed.	11.95
☐ 313-9	Old Books & Autographs 7th Ed.	11.95
☐ 298-1	Oriental Collectibles 3rd Ed.	11.95
☐ 820-3	Overstreet Comic Book 20th Ed.	14.95
☐ 522-0	Paperbacks & Magazines 1st Ed.	10.95
☐ 297-3	Paper Collectibles 5th Ed.	10.95
☐ 809-2	Peanuts® Collectibles 1st Ed.	9.95
☐ 744-4	Political Memorabilia 1st Ed.	10.95
☐ 785-1	Pottery & Porcelain (ID) 7th Ed.	12.95
☐ 524-7	Radio, TV & Movie Memorabilia 3rd Ed.	11.95
☐ 819-X	Records 9th Ed.	16.95
☐ 763-0	Royal Doulton 6th Ed.	12.95
☐ 280-9	Science Fiction & Fantasy Collectibles 2nd Ed.	10.95
☐ 747-9	Sewing Collectibles 1st Ed.	8.95
☐ 358-9	Star Trek/Star Wars Collectibles 2nd Ed.	8.95
☐ 808-4	Watches 10th Ed.	16.95
☐ 248-5	Wicker 3rd Ed.	10.95

THE OFFICIAL:

☐ 760-6	Directory to U.S. Flea Markets 2nd Ed.	5.95
☐ 365-1	Encyclopedia of Antiques 1st Ed.	9.95
☐ 369-4	Guide to Buying and Selling Antiques 1st Ed.	9.95
☐ 414-3	Identification Guide to Early American Furniture 1st Ed.	9.95
☐ 413-5	Identification Guide to Glassware 1st Ed.	9.95

☐ 412-7	Identification Guide to Pottery & Porcelain 1st Ed.	$9.95
☐ 415-1	Identification Guide to Victorian Furniture 1st Ed.	9.95

THE OFFICIAL (SMALL SIZE) PRICE GUIDES TO:

☐ 309-0	Antiques & Flea Markets 4th Ed.	4.95
☐ 269-8	Antique Jewelry 3rd Ed.	4.95
☐ 807-6	Baseball Cards 10th Ed.	5.95
☐ 647-2	Bottles 3rd Ed.	4.95
☐ 544-1	Cars & Trucks 3rd Ed.	5.95
☐ 519-0	Collectible Americana 2nd Ed.	4.95
☐ 294-9	Collectible Records 3rd Ed.	4.95
☐ 306-6	Dolls 4th Ed.	4.95
☐ 800-9	Football Cards 9th Ed.	5.95
☐ 540-9	Glassware 3rd Ed.	4.95
☐ 801-7	Hockey & Basketball Cards 1st Ed.	5.95
☐ 526-3	Hummels 4th Ed.	4.95
☐ 279-5	Military Collectibles 3rd Ed.	4.95
☐ 799-1	Overstreet Comic Book Companion 3rd Ed.	4.95
☐ 278-7	Pocket Knives 3rd Ed.	4.95
☐ 527-1	Scouting Collectibles 4th Ed.	4.95
☐ 494-1	Star Trek/Star Wars Collectibles 3rd Ed.	3.95
☐ 088-1	Toys 5th Ed.	4.95

THE OFFICIAL BLACKBOOK PRICE GUIDES OF:

☐ 823-8	U.S. Coins 29th Ed.	5.95
☐ 822-X	U.S. Paper Money 23rd Ed.	5.95
☐ 821-1	U.S. Postage Stamps 13th Ed.	5.95

THE OFFICIAL INVESTORS GUIDE TO BUYING & SELLING:

☐ 534-4	Gold, Silver & Diamonds 2nd Ed.	12.95
☐ 535-2	Gold Coins 2nd Ed.	12.95
☐ 536-0	Silver Coins 2nd Ed.	12.95
☐ 537-9	Silver Dollars 2nd Ed.	12.95

THE OFFICIAL NUMISMATIC GUIDE SERIES:

☐ 254-X	The Official Guide to Detecting Counterfeit Money 2nd Ed.	7.95
☐ 257-4	The Official Guide to Mint Errors 4th Ed.	7.95

SPECIAL INTEREST SERIES:

☐ 506-9	From Hearth to Cookstove 3rd Ed.	17.95

TOTAL		

SEE REVERSE SIDE FOR ORDERING INSTRUCTIONS

FOR IMMEDIATE DELIVERY

VISA & MASTER CARD CUSTOMERS

ORDER TOLL FREE!
1-800-733-3000

This number is for orders only; it is not tied into the customer service or business office. Customers not using charge cards must use mail for ordering since payment is required with the order—sorry, no C.O.D.'s.

OR SEND ORDERS TO

THE HOUSE OF COLLECTIBLES
201 East 50th Street
New York, New York 10022

POSTAGE & HANDLING RATES

First Book $2.00
Each Additional Copy or Title $0.50

Total from columns on order form. Quantity_____ $_____

☐ Check or money order enclosed $_____ (include postage and handling)

☐ Please charge $_____to my: ☐ MASTERCARD ☐ VISA

Charge Card Customers Not Using Our Toll Free Number
Please Fill Out The Information Below

Account No. _____Expiration Date_____
(All Digits)
Signature_____

NAME (please print)_____PHONE_____

ADDRESS_____APT. #_____

CITY_____STATE_____ZIP_____